TRADING AND INVESTING FOR BEGINNERS

STOCK TRADING BASICS, HIGH LEVEL TECHNICAL ANALYSIS, RISK MANAGEMENT AND TRADING PSYCHOLOGY.

RUBÉN VILLAHERMOSA CHAVES

This book is dedicated to my wife, Adriana,

the love of my life and my best friend.

CONTENTS

INTRODUCTION

Trading, investing: sounds appealing, right? Well, before you read on, I have to tell you that everything you have heard about how to make money on the stock market is probably false. Just think about this: Some studies claim that more than 80% of traders lose money. The reason? Trading is simply not as easy as some have led us to believe. Statistics are not on our side.

Trading in financial markets is one of the most complex professions around. It is a world controlled by large financial institutions, which allocate enormous resources and hire the best minds – engineers, physicists and mathematicians–, to appropriate money belonging to other market participants. And you're going to have to fight them. It doesn't seem like an easy task.

But not everything is doom and gloom. If you still feel you want to proceed, your only chance is to somehow level the playing field. Instead of fighting them you need to try to trade alongside them. To do this, you need to become the complete trader and develop and follow the 3 main principles that will largely determine whether you are successful or not:

1. Build a winning strategy.

2. Implement solid risk management.

3. Manage your emotions appropriately.

But that isn't all. These three main principles are the core of this book and without a doubt represent the most important content; but there is added value to be found in the first part, on financial literacy, and in the final part, on business management and practical application.

Who should read this book?

Every trader and investor who is starting from scratch and taking their first steps in stock trading. We will look at the most basic and fundamental content that you need to know in the early stages of your training as a trader or investor.

The book will also be of interest to fundamental analysts who are looking for a real approach to technical analysis by studying methodologies that I have dubbed "high-level". There is a great deal of research that suggests that the timing of the market - the moment of entry - is of significant importance, and technical analysis can help you in this task.

Technical analysis is mistakenly associated with day trading and with methods that are based on tremendously subjective or illogical principles. This book will guide the investor by explaining approaches that can give them an advantage in interpreting the information provided by financial charts.

Why do you need this knowledge?

Simply because it is your only option. As I have already mentioned, the odds are against you. You need this knowledge, period. There is no alternative if you want to approach the markets in the best possible condition. That said, this content may be essential but it is not enough. This book will lay the foundations that you simply must have at this first stage, but you must remain steadfast in your commitment moving forward. Remember that it is not an easy task.

Why this book and not any another?

The content of this book is basic. You could even easily find some of this knowledge online. The advantage of this book is that it will save you time, effort and money. I have also walked the path you are now on and I know exactly what you need to know and the best way to explain it clearly.

I have tried to avoid using technical jargon in the book simply to ensure that each and every sentence can be fully understood. As you will see, there is no filler content and each of the sentences has an eminently practical and operational meaning, in an attempt to base everything on logical reasoning.

Moreover, I think it's fair to say that this may be the most comprehensive book dedicated to beginners that you will find.

What will you learn?

This book will help you to develop the essential skills you need to trade in financial markets. Usually these are dealt with separately, but one of the major advantages of this book it that it takes a comprehensive perspective and covers all the key elements in a single, mutually reinforcing package.

We will follow this program:

- The **first** part of the book will deal with a subject that is not usually covered in books like this but is inextricably linked to trading: financial literacy. If we want to invest or trade we need money. This section will introduce some of the most important concepts for becoming more financially intelligent as well as practical recommendations to improve our finances.

- The **second** and **third** parts of the book focus on the core of the required theoretical knowledge. We will learn about the history of financial theories in order to determine the nature of markets, we will study the characteristics of the main investment products, the main types of market agents, and discover how prices are set, as well as all the fundamental concepts necessary to understand the way that markets operate.

- The **fourth** part is the key topic of the book: technical analysis. This part aims to provide the necessary knowledge to build a winning strategy, the first of the three main principles that will determine our success.

  We will cover the basics of technical analysis: chart types, the price cycle, market conditions, how to correctly draw lines etc. And we will also present the three methodologies that make up what I have dubbed a high-level technical analysis: Price Action, Volume Spread Analysis and the Wyckoff Method.

  Obviously, we won't be able to go into the minutiae of each of the proposed methods, but the most important concepts will be explained so that the reader can decide which one they should subsequently specialize in.

- The **fifth** part will deal with the second of the three fundamental principles, risk management. We will learn key concepts about money management that will help us minimize the risk of bankruptcy and we will learn to carry out more professional position management.

- The **sixth** part deals with emotional management and with it we conclude the third fundamental principle that will help us tip the balance in our favor. Essentially, we are going to focus on creating a statistical mindset which is as objective as possible. To do this, we will identify the negative emotions that distract us from our goals as well as the positive ones that bring us closer to them; and we will gain an understanding of the main cognitive biases that we may fall victim to, so that we can avoid them.

- The **seventh** part will cover certain aspects of business management that are often neglected; such as developing a trading plan, correctly recording trades, as well as recommended guidelines for periodically reviewing our performance and implementing improvements.

- In the **eighth**, and final, part of the book, we will dive into the practicalities. I will recommend some of the best tools and resources available to us that can help during real trades.

I once again want to emphasize the importance of keeping expectations low and applying common sense to what you do. Neither this book, nor any other, nor any course, mentoring session or specialization will guarantee that you become a successful trader or investor. This is a path that requires knowledge and experience. The first part –knowledge– begins here and now, with the essential content you will find in this book. By studying this, you will have laid the first foundation stone, you will have already taken the first step and you will be in a position to start studying intermediate and advanced resources. But even once you have acquired all this knowledge, this won't be enough. You will still need experience. And for this there is no possible shortcut. You can only acquire experience with hours of screen time and hard work. I wish you good luck on your journey.

PART 1. FINANCIAL LITERACY AS THE FIRST STEP TO INVESTING

The raw material used in the trading or investing business is money, so we need to start with the most basic concepts of financial literacy.

Unless you were brought up in an environment free from financial problems, the chances are you have never been taught financial literacy in your family. Financial ignorance is usually passed down from generation to generation. It goes without saying that if your parents didn't have a method for managing their finances, then obviously they couldn't pass on that knowledge to you. It may even have been a taboo subject.

The educational system deserves a special mention here. It is absolutely astonishing that a subject like personal finances, which can condition a person's adult life, is not taught in any link of the educational chain. You can come away with a specialized education in a particular field and have no idea about how to manage money. Strange.

This is why this first part of the book is going to deal with the necessary fundamentals about money. This information will probably give you a new perspective and put you in a much more advantageous position for making decisions in your day-to-day life, which will lead to an improvement in your financial situation.

With regard to money itself, it is remarkable how many people despise it and devalue it. Clearly we should not be obsessed with money, but it must be respected and recognized for what it is: a means that will allow us to achieve our basic goals. I believe money should not be made simply for the sake of accumulating wealth, but in order to build a small nest egg to ensure a good quality of life and certain financial peace of mind.

FINANCIAL LITERACY BASICS

Train Your Mind

Many people think that college, school or university is the end of the road to learning, but in reality it is just the beginning. As I have just mentioned, it is rare for someone to begin adulthood with knowledge about personal finances that enables them to make good decisions throughout their life. That is why it is your responsibility to become aware of it and train yourself in it.

There is no more absolute truth than the fact that everything that your brain stores determines the tools you have at your disposal.

If you are not satisfied with your economic reality, this is a simple reflection of what is in your mind, your training, your skills. If you are not in good financial health, you should consider the possibility of changing some of your habits. If you want to improve your results, you must first change the beliefs and habits that have led you to them. If you keep doing things in the same was as before, you will continue to obtain the same results.

You may think an investment is difficult or risky, but it might not be the case; you may simply see it that way because you don't have the knowledge to properly evaluate the opportunity. This lack of information and knowledge makes you ignorant, and that is why you have to invest in education, in learning about investment and financial intelligence.

The more financial intelligence you acquire, the easier it will be for you to recognize a good deal, or turn a bad deal into a good one. As Robert Kiyosaki says, great opportunities are not seen with your eyes, they are seen with your mind. Acquire all the knowledge you can and work with your mind instead of your body.

Assets and Liabilities

Assets and liabilities are part of the balance sheet; a financial statement about net worth that tells us what we have and what we owe.

It is the direction of the cash flow that determines whether something is an asset or a liability at the time:

- **Assets**. Products that put money in your pocket and/or that appreciate in value.

- **Liabilities**. Products that take money out of your pocket and/or that depreciate in value. These include all the expenses and debts that we are obliged to pay.

Types of asset

- Financial Instruments. Stocks, investment funds, bonds or any other asset that has the ability to appreciate or provide us with dividends.

- Property. Homes, garages, warehouses, premises etc. to rent or sell.

- Businesses. Either having shareholdings, undertakings, through franchises or through any other formula linked to this model of producing goods and services.

- Intellectual property. Patents, artistic and literary productions and in general any asset for which we own the copyright and that provides us with royalties.

- Luxury. Works of art, collectibles, precious metals and objects that are able to maintain their value over time and for which there is market in which they can be sold.

Net equity is the difference between our assets and our liabilities. It is the most reliable indicator of our financial health at any given time.

Pay your liabilities with your assets

The formula you need to achieve your desired financial freedom involves ensuring your passive income is sufficient to pay your expenses. If you want to acquire a liability, either by whim or necessity, focus first on increasing your assets so that these can cover this new cost with the cash flow they generate.

This is a very good way of forcing ourselves to continually seek new opportunities and ways to improve our income.

Do you want to buy a new cell phone? Well, find a way to buy it without using your current capital. Reinvent yourself and create a new asset that is responsible for paying for that new expense. Whether it be putting in overtime at work, executing a new project, finding new clients or improving a condition of your contract. The idea is that this expense should not result in a deficit in your current finances.

You achieve financial freedom when your assets exceed the expenses that you will incur over the course of the rest of your life. Financial peace of mind arises when your expenses are paid using your passive income.

Credit and Interest

Credit is simply the concept of borrowing to consume something now and pay for it later. This financial transaction involves two agents: the creditor or lender, who lends the money; and the debtor or borrower, who must return the money in a defined period of time.

Credit is not necessarily bad if used properly. For example, you can use a credit card and not pay any interest as long as you set up your payment process so that you pay it off fully at the end of the month.

This is something very important, which can have a significant impact on financial stability, and which many people overlook. Bear in mind that carrying over interest from one month to the next will generate the exponential growth of that debt, since it will be updated every month based on the initial balance plus the accumulated monthly interest.

Another efficient use of credit is using it to buy an asset that turns into good debt. We will discuss the concept of good debt below.

It is important to know that credit is subject to an interest rate, which is nothing more than the price of money; the percentage that you will be charged for the amount you have been loaned.

We could discuss interest rates at great length but the most important thing to know is that they directly affect us and are a factor that should therefore be taken into account when evaluating a loan.

It is important to understand the following theoretical concepts:

- A rise in interest rates penalizes consumption in the present because using money (consuming/borrowing) becomes more expensive. Therefore this scenario is more conducive to saving and consuming in the future.

- A drop in interest rates increases consumption in the present, incentivizing indebtedness and penalizing savings and consumption in the future.

Good and Bad Debt

Debt is the amount loaned plus the interest that the debtor is required to repay.

Within the scope of personal finances, which is what interests us here, we can classify debt into two types: good and bad.

Bad debt is a loan which has been used to purchase liabilities, generally in the form of an impulse buy (a new cell phone); while good debt includes the purchase of assets that will generate a cash flow for us (purchasing a home to let for which we receive rent payments, or purchasing stocks and obtaining dividends), either immediately or in the future.

It is not about not buying, but about avoiding impulse buying which can impact us negatively in the form of high interest payments in the future. If you must buy something, do so with cash, to avoid unnecessary extra costs.

Although good debt also incurs interest payments, the profitability it offers us is greater than its cost. Before deciding to purchase an asset with good debt, you should bear in mind that there are still associated risks that must be carefully assessed. Just because the financial equation for that purchase is positive does not mean that it is risk free.

The basic difference is that a purchase financed with bad debt will impact your financial situation through an outflow of money; while a purchase financed with good debt will generate a return that will cover the interest and if you've managed to get a good deal, provide you with a surplus.

A tip to keep your debt level low is to take the following approach: if you cannot cover an expense without making use of credit, it may be better not make the purchase. If you have to resort to debt to buy a cell phone, a television or any other product or service, financially speaking you probably don't have the capacity to make that purchase, and it may be more sensible to postpone it until you can pay in cash.

If you decide to get into debt, make sure the percentage doesn't exceed 30-35% of your total income. These percentages apply to the two types of debts mentioned above. The recommended percentage to allocate to bad debt is zero; but if you really must resort to it, this type of debt should not exceed 10 to 20%.

If you find it difficult to manage these percentages properly, just use common sense: only get into as much debt as you can afford to without losing sleep. Always think of the worst-case scenario when getting into debt, to the extent that if you lose the flow of return from that investment, you are still in a position to repay the debt with your main source of income. For example, if you go into debt to buy a property that you will later rent out, you must be able to cover the mortgage in the event the tenant stops paying their rent.

The most profitable and least risky investment out there is to simply pay off all your high-interest debt. It is the most intelligent financial movement, a risk-free trade that can be highly profitable.

Inflation

Inflation is a general increase in the prices of goods and services that is not limited to certain items.

It reflects a decrease in purchasing power as a consequence of the continuous printing of new currency. In other words, each time new money is printed, it subtracts value from the money already in circulation, meaning that the same product costs more over time, or in other words, that less and less can be bought with the same amount of money.

An estimated measure of inflation is the CPI (Consumer Price Index), a basket made up of all the goods and services that families consume, including:

- Daily consumables (such as food, newspapers, or gasoline).

- Durable consumer goods (such as clothing, computers, or washing machines).

- Services (such as hairdressing, insurance or property rental).

Inflation per se is not a bad thing as long as salaries rise in the same proportion as the prices of goods and services. This is the only way that purchasing power remains stable. But this is not always the case. In fact, Central Banks always try to ensure there is some inflation to drive economic progress and to avoid deflation. Deflation is a drop in prices, which can slow down consumption and economic growth.

Direct and Indirect Taxes

Taxes are cash payments that citizens are obliged by law to pay to governments without obtaining any specific nominal compensation, in order to pay for the welfare state.

Taxes are classified as

Direct

These apply to the assets and income of the individual:

- Personal Income Tax.

- Non-Resident Income Tax.

- Corporate Tax.

- Inheritance and Gift Tax.

- Wealth Tax.

- Property Tax.

- Economic Activities Tax.

- Motor Vehicle Tax.

- Local Capital Gains Tax.

Indirect

These are applied to the use of that wealth; on consumption and transfer:

- VAT or Value Added Tax.

- Transfer Tax and Stamp Duty.

- Special taxes. These taxes are only paid by people who buy or consume certain goods:

- Alcohol and alcoholic beverages

- Hydrocarbons

- Tobacco

- Vehicle registration

- Customs Duties

In addition to those mentioned, each city council, province and autonomous community also has the power to establish taxes and other fees.

All this means that taxes make up the lion's share of a person's expenses. In Spain, for example, the average citizen allocates 50% of their income to paying both direct and indirect taxes. This literally means working half the year to pay taxes. You can do the math yourself if you don't believe it.

The problem with taxes is not the taxes themselves, but the use that is made of them. It is not a question of not paying taxes since they are obviously necessary and we all benefit from them; the issue is the terrible and ineffective use that is made of them, as evidenced by the alarming cases of misappropriation of public funds we have all read about. I am referring to Spain, where I live, but wherever you are I'm sure there have been similar disgraceful cases involving our dear politicians.

Speak to an expert about reducing or minimizing the impact of taxes. When it comes to acquiring a good or service it is important to take into account the tax perspective before making any decision, comparing all possible alternatives.

Simple and Compound Interest

Compound interest occurs when the results of an investment are added to the initial capital and together they return new interest. The initial capital grows continuously since the interest generated is added and reinvested immediately.

	Simple interest	Compound interest
Formula	$C_n = C_0 \cdot (1+n \cdot i)$	$C_n = C_0 (1+i)^n$
Initial capital	$ 10.000	$ 10.000
Interest	10 %	10 %
Year 1	$ 11.000,00	$ 11.000,00
Year 5	$ 15.000,0	$ 16.105,10
Year 10	$ 20.000,0	$ 25.937,42
Year 15	$ 25.000,0	$ 41.772,48
Year 20	$ 30.000,0	$ 67.275,00

Meanwhile, in simple interest, the interest generated is not added to the initial capital when calculating the new interest for the following period since it doesn't vary. Therefore, the interest obtained in each period is always the same.

An example to differentiate between simple and compound interest: Imagine that you invest €10,000 over 20 years at 10%. Depending on the interest rate, the result varies considerably:

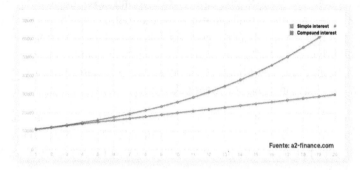

Fuente: a2-finance.com

Now you understand why many people refer to compound interest as the eighth wonder of the world or as the most powerful force in the universe thanks to its ability to exponentially multiply capital.

INCOME

Income and expenses are part of the profit and loss account. They tell us how much we are receiving and for what, and how much of our funds we are allocating and to what; as well as whether we are obtaining a profit (capacity to save) or loss (indebtedness).

Income is the source of everything. It is impossible to first save and later invest without having some form of job or occupation that provides us with an income.

Our earning capacity is the cornerstone and will largely determine our financial future.

In this sense, I believe that its vitally important to work continuously to generate new sources of income. Regardless of how much income you receive, what if that source of income disappeared? I firmly believe that being financially dependent on a single source of income is the worst possible strategy. Even the most stable job may one day disappear for all sorts of financial, legal or judicial reasons. It is important to be aware of this, especially in the globalized world in which we live today, where technological advances which can put our current occupation at risk, happen at the speed of light.

Active and Passive Income

We can essentially differentiate between two types of income depending on how much time we dedicate to obtaining it: active and passive income.

Active income

This is an inflow of money which requires a direct effort in the execution of a task. The most common form of active income is wages, where a worker receives a salary in exchange for the dedication of time and effort.

Active income has one great disadvantage and that is that it is limited. If you exchange money for time, your income will be limited to the time you can spend on the task in question. And if you don't work. you dont receive any income. Hence, it is not the best type of income.

Passive income

This is income that does not require any exclusive dedication in order to obtain it. It does not require you to exchange your time for money. It needs some initial dedication at the moment it is created or purchased, but once this phase is over, only minimal dedication, if any, is required to monitor and optimize the product or service.

Passive income is unlimited, recurring, and scalable. Unlimited because you do not exchange time for money, since this type of income continues to be generated regardless of what you do, even while you sleep. If you charge royalties for the sale of an info product, this product can be sold automatically over the internet without the need for your presence; and thanks to technology and globalization you can sell it all over the world using the same infrastructure. This is the definition of scalability. Finally, these sources of income are also recurring since you can sell a service through a periodic subscription which will provide you with a constant and recurrent source of income, again as long as your customers maintain their subscription.

Here are some examples of passive income:

- Income from renting out property.

- Royalties for intellectual property rights.

- Dividends from stocks.

- Income from the sale of goods and services online.

- Commissions for referrals. Affiliate marketing.

- Multi-level businesses.

- Advertising hosted on a website, YouTube, Twitch etc.

Guide to Creating Your Own Source of Passive Income

It all starts with identifying your passion, what you like and what you would do even if you weren't paid for it. This is the perennial problem that most people face because they have never stopped to think about what they really enjoy doing. And I don't mean watching television or hanging out with friends. That too, but here I mean something that has professional possibilities. I can give you a hint: it has to do with what you are naturally good at doing.

In my case, for example, I am passionate about the world of trading and investing, and this led me to endless hours of studying all the information that I could get hold of. I even ended up reading and reviewing books in English and that was back when I wasn't sufficiently fluent. This is a very good example because it shows that when you are passionate about something, you do whatever it takes; and in my case it was having to learn English on the fly to be able to study those books that weren't in Spanish. I did it, and it took a huge amount of effort, but it was worth it. It was passion that drove me forward. This is the level of commitment required to achieve your goals.

Once you have identified your passion, the aim is to become an expert in what you love doing. Study all the resources that are available, do your own research, and become an authority on the subject. You have to want to be the best.

When you are fully specialized, it is time to start monetizing your expertise. Whatever product or service you are going to market, it must solve a problem, something that will motivate people to buy it. If you offer enough value, the money will follow. And the more you help (the bigger the problem you solve) and the more people you help (the more reach you have), the more money you will receive.

Going back to my personal experience, I decided to become the best technical analyst specialized in the Wyckoff Method. Regardless of whether I have actually achieved this or not, all that dedication now means that within my professional community I am considered an expert in this field, which to a certain degree has enabled me to become an opinion leader. Thanks to this, I have been able to write these books and there are people, like you, who are interested in what I say (I take the opportunity to thank you for your support). Books which grant me royalties for intellectual property rights with every sale. This is an example of how I built an asset that generates passive income for me.

The options are endless. It all depends first of all on what passion you are going to try to monetize in the future. My advice is not to focus first on the product or service and then to specialize. Instead, you should specialize in what you are passionate about and then create the asset. This is the only way to ensure the excellence of that asset.

EXPENSES

Expenses include any purchase of products or services that cannot be treated as an investment. These are money outflows that cannot be recovered.

Broadly speaking, we can differentiate between good and bad expenses depending on what they are used for; and at a lower level we can differentiate between fixed, variable and superfluous expenses based on the nature of the purchase.

Good and Bad Expenses

Here we can include exactly the same content that we saw regarding the two types of debt: good and bad.

In essence, a good expense is one that is used to purchase assets that will provide us with a future return, as well as the purchase of any product or service that will improve us in some way and from which we will obtain some benefit, though not necessarily economic, such as spending on training, books, courses, tools to improve our business, improve our health, etc.

Meanwhile, bad expenses are those destined to the purchase of goods and services that do not provide us with an improvement and for which no type of return is obtained. They are expenses that are not recovered in any way and that in most cases are of an emotional, impulsive nature, such as the purchase of a cell phone just for the sake of a change or playing the lottery. Ultimately, it is spending on things that we do not need.

Fixed, Variable and Superfluous Expenses

Fixed expenses cover all those money outflows that are used to pay for products or services that are mandatory and necessary every month and which we have very little option of changing, such as rent/mortgage, utilities (water, electricity, telephone, internet), associated fees and expenses (property owners' association, taxes) etc.

Variable expenses are those over which we have some option of changing and power of decision, but that in general are still necessary for our day to day, such as spending on food, education (books, courses), clothing, transport, household, pharmacy etc.

Finally there are superfluous expenses. These include all expenses that are based more on desire than need. Examples would be spending on gifts, events, trips, restaurants, etc. Bad expenses often fall into this category, but not necessarily all superfluous expenses are bad expenses. You would have to look at what that person gets out of those expenses. The experiences enjoyed by going on trips or attending events could be classified as a bad expense but in reality they are contributing something intangible that can be very valuable.

SAVING

Saving is the first step to investing. The important thing is not how much money you make, but how much money you keep. Wealth is what you accumulate, not what you spend.

Saving is more a matter of habit than a matter of money. Developing the habit of saving is more important than the actual amount you bring in (unless the level of income is extremely low, in which case the focus should be on increasing it).

A well accepted and useful tip, which is applicable here, is to pay yourself first. This means that once you have received an income you should automatically dedicate a percentage to savings and use the rest to cover your obligations: paying debts and ordinary expenses.

Doing it the other way around and saving after paying debts and expenses is usually a bad strategy because generally there is never anything left over or the amounts are very low compared to what they could be.

Another tip is to postpone purchases to assess whether they are really necessary. Oftentimes we think we need something and buy it straight away only to find that, over time, it really wasn't that necessary after all. It ends up being stored somewhere and hardly used. If you apply the simple strategy of postponing that outlay for a few days or weeks, you will undoubtedly dispense with certain purchases that are unnecessary and based more on consumer impulse than on a need.

There are only two ways to save: reduce expenses or increase income. Ideally you should work on both. Below are some practical examples that can guide you in these matters:

How To Reduce Expenses

One half of the equation to promote savings and investment is focused on reducing expenses.

To achieve this, the strategy that will have the greatest impact on your financial health is to adopt a frugal lifestyle.

Frugality is key to wealth creation. It consists of maintaining a lifestyle below your means. But this doesn't mean that you have to become a miser or deprive yourself; rather, it has to do with making effective use of financial resources, so if you need a car, buy a good car, but not the best, not one that you know you can't afford. And do this with everything.

Obviously each segment of your life offers you different degrees of satisfaction and you may decide to be more economical in some things than in others. The important thing is to always bear in mind the premise of not wasting money.

Another way to reduce expenses is to eliminate all unnecessary fees and expenses such as those related to your telephone, gym, insurance and other subscriptions. Ask for offers to lower your fees or call the competition in search of better prices.

Taking a fresh look at these obligations and putting them in order will result in a silent transfer of money that in the long run could add up to a significant amount.

Make a list of the expenses you had last year, identify the most important ones and ask yourself how you could reduce them. One way to spend less is to go against the trend and buy items out of season, which is when you usually find good deals. For example, buying winter clothes in summer and vice versa. Buying in outlets or even second-hand products are also measures that you should consider.

Paying with cash or debit is also often an effective way to reduce expenses. And buy quality products, because in the long run it is usually cheaper than buying more economical but poorer quality products.

Another way to save is through tax breaks and deductions. There are studies that show that we renounce significant amounts of money simply by not requesting deductions that correspond to us. For example, discounts are generally offered for students, large families or for membership of certain private organizations. We may also be due certain benefits when filing our income tax returns. And there may also be benefits on offer that correspond to freelancers or business owners.

It is worth investing a small amount of time in researching this matter and it may even be worth contacting a financial and tax advisor who has the expertise to manage it in the best way possible.

How To Increase Income

This is the other half of the savings equation. For many, it is even more important than cost reduction.

As mentioned previously, having a single source of income can be very risky, whether you are a civil servant, employee, freelancer or business owner.

The first thing you can do if you are a salaried employee, if it is appropriate, it to ask for a raise. We ourselves are often responsible for limiting our income by not asking for raises, which in many cases our bosses would probably accept. If you are self-employed, you could also implement this strategy by renegotiating the economic conditions of your agreements with clients. If both parties are satisfied, asking for this shouldn't be a problem.

Another way to exploit the skills that you have and for which you receive a salary is to also work on small projects as a freelancer. Put your talents at the service of others and serve as many people as you can. If you have skills that are in high demand, you may be able to offer your services as an independent contractor and obtain extra income without having to improve your skills.

In general, regardless of whether you are working or not, ideally you should be doing something you are passionate about. It sounds utopian but this should be your goal if you want to achieve a high degree of job satisfaction and income.

You may have read this phrase many times and you may even be a little skeptical, but it is an absolute truth that if you identify your passion and manage to monetize it, it will put you in a very economically favorable position.

Emergency Fund

This is about saving money to ensure you have the capacity to cover the cost of an unexpected event that requires capital, without having to apply for a loan or dispose early of an investment.

The most important thing with regard to the emergency fund is to be clear about what is and what is not an emergency. This capital should solely and exclusively be used to deal with breakdowns, health problems, loss of employment and other similar contingencies.

This fund is not a piggy bank to be used to pay for vacations, gifts or any type of impulse purchase. A separate account should be created for these things but only after the emergency fund is in place.

As a general rule, the recommendation is to have about 6 months of normal income saved up. This will depend on each person. The important thing is that the amount is adequate depending on the personal circumstances since the fund must be able to cover practically any major financial contingency.

This money can be stored in different ways: In savings accounts, deposits or funds. The only requirement is that it must have immediate liquidity; in other words, the money must be available at short notice.

You may think that having this money sitting there doing nothing is not the best option because it will gradually lose value due to inflation. And that there is an opportunity cost in not investing it in something more profitable. But you need to be clear about the nature of this fund, and the objective is not profitability at all; but the financial peace of mind that comes from knowing that you have a certain financial safeguard on which you can call immediately.

Financial Statement Analysis

Being aware of your current position is key to protecting yourself and enabling you to make better decisions. And there is no better way to do this than to keep track of your financial statements.

The balance sheet (assets/liabilities) and the profit and loss account (income/expenses) are two financial statements that provide us with a true picture of our economic situation and that help us to make better decisions.

These concepts are used in the professional field for the analysis and valuation of companies; but they can be of tremendous help to us for our personal use, since the principles on which they are based wholly apply to the analysis of our personal finances.

Don't lie to yourself, be objective in your analysis. This is the only way to understand your current financial situation and to be able to develop a plan for achieving your goals. The aim is to understand where your income and expenses come from; as well as how much is saved and invested.

You need to know exactly how much you spend on each category of product and service. Without this kind of knowledge, it will be difficult to control your expenses. If you can't control your spending, it's unlikely you'll be able to save first and invest later.

Profit and loss account

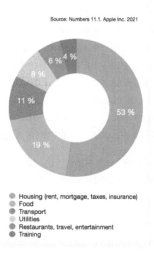

Source: Numbers 11.1. Apple Inc. 2021

Income	
Salary	3.600 €
Additional income	0 €
Total income	3.600 €

Expenses	
Housing (rent, mortgage, taxes, insurance)	1.350 €
Food	500 €
Transport	270 €
Utilities	200 €
Restaurants, travel, entertainment	150 €
Training	100 €
Total expenses	2.570 €

Profit/Loss	
Income minus expenses	1.030 €

- Housing (rent, mortgage, taxes, insurance)
- Food
- Transport
- Utilities
- Restaurants, travel, entertainment
- Training

As I said, the best way to do this is by analyzing your personal financial statements as if you were a company. You can use specific accounting software, although a simple Excel spreadsheet should be more than enough.

Below are some basic models for you to start implementing this process. There are two main aspects to this: first, the profit and loss account for which you should write down all your income and expenses; and second, the balance sheet, which should include your assets and liabilities.

Balance sheet

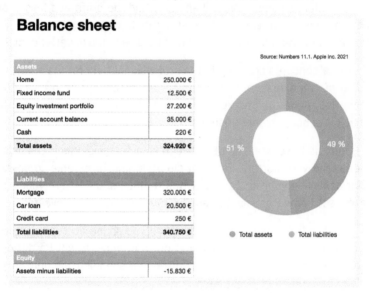

Assets	
Home	250.000 €
Fixed income fund	12.500 €
Equity investment portfolio	27.200 €
Current account balance	35.000 €
Cash	220 €
Total assets	**324.920 €**

Liabilities	
Mortgage	320.000 €
Car loan	20.500 €
Credit card	250 €
Total liabilities	**340.750 €**

Equity	
Assets minus liabilities	-15.830 €

Source: Numbers 11.1. Apple Inc. 2021

51 %   49 %

● Total assets   ● Total liabilities

The more detailed the list, the more accurate the picture you will paint of your financial position. When filling in the Assets section in the Balance Sheet, you should include any assets that have value, and try to make an objective estimate of what their sale price could be today; the purchase price isn't relevant. For example, your car is not actually an asset since it doesn't put money in your pocket; in fact it is a liability because down the line it will require certain maintenance expenses; but if you were to sell it, it would have a residual value and this is what you should include in the list. You can do this with each of your assets, although the sensible thing to do would be to take into account only those of greater economic importance.

This will allow you to analyze very quickly and visually how you are using your money, where most of the money is being spent and what percentage of your income is being saved.

Staying up to date with the analysis of your financial statements doesn't require a great deal of effort and it offers the major benefit of revealing the state of your finances. Thanks to this information, you will be able to detect possible leaks that jeopardize your financial health and eliminate them quickly. Update your accounts on the same day every month if possible.

Budgets

A budget is a preliminary list with varying time frames (annual, monthly) which is used to estimate the income we will receive and to determine how we will allocate that income to expenses, savings and investment.

To prepare one, we need to know what our income and expenses are, as well as the objectives we have set ourselves since this will determine how we distribute it across different categories.

A budget is tremendously useful for achieving the goals we have set ourselves. If you are currently at the stage where you are creating an emergency fund, most of your savings should be dedicated to this section; while if you already have this fund, you may want to start preparing your investment forecasts; and break these down into different items depending on your objectives.

Although it can vary for each family unit, a good basic model to follow is the 50/30/20 rule, which allocates the percentage of income in the following way:

- Fixed expenses: 50%

- Savings or Investment: 30%

- Variable expenses / Leisure: 20%

Obviously, the ideal thing to do is dedicate the minimum to expenses and the maximum to savings and investment. This means that if our earning capacity is high and our income far exceeds our expenses, we don't necessarily need to "invent" new expenses to account for this 50%. Ideally we would dedicate the remainder to savings and investment.

These percentages should be seen as a rule of thumb and as I say, they simply represent a framework on which to reflect. If we cannot save 20 or 30% of our income, we should endeavor to save at least 10%. The best way to achieve this is to pay ourselves first; as soon as we obtain an income, we should automatically set aside 10% of it and use the rest to cover expenses or other needs.

Some people prefer to distribute their income differently and donate a percentage of their income to causes they care about. We can set aside a percentage of the total for this type of allocation according to our interests. The idea is that this percentage should include any aspect not included in the other categories.

INVESTMENT

Investing is all about buying assets that are expected to generate future returns.

What should you invest in? As Sergio Fernández says in his book "Financial Freedom", when you yourself or other people ask you that question, the answer will always be: "in yourself, in your education, until you stop asking yourself the question".

Because to invest you need knowledge as well as money. If an investment seems very risky to you, that is basically because you don't know enough about it. So study it thoroughly until you can minimize the risk as much as possible. The risk we assume is directly proportional to our knowledge. The more knowledge you have, the more capable you will be of finding good opportunities and the greater the probability that your investments will be successful.

A very important point to keep in mind, in order to maintain realistic expectations, is that you don't have to be a full-time investor. Ideally you should start investing while still working in your main job and start to grow that other facet, your plan B, little by little.

As previously mentioned, there are different types of assets which you can invest in. The first step is to decide which type you are going to specialize in, and from there, implement strategies that allow you to obtain a high level of specialization.

Just as I recommended not having a single source of income, the same principle applies here and you should try to diversify across different investment channels. The objective is again to ensure that our financial health does not depend exclusively on the implementation of a single investment model.

What is the ideal approach? Well, continuing with what I just mentioned, the ideal thing would be to have a diversified portfolio made up of investments of all kinds: financial instruments, real estate, businesses, etc.

This book deals specifically with investments in financial assets. The goal is to provide you with the basic knowledge you need to be able to approach the market in the best possible conditions.

3 steps prior to investing

1. Work to increase income and reduce expenses.

2. Eliminate bad debt.

3. Save to create an emergency fund.

Determining Your Investor Profile

One of your first steps as an investor is to determine your investor profile. This will help you when looking for the financial products that best suit your needs.

Because investing is inherently associated with risk, it is vitally important that you know what sort of person you are, in terms of how you cope with risk.

The investor profile categorizes people depending on their degree of risk aversion. Risk aversion is an individual's preference for avoiding uncertainty and this can vary depending on many factors: financial health, earning capacity, knowledge and even prejudices, among other things.

A person who is unwilling to take major risks and who prioritizes safety is categorized as risk averse and should therefore look for investments that have lower risk and return ratios. You cannot realistically look for a higher rate without accepting an equally high risk.

Conversely, the risk prone investor is characterized by having a greater capacity to endure in difficult moments. They have a serenity that enables them to look for investments with a higher return (and risk).

When determining your profile you need to analyze your current financial situation, your financial objectives and the time available to achieve them. But this can sometimes be too theoretical; everything looks easy on paper. My recommendation is that you think about and determine what amount you consider significant and how you would feel if you were currently losing it on an investment. This simple exercise can guide you on which profile is best for you and which financial instruments to look for.

If you feel that you cannot emotionally bear a loss of a few hundred euros, you are more than likely not ready for an investment where you need to take a certain amount of risk.

If you have ever invested in a product that your bank has sold you, and have become nervous when seeing latent losses of twenty or fifty euros, your profile would be very risk averse and it may even be that investing simply isn't for you.

It is important to reflect on the risk assumed in investments and analyze whether it is compatible with your financial situation and your willingness to accept losses should they occur.

PROTECTION

This aspect of the financial equation is aimed at providing peace of mind and well-being.

The best way to protect our personal finances, at least at the outset, is by eliminating debt and ensuring we have enough liquidity to protect us from unexpected events (the emergency fund). This first level of protection can help us survive moderately severe contingencies such as accidents, theft, loss of employment, etc.

But we always need to consider the possibility of an extremely serious situation arising, one that could result in total financial collapse, such as disability or death, loss of our home and even loss of assets resulting from a civil liability claim.

To be able to cover this kind of risk, a second layer of protection is required, basically one made up of personal insurance. Insurance must be tailored depending on the age, marital status, dependent family members, income, assets, health, etc. of each person.

Asset and Civil Liability Insurance

We can divide insurance policies into those that protect your assets from the point of view of guaranteeing compensation for material losses of goods you own; and those that protect you in the event of civil liability claims that you could incur for damages to third parties deriving from actions for which you are responsible.

Some of the most important are listed below:

Asset insurance

- **Life insurance**. Offers protection against the death and disability of the insured, with their next of kin as the beneficiaries. It is important that this include cover for any outstanding loans, such as a mortgage.

- **Home insurance**. Protects against material damage that affects the structure and contents of the insured home. This type of insurance should include at least cover against fire, flood, theft and breakage of glass among other things.

- **Credit insurance**. Protects you from the risk of defaulting clients or debtors associated to commercial credit transactions carried out by your business.

- **Rent guarantee insurance**. Ensures cover against default tenants, vandalism, misappropriation.

Civil liability insurance

Insurance that protects personal assets from claims for economic, material or personal damages caused to the client as a result of errors or negligence committed in the performance of professional activity.

How To Avoid Possible Scams

This section deals with protecting capital not directly, but indirectly. I always like to say that not losing money is just as important as making it. And this section deals with the latter.

Below are a series of clues that could alert us to a possible snake oil seller or directly to a scammer.

The magic formula

Thanks to advances in technology, the internet today is flooded with a tremendous range of products and services for practically anything. Gurus have appeared out of nowhere promising us the Holy Grail for whatever it is you are looking to achieve.

The most common message used by the most aggressive salespeople involves presenting a product with a magic formula that combines success, speed and ease. As simple as that. Achieve your goals easily and in a very short time. If you ever hear this slogan promoting any particular product or service, do a runner!

It only takes a bit of common sense to reach the conclusion that this approach does not stand up to scrutiny and that it is clearly misleading and unrealistic. Mastering a subject and reaching a high degree of specialization requires many hours of study, as well as experience; the very opposite of what is promised with this approach.

Bear in mind that if something were that easy to do, everyone would be doing it and earning a lot of money. This is simply not the case.

Lifestyle

This is another common feature among those selling something with the sole objective of obtaining people's money while adding no value.

This approach uses persuasion by targeting people's basic instincts such as the desire to have a better life. Some directly involve material goods, "Do you want to have a car like this and live a dream life?", and others appeal indirectly by recording adverts with idyllic landscapes in the background. In short, it is the same strategy based on neuroscience applied to sales: apply certain stimuli to activate the emotional part of the brain and encourage impulse buying.

To a greater or lesser extent, we are all exposed to this, because a large part of these stimuli are received unconsciously. The key here to avoid potential scams is to be aware of the use of these types of strategies. No honest seller who offers you a product or service will appeal to your lifestyle to make the sale; they will try to demonstrate the differentiated value of their product, a value from which you will benefit if you buy it.

Realistic expectations

In most cases we ourselves make terrible purchasing decisions simply because we are guided by a conceptual framework that is totally wrong.

A lot of the people interested in this world of trading and investing see it as a way of making money quickly and without too much effort, which makes them susceptible to getting tangled up in the web of those sellers who target the trigger points that activate them emotionally. It's a negative feedback loop.

Keep your expectations realistic, I would say even low. It is the only way to survive in the market for any significant time. If you think that you are going to get rich here, it may be better not to even start, because you will be hugely disappointed.

I always tell anyone who asks me this not to even bother. The odds (statistically speaking) are that you will lose money. But this doesn't have to be the case. The amount of time, money, and effort it takes until you start to see the light (assuming you are on the right track) is daunting.

And I mean just being profitable in absolute terms; in other words, not losing money. Which is a long way from the idea of "making a living from trading".

This is another interesting point. Being profitable does not mean becoming rich. High returns require a lot of capital in the first place. We are talking about a few hundred thousand euros (as long as you manage your risk properly, of course). So, things are no longer as straight-forward as they seem.

The most logical and sensible approach is to start trading on the market once you have some financial stability, once you have an important source of income and certain savings, with the sole objective of trying to make them profitable. And that's it; don't start outthinking you're going to get rich here by investing.

Critical attitude

Analyze, study and compare objectively. Find out about the seller, what is their experience? If you are looking for someone to teach you about a subject, you want them to be reputable and to be able to evaluate their work in some way. Obtaining references is essential before taking that first step towards purchasing a product or service.

Also take advantage of the opinions of other customers. Nowadays it is practically impossible to control everything that an audience says, so research the opinions of other customers who have already bought the product. But cross reference these opinions because there may be a hidden agenda and they may sometimes be manipulated in some way.

Carefully analyze the seller's message. If they promise you will be able to live off your investments, ask yourself first if they live off theirs. This is one of the most basic assessment filters since it will give you a true picture of how honest this "expert" is.

Be very careful with anything that comes with the word "free"; generally if it is free it is because the product is you. Books, classes, courses, seminars etc. any means can be used to get your attention in the first place, seduce you and to ultimately try to sell you something. It is what is known in Marketing as a sales funnel. It is a process made up of different stages through which the potential client is guided with the sole objective of making the sale.

A true professional of the subject creates a school, is innovative and offers a unique never-before-seen value proposition. This is important to keep in mind because most products sold online are simply copied content from other sources with a bit of a facelift. Ask yourself if the person who is trying to sell you their product is an expert and is followed by other professionals in the sector.

When contracting any product or service, identify possible conflicts of interest. This basically applies when opening an account with a broker, contracting a banking product or even when obtaining financial advice from a professional.

Ultimately it is about maintaining a critical attitude towards life in general and trading in particular. This is an industry that is very badly abused by some and you have to tread very carefully to not fall into certain traps.

We have to do our job as consumers. We have all the means at our disposal thanks to the internet, which has broken down all the barriers. Let's take advantage of these conditions to improve our decision making.

PART 2. TRADING IN FINANCIAL MARKET: THE BASICS

This section offers an introduction to the financial markets. As with any subject matter, we first need to understand the theory before approaching the practical side of things. In this section we will study the main financial theories that will provide us with the necessary conceptual foundations, the investment products that we might come across and their characteristics, and a final more entertaining section on how prices are generated.

Financial markets are spaces in which financial instruments are traded between economic agents. This interaction between buyers and sellers, under the law of supply and demand, is what ultimately determines the price of assets.

The main objective of financial markets is to facilitate trading; in other words, to put those (be they companies or States) looking for financing to carry out their activity in contact with those who offer investment in search of a return.

As well as acting as intermediaries and promoting competitive pricing, markets provide liquidity, leading to a reduction in intermediation costs and a more efficient allocation of resources.

Types of Markets

There are different types of financial markets depending on the criteria used to evaluate them, the most important being:

According to the negotiation phase:

- **Primary**. Where new securities are issued, such as public debt or corporate bonds.

- **Secondary**. Where already issued securities are traded, such as stocks or derivatives.

According to the degree of formalization:

- **Centralized**. Public and transparent negotiation in organized markets.

- **Decentralized**. OTC (Over The Counter). Transactions occur privately, outside of centralized markets.

According to the type of asset

- **Money market**. Where money and other short-term assets such as loans, treasury bills are traded.

- **Capital market**. This includes the fixed income, variable income and derivatives markets. Here assets with a higher level of risk are traded, such as stocks, and assets with medium and long-term maturities such as debt.

According to the moment of payment:

- **Spot market.** This involves an exchange between agents in which the payment is executed instantly or, at most, within two days. In general, their use is more tangible rather than speculative. Participants tend to make use of this market based on real needs.

- **Markets based on future maturity**. These markets involve the application of future maturities to the purchase or sale of an asset; in other words, the execution of the agreement is postponed to sometime in the future. Two of the most important derivatives markets within the institutional world are the futures and options markets. They are more speculative in nature and are often used by large agents as instruments to hedge risk.

FINANCIAL THEORIES

Economists have always had a special interest in describing the behavior of financial markets in the most realistic way possible, which has led to a series of theories being postulated for this purpose.

Based on the rationality or irrationality of the agents, all the hypotheses were aimed at defending the efficiency or inefficiency of the market with respect to information with the ability to influence the asset price (that which already exists and that which will be generated).

The first major accepted theory was the efficient market hypothesis, after which a new way of thinking emerged, the theory of behavioral finance. More recently a new approach has been postulated: the adaptive market hypothesis. I will try to explain the most important points of each of them below.

The Efficient Market Hypothesis (EMH)

Put forward by Eugene Fama in the 1960s, its underlying principle is the rationality of market agents and therefore the efficiency of market prices in reflecting all available information.

The concept of efficiency is based on the idea of random walk theory (Burton G. Malkiel, "A Random Walk Down Wall Street"); a model which demonstrates that price evolves in the form of random and unpredictable movements, making it impossible, according to this hypothesis, to identify patterns of behavior that might produce opportunities to obtain returns on a recurring basis.

The reasoning is that when new information that could change the intrinsic value of a particular asset appears, the news spreads so quickly that it is incorporated into the price almost immediately making it impossible to take advantage of the new information.

According to this hypothesis, neither fundamental analysis nor technical analysis are useful in providing the investor with an advantage with which to generate returns above what could be obtained randomly.

There are different forms of this hypothesis:

- **Weak form**: Prices reflect all historical information. In this form, the hypothesis disregards the usefulness of Technical Analysis as a tool for predicting future price movements.

- **Semi-strong form**: Prices reflect, in addition to historical information, all current publicly available information. In this form, the hypothesis disregards the usefulness of Fundamental Analysis, since public information already includes any estimates that might be generated from the analysis of financial statements.

- **Strong form**: Prices include all the information available past and present, both public and private.

Over time and in view of the extraordinary, above market average returns that some investors have consistently managed to generate, it has been empirically demonstrated that the postulates of said hypothesis may not be completely true and doubts have been casted on whether market prices fully reflect all available information.

Another behavioral factor which suggests that this theory is not entirely adequate is that most irrational of actions that sometimes occurs in the market: a bubble. If agents were really rational in their actions these bubbles would not appear. It seems logical to think that as long as human beings continue to be an important part of the decision-making process when it comes to intervening in financial markets, bubbles, as well as other emotionally biased behaviors, will continue to occur.

Behavioral Finance (BF) Theory

At the beginning of the 21st century, the efficient market hypothesis began to increasingly lose influence due to the empirical evidence of the existence of anomalies.

Anomalies are inefficiencies; patterns of price behavior that offer opportunities for obtaining returns.

Many financial economists began to emphasize the psychological and behavioral elements that affect financial market participants and a new alternative theoretical framework known as Behavioral Finance (BF) emerged.

This theory studies the influence of psychology on the behavior of agents. It is based on the fact that agents are not perfectly rational; the behavioral biases and cognitive limitations of agents lead them to act in a certain way, resulting in inefficiencies emerging in the price formation process.

It focuses on how agents interpret information and make their decisions based on this; decisions that are not always based on impartial reasoning.

Contrary to what the Efficient Market Hypothesis postulates, according to Behavioral Finance, the pricing of assets is not random, rather it is unpredictable because the reaction of agents to newly generated information is also unpredictable.

Behavioral finance is comprised of a series of overarching elements that encompass most of the irrational behaviors of agents, as well as a series of biases that govern decision-making to a lesser extent:

- **Mental accounting**. This refers to the fact that each agent allocates their capital based on their own preferences, to whatever offers them the greatest utility. These preferences will differ depending on a multitude of factors.

- **Herd behavior**. We tend to mimic the behavior of the majority, to the extent that we may disregard our own independent evaluations. This is what causes large rises and falls in the market, such as bubbles.

- **Emotions**. Decision making can be skewed by extreme emotions such as anxiety, anger, fear, or excitement.

- **Overconfidence**. The tendency to overestimate our skills, knowledge and capabilities, which can cause us to make incorrect assessments.

- **Confirmation bias**. The tendency to seek out and accept information that is in line with our beliefs. If we believe that a stock is going to rise, we will look for all the information that confirms our hypothesis, even if it has no basis in fact.

- **Experience bias**. Our most recent experiences hugely influence our future decision-making.

- **Loss aversion**. In general terms, this involves prioritizing avoiding loss over obtaining profits, which could lead us to discard an investment with a rationally acceptable level of risk.

- **Familiarity bias**. The tendency to invest in what we know, which can lead to inefficient diversification.

Many financial economists still dismiss this theory of behavioral finance, alluding to a lack of a philosophical and theoretical basis; in addition to the absence of scientific studies to back it up.

The Adaptive Market Hypothesis (AMH)

Presented by economist Andrew Lo in 2004, this theory adopts a more holistic view of markets, by trying to reconcile insights from the efficient market hypothesis with behavioral finance and psychology. It does not assume that the previous two theories are wrong, but incomplete.

In the author's words: "Behavioral anomalies and efficient markets are opposite sides of the same coin: they reflect the dual nature of human behavior". The fact is sometimes we're rational and sometimes we're emotional. Usually we're a bit of both".

AMH is based on the evolution and adaptability of agents. This hypothesis implies that behaviors are constructed and shaped by the continuous interaction of the agent's own internal reasoning, together with the external conditions of the current environment.

This new approach is situated somewhere between the two previous theories: the agent is not assumed to be rational or irrational. Instead, depending on market conditions, agents will act in one way or another. In a stable environment agents will act more rationally, while in an unstable, volatile environment, with excessive uncertainty, different behavioral biases will be activated that will lead them to act in a more irrational way, in order to overcome the challenges they face.

This theory does not assume that the market is either efficient or inefficient. Rather it depends on the moment, due to the flow of information and the importance of a changing environment.

We are not all the same, nor do we react in the same way. Moreover, the same person may react differently to the same event depending on the situation. It is also worth emphasizing that each person behaves differently depending on their appetite for risk, and the degree of this will also be influenced to a great extent by the context of the market at the time.

The particular conditions of the market and our own situation as traders all come into play here; and both evolve over time.

This theory has been generally accepted in the financial world, especially by managers and investors who trade daily in the financial markets, and who recognize that adaptation is the key to survival. Meanwhile, in academic circles, this theory is viewed with some skepticism, mainly because it has not been presented in a purely mathematical and quantitative way.

MAIN FINANCIAL INVESTMENT PRODUCTS

Financial investment products are instruments which are transferred into funds by economic agents, in other words, an exchange of resources for assets.

But the issuer also transfers the risk inherent in the asset. And this is one of the characteristics of financial assets: risk. This, together with liquidity and profitability, gives rise to the different categories of assets that can be found on the markets.

As a general rule, products that offer higher profitability also have higher risk and lower liquidity; and in contrast, the lower the profitability, the lower the risk and the higher the liquidity.

Fixed Income

These are negotiable securities issued by companies and public institutions with the peculiarity that the return that said investment will generate if it is held until maturity can be estimated in advance, since issuers are obliged to pay the amount stipulated during the previously established period.

However, these securities are not risk-free. The final return may differ from what is initially expected, depending on the structural characteristics of each fixed income security. This is because some fixed income securities are subject to variable interest rates, which are adjusted periodically.

Examples of fixed income products include treasury bills, government bonds and obligations, as well as any type of debt from public bodies. Private sector products include promissory notes, corporate bonds, covered bonds, obligations, etc.

These types of assets can be useful as a means of preserving capital and in order to obtain a predictable return.

VARIABLE INCOME

The fundamental characteristic of this type of asset is that it is impossible to know at the time of purchase what the future yield will be and even whether the initial capital will be returned, making these considerably more risky than fixed income products.

Stocks

Stocks are the star variable income product. Stocks are securities that grant the holders a proportional part of the ownership of a company.

Stocks are traded on regulated cash markets known as Stock Exchanges.

Investing in stocks can generate a return in two ways:

- **Evolution of the stock price**. A return may be generated from a rise in the stock price as a result of the company's appreciation. Keep in mind that any gains or losses only become effective when the stock is finally sold, not before.

- **Payment of dividends**. This involves the distribution of profits obtained by the company among its shareholders. It is an appealing form of passive income but it requires a large capital investment if the earnings are to be significant.

Types of stocks:

- **Growth stocks**. These rarely pay dividends and investors buy them in the hope that they will earn money through capital gains.

- **Income stocks.** Investors buy them primarily for the dividends they consistently pay.

- **Value stocks**. These can be growth or income securities. They have a low price-earnings ratio, which means that they are cheap in accounting terms. They are acquired in the hope that the market will eventually recognize their value and the price will rebound.

- **Blue-chips**. These are well-known, large cap companies with a strong history of growth, offering the investor confidence and stability. They generally pay dividends.

Another way to categorize stocks is based on their capitalization. Capitalization is the total value of the company. It is obtained by multiplying the stock price by the total stock outstanding. This allows us to distinguish between three main categories:

- **Large-cap stocks**. These are the largest and most stable companies with a capitalization of more than 10 billion US dollars. They tend to be traded on the main stock market indexes.

- **Mid-cap stocks**. They usually have a capitalization of between 2 and 10 billion dollars. They offer better growth potential compared to large caps, but in return they also present a greater risk as they do not yet have as much stability.

- **Small-cap stocks**. Companies whose market value is somewhere between 300 million and 2 billion dollars. These characteristically have high growth potential and high risk and volatility.

Investment Funds

Investment funds are participation based collective investment institutions whose price or market value is the net asset value calculated by dividing the total equity of the fund by the number of stocks outstanding.

The most advantageous and characteristic aspect of investment funds is the way they are taxed, since any profit or loss does not become effective for the investor until they collect the definitive payment, allowing tax-free transfers between funds (disbursement from a fund for subscription to another fund).

There is a wide range of investment funds depending on the financial assets that comprise them: monetary, fixed income, variable income, mixed, passive management, absolute return, global, among others.

Exchange traded funds (ETFs)

These are investment funds which are traded on secondary markets, in the same way as stocks or derivatives.

This gives this kind of fund a huge advantage over traditional funds, since it offers total flexibility when buying and selling (real-time quotes) while in traditional funds the transactions are executed according to the market value, which is determined at the close of the day.

ETFs are index funds whose objective is to replicate as accurately as possible the evolution of the index on which they are based.

As well as these funds that follow the evolution of the market, the ETF range also includes others of an inverse nature and others with different leverages; offering us total accessibility to the market.

Derivatives

Derivatives are instruments whose value derives from the evolution of other financial assets such as stocks, as well as tangible (real) assets such as raw materials or precious metals. These other assets, from which the derivatives are created are known as underlying assets.

Although these types of products are also often used to take advantage of directional pricing, they are mainly used by large institutions to reduce the risk of price movements in their portfolios through so-called hedging trades.

Hedging is nothing more than taking an equivalent position in the opposite direction to the one you already have in a spot market. This allows you to offset any potential loss in that initial position with a potential gain in this open position with a derivative. This type of strategy is possible because prices in the spot and derivatives markets are fully correlated, moving in unison, thanks to arbitration mechanisms.

Clearing House

A clearing house is a financial institution that is responsible for ensuring that the obligations of the agents are fulfilled. In order to do this, guarantees must first be provided as a means of reducing the counterparty risk (the possibility of a breach of the acquired obligation). These guarantees act as a deposit, which is recovered when the position is closed.

If one of the two parties does not comply with its obligation, it is the clearing house that bears the losses generated by that defaulting party.

The main drawback of clearing houses is that the guarantees required are usually high, which leads many agents to negotiate in non-centralized markets (OTC) which offer easier accessibility, as they require smaller guarantees.

Main derivative instruments:

Futures

The futures market is an organized (centralized) market where agents agree to the obligatory exchange of a specified quantity of an asset at a future date and at a specified price.

Type of trade	Sentiment	Expectation
Buying a Future	Bullish	That the price will go up
Selling a Future	Bearish	That the price will go down

Contracts can be settled in two ways: through an offset transaction, which involves selling in the event that a purchase contract has been opened (and vice versa); or through the physical delivery of the underlying asset upon expiry of the contract, a settlement that occurs rarely.

Futures are subject to expiration dates. The expiration date establishes the useful life of the contract. Generally, trading takes place on the contract with the nearest expiration date, unless there are only a few days left on it and the next contract with a later expiration is already trading at a higher volume.

When the expiration date is reached, the position is closed automatically. To keep it open, a manual rollover must be performed, which implies transferring the position to the next expiration. In essence it is a simultaneous purchase and sale transaction.

Options

Options are also listed on a centralized market where, unlike Futures, there is an obligation to fulfill the agreement. Options contracts grant the buyer the right, but not the obligation, to execute the purchase or sale of the traded asset on the expiration date. The selling party, however, is obliged to buy or sell if the buyer executes this right.

The role assumed by each party in the contract is of vital importance, since they have substantially differential conditions. While the buyer always has limited losses and unlimited gains, the seller is subject to unlimited losses and limited gains.

This is because the buyer only has rights, which means that their loss is limited to the value of the premium (option price), while the seller always collects the premium (whether the contract is finally exercised or not) but the nature of their role means they are obliged to bear potentially unlimited losses (which would be the buyer's unlimited gains).

Types of options

- **CALL**. Right to buy.

- **PUT**. Right to sell.

Type of trade	Sentiment	Expectation
Buying a Call	Bullish	That the price will go up
Buying a Put	Bearish	That the price will go down
Selling a Call	Sideways/Bearish	That the price will not go up
Selling a Put	Sideways/Bullish	That the price will not go down

Classification of options depending on the situation

- An option is "**In the money**" if the buyer makes a profit when exercising it. The price of the underlying asset is higher in the case of a CALL and lower in the case of a PUT.

- An option is "**Out of the money**" if no profit is made when exercising it. The price of the underlying asset is lower than the strike price of the CALL or higher in the case of a PUT.

- An option is "**At the money**" if it is on the edge of generating a profit or loss because the strike price and the spot price of the underlying asset are almost identical.

Other derivatives

- **Warrants**. These are products that incorporate the right, but not the obligation, to buy or sell the underlying asset on the expiration date

- **Forward**. A private contract between two agents whose transaction expiration is postponed to a specific future date and is executed in a non-centralized market. In essence, it is the same as a futures contract with the exception that in Forwards the agents set the conditions according to their needs, whereas in Futures the conditions are standardized.

- **Swap**. A private contract executed in a non-centralized market through which cash flows are exchanged at a future date.

- **CFDs**. Contracts for Difference. These are contracts between two parties, executed in non-centralized markets, which can generate profits from the price movement of the underlying asset, without the need to own it. They are Spot markets whose expiration is immediate.

Stock Market Indexes

An index is a product made up of pool of listed assets that meet certain characteristics.

An index is comprised in two main ways:

- **Depending on the price**. Through the arithmetic mean of the price of the securities that comprise it. This involves adding the price of all the securities and dividing it by the total number of securities.

- **Depending on the value**. This is the most commonly used method. It is based on the capitalization of each security, with each one having a greater or lesser influence on the evolution of the price of the index depending on its market value.

This is very useful for understanding the general behavior of that group of assets and for analyzing its comparative strengths and weaknesses.

Moreover, since indexes are used as a benchmark or reference point, managers and investors often take them into account when evaluating yield. Say you have obtained an 8% return this year. Does that sound good? Well it depends: if your benchmark index shows a 30% return, then your yield hasn't been so good.

For the vast majority of investors, a benchmark index can be tremendously useful as an investment instrument, since it includes all the securities that comprise it. This means that managers, or we as investors, don't have to worry about selecting the securities we think are going to generate the highest return.

Below is a list of some of the major stock market indexes:

Index	Country / Zone	Companies
S&P500	USA	500
Dow Jones	USA	30
Nasdaq 100	USA	100
FTSE 100	UK	100
CAC 40	France	40
DAX 30	Germany	30
FTSE MIB	Italy	40
IBEX 35	Spain	35
Eurostoxx 50	Europe	50
Nikkei 225	Japan	225
Bovespa	Brazil	50

The best known and most important benchmark index is the S&P500 (Standard & Poor's 500), made up of the 500 companies with the largest market value listed on the US stock market. The evolution of this index is taken as the best indicator of US equities, and one of the most reliable indicators for assessing the health of the economy.

There are several ways of investing in these types of products; from spot trading, investment funds or ETFs, to derivatives.

Foreign Exchange

The currency or Forex (Foreign Exchange) market is the financial market that records the most transactions, making it the largest in the world.

Apart from its extreme liquidity, its main characteristic is its accessibility, since it is open 24 hours a day (only closed on weekends).

Agents use it to exchange currency. And to do so, this market is structured around currency pairs. These pairs are made up of the base currency (first) and the quote currency (second).

The main currencies based on trading volume are as follows:

Ranking	Currency	% daily trades
1	US dollar	88,3 %
2	Euro	32,3 %
3	Japanese yen	16,8 %
4	Pound sterling	12,8 %
5	Australian dollar	6,8 %
6	Canadian dollar	5 %
7	Swiss franc	5 %
8	Chinese yuan	4,3 %
9	Hong Kong dollar	3,5 %
10	New Zealand Dollar	2,1 %

Currency pairs are classified as:

Main or Major

These are the most traded. They contain the US dollar as the base or quoted currency.

Symbol	Foreign exchange
EUR/USD	Euro / US Dollar
GBP/USD	Pound sterling / US dollar
USD/JPY	Australian dollar / US dollar
AUD/USD	Australian dollar / US dollar
NZD/USD	New Zealand dollar / US dollar
USD/CAD	US dollar / Canadian dollar
USD/CHF	US dollar / Swiss franc

Cross or Minor

They are also considerably liquid. They are made up of major currencies but do not include the US dollar. Some of the most important are:

Symbol	Foreign exchange
EUR/GBP	Euro / Pound sterling
EUR/AUD	Euro / Australian Dollar
EUR/NZD	Euro / New Zealand Dollar
EUR/JPY	Euro / Japanese Yen
EUR/CAD	Euro / Canadian dollar
EUR/CHF	Euro / Swiss Franc
GBP/AUD	Pound sterling / Australian dollar
GBP/NZD	Pound sterling / New Zealand dollar
GBP/JPY	Pound sterling / Japanese yen
GBP/CAD	Pound sterling / Canadian dollar
GBP/CHF	Pound sterling / Swiss franc
AUD/NZD	Australian dollar / New Zealand dollar
AUD/JPY	Australian dollar / Japanese yen
AUD/CAD	Australian dollar / Canadian dollar
AUD/CHF	Australian dollar / Swiss franc
NZD/JPY	New Zealand dollar / Japanese yen
NZD/CAD	New Zealand dollar / Canadian dollar
NZD/CHF	New Zealand dollar / Swiss franc
CAD/JPY	Canadian dollar / Japanese yen
CAD/CHF	Canadian dollar / Swiss franc
CHF/JPY	Swiss franc / Japanese yen

Exotic

Composed of a major currency and another from an emerging country or one with a weaker economy. Some of the most important are:

Symbol	Foreign exchange
USD/HKD	United States dollar / Hong Kong dollar
USD/SGD	US dollar / Singapore dollar
USD/DKK	US dollar / Danish krone
USD/SEK	US dollar / Swedish krona
USD/NOK	US dollar / Norwegian krone
USD/ZAR	US dollar / South African Rand
USD/MXN	US dollar / Mexican peso
USD/RUB	US dollar / Russian ruble
EUR/TRY	Euro / Turkish lira

The foreign exchange market is essentially affected by significant political and economic factors such as monetary policies, interest rates, inflation, unemployment, deficits, etc.

At a trading level and from a speculative point of view, it is important to understand that if we buy EUR/USD we are expecting the par value to rise, which basically means a strong euro and a weak US dollar. Conversely, if we sell or go short on EUR/USD we would profit if the price fell, indicating a weak euro and a strong US dollar.

The 10 most traded currency pairs in 2020 according to Statista were:

Ranking	Currency	% total trades
1	EUR/USD	27,95 %
2	USD/JPY	13,34 %
3	GBP/USD	11,27 %
4	AUD/USD	6,37 %
5	USD/CAD	5,22 %
6	USD/CHF	4,63 %
7	NZD/USD	4,08 %
8	EUR/JPY	3,93 %
9	GBP/JPY	3,57 %
10	EUR/GBP	2,78 %

Source: Statista. Leading forex currency pairs in 2020, by share of total trades

There are different standardized measures of amounts traded:

• Lot. 100,000 units of the main currency.

• Mini lot. 10,000 units of the main currency.

• Micro lot. 1000 units of the main currency.

Cryptocurrencies

Cryptocurrencies are a type of alternative, virtual currency.

One of their main characteristics is their use of cryptography as a means of securely guaranteeing transactions.

Their decentralized nature is another major advantage, since they are not subject to any company or government controlling their operation or structure. Moreover, thanks to blockchain technology there are no interme-diaries, which significantly reduces transaction costs.

There are currently thousands of cryptocurrencies, most of them with no real use. However there are a few with well-structured projects behind them, which aim to become a means of payment, unit of account and/or a means of storing value, the best known of which is Bitcoin.

Ranking	Cryptocurrency	Symbol	Capitalization (in millions of dollars)
1	Bitcoin	BTC	781,8
2	Ethereum	ETH	287,4
3	Tether	USDT	61,8
4	Binance Coin	BNB	54,2
5	Cardano	ADA	42,1
6	XRP	XRP	34,9
7	USD Coin	USDC	27,3
8	Dogecoin	DOGE	27,1
9	Polkadot	DOT	15,7
10	Uniswap	UNI	12,4

Source: Coinmarketcap.com. Agosto 2021

Bitcoin

This was the first cryptocurrency to come to light in 2009, presented by Satoshi Nakamoto in a paper that would impact the course of the world's economy.

It was presented as an alternative to the monetary system; a way to tackle the inflation generated by the monetary policies of Central Banks on traditional currencies. This monetary expansion was based on the uncontro-lled printing of new money, resulting in a continuous loss of value for these currencies.

Bitcoin proposes a new paradigm by trying to offer the same thing that traditional currencies offer with the significant advantage of eliminating potential inflation by limiting the maximum number of units put into circula-tion. In other words, new bitcoins cannot be generated from existing ones. There is only what is in circulation.

Raw Materials

Also known as commodities or basic goods. They are generally treated as inputs for commercial use, to manufacture other products.

There are different groups:

- **Metals**. Gold, silver, copper, platinum, aluminum, palladium.

- **Energy** Oil, Coal, Natural Gas.

- **Agricultural products and livestock**. Wheat, corn, oats, barley, soybeans, cocoa, coffee, sugar, pork, live or feeder cattle.

As well as physically purchasing the asset, we can also invest in raw materials through financial products such as Investment Funds, ETFs, Futures, etc.

TYPES OF PARTICIPANTS

A whole host of agents participate in the financial markets, trading in different ways based on their needs and requirements at that specific time.

We are in a better position to make trading and investment decisions if we know those that have the ability to influence price movements.

Market participants are traditionally divided into two broad categories depending on their objectives:

Hedgers

These are involved in the execution of financial trades aimed at canceling or reducing risk. These trades consist of purchasing or selling derivative products (such as futures and options) to manage the risk created by fluctuations in the price of the underlying asset.

While it is true that the main objective of hedging is to limit risk, it can also be used to secure a latent profit or preserve the value of a fixed asset.

These traders don't care in which direction the price goes, since this is not part of their core business. They do not trade with any directional intention, but with a more long-term vision.

Although there are different ways of hedging, the most traditional one focuses on the producer:

An example would be an airline company that buys oil futures as a way of balancing its fuel costs.

Another example would be a large international import and export company that purchases foreign exchange to hedge against possible price changes.

This makes it easier for companies to manage price risk and stabilizes the cost passed on to the end user.

Market makers would also be included in this category since they might go to the market, depending on their needs, in order to ensure the neutral risk of all their positions as a whole.

Speculators

Unlike hedgers, who basically trade to reduce their exposure to risk, speculative traders actively take on risk when they open their positions.

If, given the current market conditions, they believe that the price of the asset in question is cheap, they will buy. An vice versa if they consider it to be expensive. The sole aim is to obtain a profit from the price movement.

This category includes hedge funds, investment funds, trading firms and in general any institution that trades directionally in the market to seek profitability.

They trade under all sorts of different time frames and also execute trades using high-frequency algorithms. Their participation is vital since they provide most of the liquidity in the market, promoting its efficiency.

They are the most active players in the financial market. They basically focus on finding liquidity zones as, due to the large volumes they move, they need to find a counterparty to match their orders.

There is a very common misconception that all institutions are profitable. Many of these institutions are the preferred prey of agents in financial markets, because they move significant amounts of money and may have a weak trading model.

Although they are not purely speculative, some options traders could be included in this category as, if they have a large open position in the options market, it is very likely that they will also go to the futures market to try to defend them if necessary.

Other Types of Participants

In addition to hedgers and speculators, there are other players involved in market transactions.

Brokers

These are the financial institutions which act as intermediaries in the negotiations carried out by the participants.

As individuals, we cannot go directly to a financial market and make a transaction; we must approach a Broker to put us in a position to participate in the market.

Difference between Brokers and Dealers

- **Brokers** are merely intermediaries in charge of buying or selling assets under the instructions of their clients (on their behalf), for which they charge a fee.

- **Dealers**, as well as performing this role as intermediaries, they also have the power to buy or sell assets on their own behalf, and can act as direct counterparties to their clients.

Types of Broker

- **Dealing Desk**. This is where market makers manage the negotiations at their own dealing desk, therefore acting as a counterparty to their clients. In other words, the orders of their clients do not reach the real market where another participant would act as a counterparty, rather it is the broker itself that acts as the other party in the trade. The problem with this way of trading is that the broker's profits depend on the trader's performance because if the trader wins they lose and vice versa. This could lead to conflicts of interest for brokers who might potentially carry out unethical trades on price movements when forced to accept major losses.

- **No Dealing Desk**. Here there is no dealing desk involved. These Brokers go directly to the market to match the orders of their clients, acting as genuine intermediaries. Their profit is not related to the result of their clients' trades, eliminating the possibility of any conflict of interest. There are basically two types of NDD broker:

  - **ECN Brokers** (Electronic Communication Network). They connect traders with all market players.

  - **STP Brokers** (Straight Through Processing). They connect traders directly with their liquidity providers.

Market Makers

Market makers are financial entities, designated by the regulators of the market which they serve. Their function is to provide liquidity, continuously quoting both buy and sell prices on assets to ensure that all participants have their counterparty.

They exist for all types of markets: fixed income, variable income, derivatives and foreign exchange.

Their participation is very important since they are responsible for a significant amount of the liquidity that is provided in the markets, which enables large traders to participate without their actions having a substantial effect on the price.

They are also expected to act as price stabilizers in times of extreme volatility, when there is typically no counterparty in the market.

Market makers usually make a profit by sticking to the spread; the difference between the bid and ask prices.

HOW PRICES ARE FORMED

Prices are set through the continuous interaction between supply and demand; the supply being those who are willing to sell, and the demand those who are willing to buy.

This interaction starts from the basic and fundamental premise that for someone to buy, there must be someone willing to sell to them. In other words, there are always the same number of buyers and sellers in all markets and transactions.

Each buyer (demand) bids for a certain quantity at a certain price, and each seller (supply) offers or "asks" for a certain quantity at a certain price. When the buyer and seller agree, a transaction is executed.

The reasons behind both participants' decision to buy and sell can be endless: perhaps the seller needs the money, or one of the participants has obtained some important information about the asset, or they simply need to increase or reduce their exposure in that market as a way of managing their portfolio risk. Regardless of the reason, the price is established when all this information is collected, digested and acted upon through supply and demand.

Ultimately, for the market to rise, buyers have to be more aggressive than sellers; and for it to fall, the sellers will have to act with greater determination and drive than the buyers.

The Price Discovery Process

As mentioned previously, the main function of a financial market is to facilitate negotiation between its agents. To do this, the market will always seek to reach a point of equilibrium: that price level at which buyers and sellers are willing to negotiate. This basic principle, which governs how prices are established is determined by the law of supply and demand.

The law of supply and demand states that given certain prices and quantities, an increase in price will cause a decrease in demand and an increase in supply; and that a fall in price will cause a decrease in supply and an increase in demand.

To put it another way, as the price rises, there will be fewer and fewer buyers willing to continue buying, while sellers will become more motivated to sell (because both begin to see the price as expensive). Conversely, as the price falls, the seller's interest decreases and the buyers' increases (because both begin to see the price as cheap).

In today's markets, continuous supply/demand and buyer/seller interaction is based on a process of price discovery, which attempts to determine the market equilibrium price.

Markets reach different price levels in order to assess the interest or lack of interest generated for participants. If the market reaches a point where there are no participants interested in trading, either because they consider the price to be expensive or cheap, it will quickly return to a new zone in which these agents want to continue trading.

At a certain point in time, the price of an asset may begin to rise, due to a change in the perception and valuations of the agents, regardless of the origin of said change. The fact that the price continues to rise means that there are still participants interested in trading in that zone; and in particular, that there are buyers who have the initiative and aggressiveness to continue buying even when the price rises, mainly because they expect the price to continue rising.

What happens when you reach a price ceiling? What happens is that the price discovery process has come to an end: buyers are no longer interested in continuing to buy, possibly because they no longer see it as being cheap; and at the same time sellers are faced with a price rise that they consider excessive, presenting them with an interesting opportunity to sell in the expectation that the price will start to fall.

This process is repeated continuously over and over again in every single price movement. It is about discovering what interest the market participants have with respect to the level at which the asset is trading.

The Electronic Trading System

Financial markets have changed very quickly. In the beginning, financial trades were carried out physically by the traders who worked on the stock exchanges. If you wanted to buy or sell you had to go through them.

Little by little, access to financial markets was democratized, first by the possibility of carrying out transactions by telephone and subsequently, with the arrival of the Internet, enabling trades to be carried out entirely electronically through global routing systems.

This represents a huge turning point. Today anyone with a computer and internet connection can participate in the financial markets from their home, through trading and investment platforms. This globalization of the markets has given rise to an interconnection that allows us to buy and sell all types of assets regardless of where they are located.

Technological advances have given way to a new form of interaction between agents; and this electronification of the markets has made it possible to improve the efficiency of trading, making it much cheaper and faster, while also allowing easy access to the general public.

Electronic trading has helped level the playing field for the individual trader, by improving access to information on prices and trades. The speed and ease of execution of the trades, combined with the application of modern risk management, allow the individual trader to access markets and strategies that were previously reserved for institutions.

Randomness or Determinism

Randomness is based on the premise of market efficiency. Determinism (non-randomness) is based on its inefficiency.

The random market approach, as we have already seen, implies that the current price already reflects all the information of the events that occurred in the past and even of the events that the market expects to take place in the future. That is, all the information about the asset is entirely discounted and therefore it is not possible to predict the future price action.

The deterministic market approach suggests that price movements are influenced by external factors, so by knowing what these factors are, the future price action can be predicted. Therefore profits can be obtained by correctly interpreting the market.

When we talk about randomness, we refer to the fact that there is no logical intent behind the movement of the market; it is simply a price fluctuation. Randomness is born of the innumerable variables that exist in the market. No one can possibly know how the rest of the market participants are going to act. If someone knew, they would implement a deterministic system to predict the right outcome every single time.

On the one hand, if the Efficient Market Hypothesis and the randomness of the market were valid, no one would be able to obtain profits on a recurring basis. And history has shown that this is not the case. We all know big players in the financial markets who have managed to win with different approaches (technical, fundamental and quantitative).

On the other hand, financial markets cannot be modeled as a totally deterministic process in which there is no randomness. This would result in strategies with 100% probability of success and this (as far as we know) is not the case.

We are, therefore, led to the conclusion that financial markets are made up of a percentage of randomness and a percentage of determinism, though we cannot attribute a proportion to each.

This theory is supported by the Adaptive Market Hypothesis (AMH) which shows the efficiency of financial markets not as a characteristic that either exists or doesn't exist, but as a quality that varies according to market conditions (the environment, context), which are determined by the interactions between agents.

The same author of the Adaptive Markets Hypothesis, Professor Andrew Lo, published in 1988 a study with the title "Stock Market Prices Do Not Follow Random Walks: Evidence from a Simple Specification Test" which concluded, by using a simple mathematical model, that between September 1962 and December 1985, stock market returns were not random.

These tests against randomness show that prices can show deterministic behavior at certain times, which can offer us some kind of predictive power and, therefore, allow us to see an anomaly. The task of the trader is to identify and exploit this advantage.

PART 3. TRADING AND INVESTING USING COMMON SENSE

T he sole objective of trading in financial markets, whether you are trading or investing, is to obtain a return on your allocated capital, while maintaining, where possible, a controlled risk.

There are different ways of playing the market. In this part of the book we will broadly address the different available analyses, trades and strategies in which we can specialize, to tip the chances of success in our favor. We will also review some of the most important concepts we need to know, as well as useful information for the trader or investor.

How Can You Make Money in the Financial Markets?

The main way a particular financial asset can make us money is **through its price movement**, be that up or down.

If, based on our analysis, we expect the price of an asset to rise, we can buy that asset in order to later sell it at a higher price and obtain the difference as profit.

Similarly, we can profit from a fall in prices. This is what is known as selling short, or simply "shorting". We will address this concept later, but it basically involves selling an asset in the belief that its price will fall only to then buy it again later, keeping the difference as profit.

The underlying reason why price movements occur is due to discrepancies in current price valuations by agents. In other words, if the price of an asset is low according to the valuations of the participants in that market, they will want to take advantage of that discount and will buy, making it rise until it reaches a new, higher, equilibrium price.

This is the classic type of trade where you can make money from a price increase. But as I mentioned, it is also possible to make money from a fall in price. If market agents believe an asset is expensive, they will sell it, causing the price to fall until it reaches levels which they consider to be fair according to their valuations.

Additionally, in the case of stocks, it is also possible to earn money **by receiving dividends**. As explained previously, dividends are part of the company's profits, distributed among all its shareholders. Here the investor seeks to build a portfolio with stocks that provide high dividends so that, together, they offer a moderate long-term return. The advantage of this form of investing is that the moment of entry is not important. Basically the main goal is not the revaluation of the asset, but the security offered by the return of a stable dividend.

The fundamental disadvantage of dividend investing is that it requires large amounts of capital to deliver a significant return. With an average dividend of 5%, in order to obtain €20,000 per year you would need to invest €400,000, which could imply a serious opportunity cost. This is why it is not a highly recommended strategy for those who do not have a large amount of capital. It is more suitable for those who have a great deal of wealth and are looking to stabilize their portfolio in some way.

In general, the way to earn money in financial markets is not very different from that of other markets, such as real estate, in which a property owner can obtain returns in two ways: either by renting (the equivalent of receiving dividends in the stock market), or through the capital gains earned from the purchase and sale of the property (revaluation of the price).

Difference Between Trading and Investing

When we talk about trading or investing, in essence we are talking about the same thing, since both approaches are based on obtaining a return on capital.

The only notable difference has to do with the time frame used in each approach; trading involves shorter-term trades (from minutes to days), while in investing, the trade covers a much longer time period (weeks to years).

Many investors see traders as evil speculators. In reality they both apply the same underlying logic: taking advantage of a potential anomaly. The only difference between the two approaches is the tool used to identify this possible inefficiency.

While trading is more associated with Technical Analysis, investing is more associated with Fundamental Analysis. This is a general rule which doesn't necessarily apply in all cases, since it would be perfectly valid and useful to perform a technical analysis on an investment that is part of a longer-term trade.

Many investors try to distance themselves from traders by alluding to the fact that their investment theses are based on in-depth studies, which they use to obtain a fair valuation of the price of the stock. Although it is true that their analysis offers them a great deal of knowledge about the company in question, allowing them to invest in long-term projects with confidence, the end remains the same: capital appreciation.

DIFFERENT TYPES OF ANALYSIS FOR TRADING

Before we start trading in the financial markets we must decide what type of approach we are going to use when performing our analyses. There are three main methods of analysis: fundamental, technical and quantitative; each one incorporating different analytical tools.

This section will explain the fundamental principles on which each of these is based, so that the reader can decide what type of analysis methodology best suits their personality, and which they may later choose to specialize in.

The same debate has been raging for decades: which method is better, fundamental or technical analysis? Each one focuses on analyzing different information and the truth is that they are not mutually exclusive. In fact many large investors tend to combine them, using fundamental analysis to determine what to buy and technical analysis to determine when to buy.

Ultimately, deciding to use one approach or the other is a decision for the trader to make based on their knowledge and personality. As always, it is the trader's job to independently evaluate and draw their own conclusions.

Technical Analysis

Technical analysis focuses on studying market actions; in other words, the interaction between buyers and sellers. This interaction is ultimately reflected in the two main sources of information that govern the rest of the analytical tools: price and volume.

The technical analyst evaluates the movements of the price and/or the volume of trading to understand the state of the market and to forecast which way the price is most likely to go in the future.

Principles of Technical Analysis

All the hypotheses formulated by technical analysis are based on three basic principles:

1. The market discounts everything

This is the cornerstone of technical analysis. This is based on the premise that everything that can affect the market is already reflected by the price: both public and private, current and even future information; as well as the behavioral biases of its participants.

Technical analysis is not concerned with understanding the fundamental reasons why the price of an asset may go up or down. It takes into account that the chart is not the cause of price movements; but that all the economic and emotional fundamentals are reflected in it.

We can assume, then, that if everything that affects the market is represented in the price, the only thing that needs to be analyzed to understand the complete history of what is happening in that market is its chart.

2. Prices move in trends

A fundamental concept for technical analysts and on which many strategies are based. The idea is that the market develops trends (upward and downward) and that it generally tends to continue in this direction until there are clear signs of intent to move in the opposite direction.

Implicitly, this principle is also related to the inertia of the market. In physics, we are told that bodies tend to remain in their existing state unless that state is changed by an external force. This hypothesis suggests that the market is most likely to remain in its current state: if we are in a bull market, it is most likely that prices will continue to rise; and if we are in a bear market, the probability is that prices will continue to decline.

Therefore, when making forecasts, this principle suggests we should act on the basis that the current market context will continue, rather than moving in a different direction.

<u>3. History repeats itself</u>

This is based on the assumption that the market is expected to behave in the future in the same way as it has in the past.

This assumption of future behavior follows the logic of inductive or inferential statistics, which is used to analyze and study past data (the chart) in order to model behaviors (patterns) and try to predict future performance.

Over time, the repetitive nature of price movements has led to the identification of chart patterns to which a certain predictive capacity can be attributed.

It should be noted, however, that it is impossible for two completely equal actions to occur in the market. For this to happen you would need the same participants who carried out the first action to behave in exactly the same way the second time around, which is impossible. For this reason a certain amount of flexibility must be applied in the development of these behaviors or patterns in this principle.

The pros of Technical Analysis

The main advantage of technical analysis is that a simple glance at the stock chart can reveal all the fundamental valuations as well as the rational or irrational behaviors of participants.

The number of participants and their motivations or needs are almost infinite. Each and every one of the factors that influence market price are summarized and represented in the chart, to the extent that the technical analyst doesn't need to assess the reasons why the market is trading at those price levels, since these are indeterminable, due to the large number of influencing variables.

Another very positive aspect is that, in general terms, technical analysis approaches are universal. Their tools can be applied to all assets, universally. This allows the trader to analyze several assets at once and, therefore, to be in a position to overhaul their entire portfolio if necessary.

This universality can also be understood as fractality. Fractality refers to the fact that the market behaves in the same way, regardless of time frame. This allows the trader to apply the same tools and principles in different time frames (short, medium and long term), depending on their particular characteristics and personality.

The cons of Technical Analysis

Most technical analysis methods taught are not based on real underlying logic or sound principles, hence its bad reputation among many other types of investors.

Most technical analysis approaches date back decades (one of the most popular books on technical analysis, "Technical Analysis of Stock Trends" by Edwards and Magee, was published in 1948), when the financial market ecosystem was very different to how it is now. Today, in all markets large amounts of capital are constantly being moved and technology has taken huge leaps forward. This has led to a competitiveness never before seen, which calls into question the real usefulness of old technical analysis techniques based on the subjective drawing of simple lines on the chart or on an almost mystical expectation of how certain behavioral patterns will develop.

In addition to deciding which tools to use, the fundamental disadvantage of technical analysis has to do with the subjectivity inherent in its analysis. No matter how much knowledge the trader has and no matter how precisely this is applied, a certain amount of subjectivity will be involved, to a greater or lesser extent. This means, for example, that two traders using the same tools can come up with two completely opposed scenarios, when in theory they should actually be seeing the same thing.

Subjectivity can sometimes be positive, especially for those who have a lot of experience in the markets. It allows us to subconsciously pick up on details as a result of this know how. However, this discretionary aspect will most likely be detrimental to the interests of the trader. A trader should always try to ensure their analyses are as objective as possible However, removing the element of emotionality can be tremendously complicated. Our emotions can play tricks on us and make us see things that don't really exist and which only we see. And this perception will most likely be in line with what we want the particular asset to do.

Fundamental Analysis

Fundamental analysis involves the comprehensive investigation of the economy, the sector, the competition and the company itself; as well as national or international policies; and ultimately, any factor that has the ability to positively or negatively impact the valuation of the company in question.

All this with the aim of detecting exploitable anomalies or inefficiencies in the form of undervalued stocks, in order to obtain a potential future yield if the analysis is correct.

Fundamental analysis basically covers two categories:

- **Financial statements.** Quantitative analysis of the income, expenses, assets, liabilities and all other financial aspects of the company.

- **Intangible elements**. Qualitative analysis to measure the impact of intangible aspects such as the brand, the impact on society, the dealings with clients and employees, the management history of the team of directors, competitive advantage, the business model, etc.

These elements may not seem important, but they are increasingly relevant in today's markets, in some cases having a significant impact on an increase or decrease in the value of the company.

Key financial ratios:

Investors use different tools to come up with a valuation. Below are some of the most important ratios that can be analyzed and offer information about the past performance and future forecasts of a company:

Price to Earnings Ratio (PER)

This measures the relationship between the share price and the earnings per share. It helps to identify if a company is undervalued or overvalued.

- PER = (Share price / Earnings per share)

- A PER of 15 means that it will take 15 years for the initial investment to be recouped, assuming the profit remains stable.

Earnings per Share (EPS)

This measures the net profit per share. It indicates how much of the company's profit is allocated to each share.

- EPS = Net profit / number of shares

- An EPS of 0.05 means that investors would receive $0.05 for each share they own.

Dividend Yield

This measures the annual dividend payment of a company in relation to the price of its shares. It indicates the value of dividend payments that shareholders receive for each dollar of company shares they own.

- Dividend Yield = (Dividend per share / Share price) * 100

- A 5% percentage means that investors receive $0.05 for every dollar they have invested in the company.

Price to Book Value (P/B)

It measures the price of a company's shares relative to its book value. It indicates the price that investors must pay for each dollar of book value.

- P/B = (Share price / book value per share)

- A P/B of 3 means that investors pay $3 for every dollar of book value of shareholders' equity.

Return on Equity (ROE)

This measures the ability of a company to generate profits relative to its shareholders' equity. It indicates how much profit is generated for each dollar of shareholders' equity.

- ROE = (Net Income / shareholders' equity) * 100

- An ROE of 5% means that for every dollar of shareholders' equity, 0.05 cents of profit can be generated.

Debt to Equity (D/E)

This measures a company's debt relative to its shareholders' equity. It indicates the degree to which its operations are financed with debt and if the shareholders' equity can cover the total liabilities.

- D/E = (Total liabilities / Shareholders' equity)

- A D/E of 2 means that the company has twice as much debt as it has shareholders' equity; in other words, that its equity would not be able to cover its debt.

Investment strategies

Value investing

This investment philosophy is based on determining the intrinsic value of a company; in other words, the value of the company's assets and its capacity to generate cash flow.

This intrinsic value would be the value of the company in the event of its liquidation. In accounting terms, these types of shares are cheap. They are acquired with the expectation that the market will finally recognize their value and the price will rise.

Determining the intrinsic value of a company allows us to identify possible discrepancies between value and price. If the market price is below the intrinsic value, then the market will be considered undervalued, offering a buying opportunity. Conversely, if the price is above the estimated value, the market will be deemed overvalued and a fall in price should be expected.

When value investing, traders look for companies with low levels of debt, a good competitive advantage, that are susceptible to becoming part of a merger or acquisition and with low fundamental ratios.

<u>Growth investing</u>

Growth investing places more importance on the future potential of the company than on its current price and intrinsic value; in other words, companies that according to their price and/or value are overvalued could be deemed good buying opportunities, provided they have significant potential to continue growing in the future.

These types of companies tend to have a dominant position, with a large market share and a good competitive advantage in their products or services, as well as a solid business and global expansion model.

When growth investing, traders look for companies with ratios that demonstrate the efficiency of the management team in the use of assets, income and expenses; as well as fundamental ratios that imply reasonable prices.

The pros of Fundamental Analysis

Fundamental analysis reveals the direction of the market. With no irrational cognitive biases involved, it is the health of the company and its future projection which will make the price rise. And this valuation can only be determined by analyzing the company's financial statements.

The main advantage of fundamental analysis is that, in the best case in which the analyst has the adequate knowledge and tools to allow them to carry out a thorough and objective analysis, it puts them in a position to know the real value of the company and to identify excellent investment opportunities.

A good investment can offer an extraordinary return, especially if the company has great potential and its stocks are bought in the early stages of its growth phase.

Moreover, fundamental analyses are valid long term, as company valuations do not radically change from one day to the next.

The cons of Fundamental Analysis

Fundamental analysis is based on trying to assess the value of the asset in question as objectively as possible. But this task can become more difficult depending on the nature of the asset. It also requires an exercise in faith; to trust that the data provided by the company is a true and fair view of its situation (this is not the case when there is fraud). This difficulty and the opacity of certain information can mean that a fundamental valuation is not entirely objective and any profit estimates may not be correct.

The trader must also have sufficient knowledge, means and resources to carry out the appropriate investigations. Many investors mistakenly believe that taking into account some of the most important fundamental ratios and making a few small comparisons is enough to arrive at a fair valuation of the company. Nothing could be further from the truth; high levels of know-how are required to carry out an objective and accurate assessment of the situation of the company based on financial statements and other, intangible, elements.

Although perhaps the most negative aspect of the fundamental approach is the opportunity cost that may be involved. The investor may have performed an objective valuation and identified a good opportunity to buy a security that is undervalued according to the market. They may invest their capital in that security, but it is then up to the market to adjust the value and price, and there is no possible way to estimate how long this may take.

The company may react quickly and reach the price levels projected in the analysis; but weeks, months and even years may pass without this happening. This creates a huge opportunity cost for the investor, who has invested capital for which they are not obtaining a return either from that investment, or from another possible investment in which they might have invested were the capital still available to them.

In other words, it is no longer just about what you are not earning because the market "does not agree with you" but also about what you are failing to earn by not being able to invest your capital in some other identified opportunity. This is known as an opportunity cost.

Quantitative Analysis

Trading or investing through quantitative analysis is based on the use of scientific methods in the study of financial markets. This approach applies mathematical and statistical models to market behavior, to try to identify and take advantage of anomalies or inefficiencies.

Quantitative Analysis feeds on the technical and/or fundamental approaches. In order to obtain statistically significant conclusions, we hypothesize and carry out a process of data collection, analysis, and optimization.

Trading based on quantitative analysis aims to develop systems with a positive mathematical expectation (or advantage). In other words, it aims to create 100% objective strategies, the application of which invariably puts the odds in our favor and allows us to obtain long-term market profitability.

The most important thing when studying this interpretation of the market is the mindset that it provides us with; although you are presented with a winning system, you will be skeptical and will need to double check yourself. This is priceless.

In addition to this complete change of mindset, trading systems based on quantitative analysis offer the following advantages:

The pros of Quantitative Analysis

Complete knowledge of the strategy

We can all agree that past results do not guarantee future results; but it is also true that we are better off going into a market with a strategy that has been proven to work in offering a good return.

Knowledge of the system is the key to unlocking all other advantages. Moving in an environment in which everything is quantified and you know what to expect will take your trading up a few notches.

Having knowledge of data such as the Drawdown (greatest accumulated loss), the largest number of trading losses, the probability distribution of trades, the number of consecutive months of losses... and, in general, of all the negative figures reflected in historical data, provide you with greater confidence when implementing your system. Moreover, this information will help you to decide on how to implement important aspects such as risk management.

Reduction of stress

Following on from the previous point, if having a detailed understanding of this data offers anything, it is that ultimately, it makes trading and your day-to-day operations more stress-free. The thrill of "being right" in your analysis disappears.

The number of potential winning systems that you will have discarded because you are going through a simple Drawdown period... Losing streaks when playing the market are inevitable, so ensuring you have measured the environments in which you can implement your strategy, once again, gives you an advantage.

If you take a discretionary approach to trading and you don't have this data quantified, after an insignificant streak of five of six trading losses you may psychologically breakdown. In truth, this makes no sense, unless the statistics tell you otherwise. The problem is that we generally don't have that knowledge; we don't know if this number of losses is significant or not. For this reason, quantifying it will help psychologically during your toughest moments.

Reduction or elimination of the human factor

Of all the parts that make up a trading system, the human factor is by far the weakest link. For this reason alone, any measure aimed at reducing or eliminating it is positive.

The main reason why the system does not always function under the same conditions is the traders themselves. If it ultimately falls on the trader to take all decisions, elements such as intuition and hunches come into play; therefore trying to draw objective conclusions about subjective factors is completely illogical.

By definition, any strategy based on quantitative analysis could be executed with or without human intervention. These systems, made up entirely of an objective set of rules, would only require human intervention (if at all) at the moment of executing the entry orders.

Having well-defined rules means that it is possible to completely automate the strategy with programming. This is another huge advantage, although there are some traders who prefer to execute the signals manually.

Developing an automatic trading system allows you to completely eliminate the human factor and, therefore, gives you more free time.

The cons of Quantitative Analysis

In reality there are no disadvantages. In fact, developing strategies based on quantitative analysis, if done correctly, is the best way to play the financial markets, mainly because of the advantages outlined above.

The one thing worth noting is the tremendous difficulty involved in the optimal development of strategies. It is a complex process in which the slightest mistake can spoil all your hard work.

You need good data to work with, have ideas based on real underlying logic with which you can create a working hypothesis, have extensive knowledge to be able to optimize and validate the strategy, have a fundamental understanding of capital and risk management and also a solid foundation of statistical and mathematical knowledge.

How to develop quantitative strategies

The basic process for developing trading strategies based on quantitative analysis is as follows:

1. Propose a working hypothesis.

2. Codify the idea so that its logic is 100% objective.

3. Test the strategy using historical (in-sample) data to check against its past performance.

4. Optimize the model by identifying the parameters that improve performance and those that negatively affect it.

5. Validate the strategy on out-of-sample data to verify performance using unprocessed data.

6. Create the final model and put it to work, initially in demo mode and then live.

FUNDAMENTAL CONCEPTS

Time Frames

One way to categorize traders is based on the time frame they trade in.

A time frame is a graphical representation of a financial asset over a certain period of time. The same asset, depending on the time frame in which you observe it, will show different behavior.

As a general rule, traders make use of multiple time frames when analyzing and proposing scenarios. Multiple time frame analysis deals with the use of several time frames for the same asset in order to achieve a more complete analysis.

Longer time frames (major trends) have a greater influence on the other time frames (minor trends).

This concept of multiple time frames is based on the fractality of the market; a theory introduced by the mathematician Benoît Mandelbrot which states that a geometric object with a basic, fragmented or apparently irregular structure is repeated at different scales.

Applied to financial markets, this theory suggests that, regardless of the time frame being tracked, price movements will always repeat themselves, across the board.

The concept of fractality goes hand in hand with the different types of traders:

- **Short-term** trading: scalper and day trader

- **Medium-term** trading: swing trader

- **Long-term** trading: position trader or investor

The table below summarizes the most important characteristics of the different types of traders that can be classified according to the type of trades they execute.

Trading approach	Time frame	Progression	Duration	Leverage	Difficulty
Scalping	Seconds / Minutes	Very short	Seconds / Minutes	Very high	Extreme
Day Trading	Minutes / Hours	Short	Minutes / Hours *less than a week	Considerable	Very high
Swing Trading	Hours / Daily	Medium	Days / Weeks *more than one day	Low	High
Position Trading / Investing	Daily / Weekly	Long	Months / Years	Very low or none	Medium

It should be noted that they are not mutually exclusive. In other words, over time the more experienced trader will be able to discern when a particular transaction is valid for one type of trading and when it is valid for another. And different open positions can be held on the same asset (bought and sold at the same time) depending on the progression the trader is looking for. But this is already quite advanced, we should return to that later.

The following chart shows the main movement (red) which is the main progression or trend that a Position trader or investor would look for; the fractal immediately below (green) would be the intermediate progression that a Swing trader would look for; the one immediately below that (blue) is the movement that a Day trader would look for.

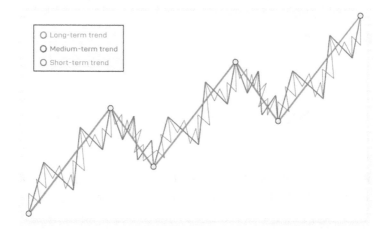

There is no ideal time frame in which to trade. Everything will depend on the type of trader you decide to be. This decision will determine which time frames to choose.

The following table shows a typical example of how multiple time frames are used based on the type of trader you decide to be. To do this, I have selected three time frames:

Time frame	Scalping	Day Trading	Swing Trading	Position Trading / Investing
Long-term Context analysis	15 minutes	1 hour	Diario	Weekly
Intermediate Decision making	5 minutes	15 minutes	4 hour	Daily
Short-term calibration	Seconds	5 minutes	1 hour	8 hour

- **Long-term time frame** for the purpose of analyzing the chart to identify the general context. This provides you with excellent points of reference for identifying macro decision-making zones.

- **Intermediate time frame** used to take decisions (to look for the entry trigger, the exit and to manage the position). The most exhaustive technical analysis is carried out based on this time frame, as this is the one that will provide you with your trading signals.

- **Short-term time frame** (optional) to refine the entry and exit as much as possible once the signal has been emitted on the intermediate graph.

You need to understand these multiple time frames and always prioritize the longest time frame over the shortest. Understanding the context is of paramount importance.

Long and Short Positions

"Long" or "short" are financial terms which you need to understand and which simply refer to the direction in which we position ourselves.

Long

A position in which the trader purchases an asset in the expectation its price will rise. It is used as a synonym for buying and is sometimes referred to as "going long", which means that the trader has bought that asset.

If, based on our analysis we think that a certain asset will go up in price, we can try to take advantage of this potential upward movement with different instruments:

- Buying stocks, futures or other derivatives such as CFDs, investment funds, ETFs, etc.

- Buying CALL options.

Short

A position in which the trader sells an asset in the expectation its price will go down.

It is possible to sell a financial asset without having previously bought it, since what is sold is the position in the contract, for which the seller assumes an obligation. This is what is known in the market as "going short".

There are different ways of taking a short position on an asset:

- Selling futures or other financial derivatives.

- Buying PUT options.

- Buying inverse ETFs, which replicate the opposite behavior of the underlying asset. In other words, if we want to take a short position because we believe that the price of a market is going to fall, we can buy the inverse ETF, whose value will decrease when the underlying asset's value increases.

In the case of stocks, the operation is somewhat more complex but easily understandable. It is known as short selling. In this case, clicking on sell means we borrow the stocks from the broker and later (when we close the position) we return the same amount but (hopefully) at a lower price, with the difference paid to us as profit.

If, believing the price of a security is going to fall, we short sell its stocks that are trading at $50 and later buy them back at $40, at the close of the trade we will have earned $10 for each share. But we need to be careful; if the share price increases above the price we sold at, we will incur a loss.

Types of Trading

Traders can use different types of trading strategies depending on what they base their decision-making on:

Discretionary

Discretionary trading is based on elements that are not quantitatively measurable. These include intuition, hunches, expectations and other subjective perceptions.

Systematic

When we talk about systematic (algorithmic) trading, we refer to a form of trading or investment that is based on well-defined rules. This type of trading can be carried out both manually and automatically. The key is that the decision-making process is entirely predefined.

Quantitative

A systematic strategy may or may not be quantitative. For it to be the latter, said quantitative analysis model must have previously undergone a statistical study or Backtest. This simply involves verifying that the model is profitable in the long term, using historical data and a process of optimization and validation, and ensuring that it therefore has a certain statistical advantage.

Automatic

It is also worth knowing what automatic trading is. This involves the codification of objective rules in the form of a computer program (robot or bot) which can then run completely independently when the established rules are met.

High-Frequency trading

The terms Algorithmic Trading and High-Frequency Trading are often mistakenly used interchangeably.

While it is true that HFT is executed using algorithms, these are very different to the algorithms that we have access to as retail traders.

The key difference between the two terms is their speed. Whereas HFT algorithms operate in terms of microseconds (and even faster), the algorithms that a retail trader might program are said to be low or medium frequency.

Another aspect that distinguishes them is their complexity. Bear in mind that the developers of this type of algorithm (HFT) have almost unlimited knowledge, means and resources.

At the end of the day, they are in a different league. A programmer who develops a low-frequency algorithm isn't trying to compete with HFT algorithms; it would be pointless. The kinds of anomalies that one and the other fight for are completely different. The only thing they have in common is that they are directed by computer code.

Strategies

There are many types of strategies that can be adopted when trading in financial markets, depending on the nature of your approach to price movement.

This section includes concepts that are a little more advanced than you would expect to find in a book such as this, but I think it is worth explaining.

Below are two of the most important categories used by the major traders.

Directional Strategies

Directional strategies involve successfully betting on a price direction to make a profit.

These are the conventional strategies that we all know which involve taking a long position if the price is expected to rise to try to take advantage of the movement; and taking a short position if the price is expected to fall.

Arbitrage Strategies

Arbitrage is a form of trading that tries to exploit market imperfections by profiting from the price differences between strongly correlated instruments.

There are different ways this can be applied. It can be used on the same asset listed in different locations; or on the same asset listed in different markets (derivatives market and spot market).Since the markets are highly correlated, the strategy consists of buying the one with the lowest value and at the same time selling the one that is trading at a higher price in the hope that the markets will soon adjust, thus generating a profit.

One of the keys to this strategy is that the transactions must occur simultaneously, to avoid exposure to the risk that prices may change in one of the markets before both transactions are completed. This is why this type of strategy is basically quantitative in nature, developed using mathematical and statistical models and executed using high-frequency algorithms.

Orders

There are basically four different types of orders involved when participating in the market.

Market

An aggressive order that is executed when the best purchase and sale price is available (Best BID/ASK). An immediate order, guaranteeing the execution of the order but not the specific price at which it has been executed, due to constant change in price and the application of the Spread. Once the order is launched it cannot be canceled, since it is executed automatically.

These types of orders are known as "sweeps" since all available liquidity is consumed when they are executed, even if the order has to be partially completed, in blocks at different price levels, until the full order has been completed. This may incur higher transaction costs.

Limit

A passive order that is executed at a specific price. Entry or exit at that particular price is guaranteed but execution is not guaranteed. In other words, the price might never reach the desired level and therefore the order might not be executed, or might only be partially executed. It can be canceled at any time, as long it hasn't been executed.

Stop

A passive order that is executed at a specific price. When this price is reached, it becomes a market order and is therefore executed at the best available price (Best BID/ASK).

Stop-Limit

This combines the characteristics of Limit and Stop orders. Once a certain price level is reached (function of a Stop order), an order is generated at a specific level (function of a Limit order). Operationally it works in the same way as Limit orders.

These four types of orders are used to both enter and exit a trade. When an open (buying or selling) position is closed, there are basically two possible results: profit or loss.

To close a trade at a profit we use a Take Profit order. To close it at a loss we use the Stop Loss order. Let's clarify this further, because it is not as simple as it sounds. Take Profit and Stop Loss are really the same as the previously explained orders. They are simply given a different name at the close of the position in order to distinguish between the results of the trade.

Take Profit

We use this to exit the market at a profit and it will always be the reverse of the order used previously when opening the position. In other words if our open position was a purchase, the Take Profit will be an order to sell; and if we opened a short position (sell), the Take Profit would now be an order to buy.

As we will see later, in order to exit the market, someone must act as a counterparty; and the order of that counterparty will be the reverse of our own order.

Stop Loss

This tool is used to accept a loss and exit when the market is going against us. The nature of this type of order will also be the reverse of our initial order, just like with Take Profit: if we have a long position, the Stop Loss will be a sale; and if we have a short position the Stop Loss will be a purchase.

Following on from the four types of orders we have just seen, the list below describes the full range of basic orders available according to intention and use:

✤ **Buy Market**. Aggressive order at the current price. Used for:

- Entering the market to buy.
- Closing a sell position (either at a profit or loss).

✤ **Buy Stop**. Pending order above the current price. Used for:

- Entering the market to buy.
- Closing a sell position (due to a Stop Loss)

✤ **Buy Limit**. Pending order below the current price. Used for:

- Entering the market to buy.
- Closing a sell position (due to a Take Profit)

✤ **Buy Stop Limit**. Pending order below the price after reaching a certain limit. Used for:

- Entering the market to buy.
- Closing a sell position (due to a Take Profit)

✤ **Sell Market**. Aggressive order at the current price. Used for:

- Entering the market to sell.
- Closing a buy position (either at a profit or loss).

✤ **Sell Stop.** Pending order below the current price. Used for:

- Entering the market to sell.
- Closing a buy position (due to a Stop Loss)

✤ **Sell Limit**. Pending order above the current price. Used for:

- Entering the market to sell.
- Closing a buy position (due to a Take Profit)

✤ **Sell Stop Limit**. Pending order above the price after reaching a certain limit. Used for:

- Entering the market to sell.
- Closing a buy position (due to a Take Profit)

Fluctuation Units

To be able to manage capital and risk when trading, we need to understand the fluctuation units and how they impact our profits and losses.

Fluctuation units simply describe changes in prices. Different units of measurement are used depending on the market, each with their own significance:

Point

This is the largest change in prices that can occur. It represents a minimum change to the left of the decimal point of the quote. Points are made up of Ticks.

If the price of a stock changes from $30 to $31, this price is said to have increased by one point.

If, for example, the price of E-mini S&P 500 futures moves from 2800.00 to 2801.00 this would also be considered a price increase of one point.

Tick

A tick is the smallest amount of fluctuation that can occur to the right of the decimal point. The size of the tick varies depending on the asset, for some instruments it can be measured in increments of 0.0001 (for example certain currencies) while other instruments can be measured in increments of 0.25 (such as E-mini S&P 500 futures), or 0-10 (such as $GC Gold futures).

The size of the tick determines how many ticks it takes to increase the point.

One tick on an E-mini S&P 500 contract is equivalent to 0.25 of a point. Since one point of the index is valued at $50 in the E-mini contract, one tick would be equivalent to $12.50.

One tick on the Gold contract is equal to $10 since a point of the contract is worth $100.

Pip

Acronym for Percentage in Point. The pip represents the smallest change to the right of the decimal, and is a unit of measurement used exclusively for the foreign exchange, or forex, market.

For all currency pairs it corresponds to the fourth decimal place, except for those that involve the Japanese Yen (JPY) in which case it corresponds to the second decimal place.

A change in EUR/USD from 1.3100 to 1.3101 would imply an increase of 1 pip (0.0001).

A change in USD/JPY from 130.00 to 130.01 would also imply an increase of 1 pip.

There are also fractional pips or pipettes, which are the fifth decimal place (for pairs that do not involve the Yen) or the third (for those that do involve the Yen). 10 pipettes would equal 1 pip.

The value of one pip for a single lot is 100,000 x 0.0001 = $10.

BID/ASK, Spread, Liquidity, Volume and Slippage

In financial markets there is no one single price. This may seem obvious, but it is something that a lot of people don't understand. When a participant goes to the market, they will be presented with two prices: the purchase price and the sale price.

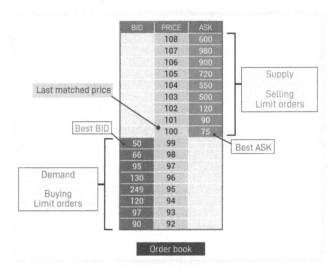

BID

The BID column is the part of the order book where buyers go to place their order (buy limit orders) and where sellers go to match their sell orders. The highest price within the BID column is known as the Best BID and represents the best price at which the security can be sold.

ASK

The ASK column is the part of the order book where sellers go to place their pending sell orders (offer) and where buyers go to find the counterparty for their purchases. The lowest price within the ASK column is known as the Best ASK and represents the best price at which the asset can be bought.

Spread

This is the difference between the BID and ASK prices at any given moment.

It is an indicator of the liquidity of said asset. The lower the Spread, the more liquid the asset.

Keeping the spread under control is vitally important, as it can greatly impact the yield. You should be aware that there may be critical moments, such as just before the announcement of important news, in which liquidity decreases and the spread increases significantly. This may mean that the price observed prior to the execution of our order does not correspond to the actual price of the trade, a factor known as slippage.

Liquidity and volume

Liquidity refers to the ease with which an asset can be bought or sold without its market price being affected.

Volume refers to the number of stocks, contracts, or units that have been traded at a given moment.

Although they are different concepts, liquidity and volume are strongly related. High volume indicates a high level of liquidity. This is an easy concept to understand; the more trading that goes on in a market, the easier it is for assets to be bought and sold.

By contrast, a market with low liquidity suggests there is little agent interest from agents, as evidenced by a low volume of trades.

A word of advice: the more liquid the assets you trade the better as it is less likely that a large trader will be able to individually impact the price.

It is therefore a measure to avoid possible manipulation. If you are trading an asset that trades at very little volume, a large institution will most likely be able to move the price with relative ease. These environments should be avoided.

Slippage

Slippage refers to the difference between the expected price of a trade and the price at which the trade is executed. When we click and send our order from our platform, it may not be executed at the price that we saw on the screen at the moment we clicked. That difference between the price we saw and the one that has actually been executed is known as slippage.

This phenomenon occurs mainly during periods of greater volatility and when large market orders are used, causing the price to move up or down through different price levels in search of the liquidity needed to match that order if there is not enough volume in a single price level.

Although slippage is normally associated with a negative market event, a situation that occurs due to the dynamics of the flow of orders, it can occur in our favor and indirectly benefit us.

Volatility

Volatility is a statistical measure of the dispersion of returns for a given asset and is obtained by analyzing the standard deviation or the variance between the returns from that same asset.

It is usually associated with big swings in the market and that is why it is a key factor in the options market. It is associated with a specific time period; generally daily, weekly, monthly or annually.

This indicator is linked to risk, since volatile assets are considered riskier due to the degree of uncertainty arising from the asset's variable movements. A high level of volatility suggests that a significant change in value is possible in a short period of time. By contrast, low volatility is associated with lower risk thanks to the stability provided by a low fluctuation of movements.

VIX volatility index

The volatility of the market can be analyzed using this index. It measures the implied volatility of the US stock market derived from the quoted prices of the S&P500 CALL and PUT options.

We can use this to analyze the sentiment or expectations of the market, measure the degree of short term uncertainty in the market, predict the volatility of the returns on financial assets and provide useful information to market participants and regulators.

The VIX is known as the "fear index" because high index levels coincide with market extremes.

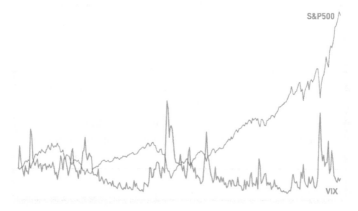

Recent studies analyzing the relationship of the VIX and the S&P500 showed that there is a negative correlation. High VIX levels usually indicate an oversold market and coincide with market lows, which offer good opportunities for seeking out long positions. Conversely, low index levels signal an overbought market and usually coincide with a market ceiling, which would be a good time to seek out short positions.

Leverage

Leveraged or margin trading is a mechanism through which the trader can obtain greater exposure in the market by paying only a part of the total value of the position. It is a type of loan in which the broker lends us capital so we can increase the size of our position.

This tool is a double-edged sword since it allows us to acquire a greater proportion of the asset we want, putting us in a position to obtain much higher profits –but also losses– than we would otherwise obtain with a spot trade or one without any leverage.

Brokers generally allow the trader to decide the amount of leverage they want. Leverage ratios can be around 20 or 30 to 1, all the way up to 300 or more. A ratio of 30:1 means that the broker lets us borrow 30 times the capital that we have available in our account.

The recommendation, especially when starting out, is not to use leverage or to keep it as low as possible because this type of trading involves a higher risk and requires more advanced knowledge in correct capital management.

If we open a position using leverage and this position incurs losses, our margin of coverage will gradually be consumed (our exposure to the market based on the capital in our account). In the event that said margin falls below the minimum required to maintain the position, the broker will issue a **margin CALL**. This is a notice warning us that our exposure is excessive and that we are taking on a risk in the market that is higher than allowed. At that point, if we do not reduce our exposure by closing a position, the broker will automatically do so as a risk control measure.

High Impact News

One of the best tools available to us is a news calendar, specifically one showing news that can significantly impact the price of the asset which we are interested in trading.

A huge amount of news is constantly being broadcast so you need to filter out and take into account only the most relevant items.

Depending on which market you want to trade in, certain news items will be more relevant than others. For example, if you invest in stocks, you will be most interested in the financial results of companies, which are usually presented on a quarterly basis.

Time	Cur.	Imp.	Event	Actual	Forecast	Previous
			Monday, January 3, 2022			
10:00	USD	★ ★ ★	ISM Manufacturing PMI (Dec)		60.2	61.1
			Tuesday, January 4, 2022			
10:00	USD	★ ★ ★	ISM Manufacturing PMI (Dec)		60.2	61.1
10:00	USD	★ ★ ★	JOLTs Job Openings (Nov)			11.033M
			Wednesday, January 5, 2022			
08:15	USD	★ ★ ★	ADP Nonfarm Employment Change (Dec)		413K	534K
10:00	USD	★ ★ ★	ISM Non-Manufacturing PMI (Dec)		67.0	69.1
			Thursday, January 6, 2022			
10:00	USD	★ ★ ★	ISM Non-Manufacturing PMI (Dec)		66.8	69.1
			Friday, January 7, 2022			
05:00	EUR	★ ★ ★	CPI (YoY) (Dec)		4.7%	4.9%
08:30	USD	★ ★ ★	Nonfarm Payrolls (Dec)		400K	210K
08:30	USD	★ ★ ★	Unemployment Rate (Dec)		4.1%	4.2%

Source: Investing.com

As well as the news specifically related to each asset, the following types of economic data can have a huge impact on the economy as a whole:

Interest rates

The interest rates set by Central Banks are of vital significance. As we discussed in the section on financial literacy, an interest rate is nothing more than the price of money, which largely determines the preferences of the main market agents when deciding whether to consume now or in the future.

The most relevant are those that affect the main currencies, such as the US dollar and the euro.

The Central Bank of the United States is known as the Federal Reserve (FED). It is a public-private institution that is responsible for the country's monetary policy, as well as supervising the country's banks, to ensure financial stability, economic growth and full employment.

The European Central Bank (ECB) is the bank of the European Union countries whose common currency is the Euro. In addition to ensuring the security of the system, these banks help maintain price stability and keep inflation under control.

Consumer Price Index (CPI)

The CPI is a statistical measure that reflects the price changes of a basket of basic consumer goods and services in a given period of time. This index tries to evaluate changes compared to the previous cost, in relative terms.

The goods and services included in this basket are basic products that the average consumer buys on a regular basis.

Thanks to its fundamental characteristics, it is an excellent tool for measuring inflation in a given country.

Gross Domestic Product (GDP)

GDP measures the monetary value of all the goods and services produced by a country or geographic region in a given period of time, which makes it an excellent indicator of the health of that economy.

It is important to note that it only includes goods and services produced within the country, regardless of the nationality of the producer.

As with all other indicators, it is important to compare its evolution with respect to the previous figure, in order to assess whether the country is actually growing economically.

Employment reports

These reports publish the number of jobs created or lost in the previous month as well as the proportion of people who are unemployed but actively looking for work.

The most important is undoubtedly the US Non-Farm Payrolls (NFP). This ratio measures the rate of job creation in the United States (excluding agricultural jobs). It is published on the first Friday of each month at 8.30 am (NYSE time).

This is the most important news item, because it represents around 80% of the workers involved in generating the US GDP and, for this reason, it offers a true reflection of the country's employment situation.

Positive reports suggest that companies are growing and hiring more, which will have a positive impact on the economy as more people will have more money to spend.

Other dates that should be monitored closely are public holidays during which the markets are closed. As well as common celebrations such as Christmas, New Year and religious holidays (Easter, All Saints' Day), each country has its own holidays on different dates; such as National Holidays and Labor Day, among others.

One of the most commonly used platforms for keeping all this information up to date is provided by Investing, which you can access at the following address: https://investing.com/economic-calendar

This platform is very complete. It centralizes all the content, allowing you to access it quickly and intuitively. It also has a filter tool so you can narrow down your search for information, making it even more accessible.

Trading Hours

It is important to know the trading hours of stock exchanges in order to structure your operations around your geographical location.

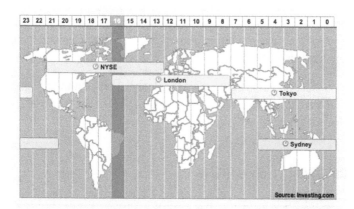

The electronification of markets now allows for the possibility of trading 24 hours a day in markets such as the foreign exchange market, which is open from 10 pm on Sunday to 9 pm on Friday (GMT); from the opening in Sydney to the close in New York thanks to the Globex session.

There are 3 main sessions in the Forex market which account for most of its volume, and that are related to the opening and closing of the main stock markets: London (Europe), New York (America) and Tokyo (Asia).

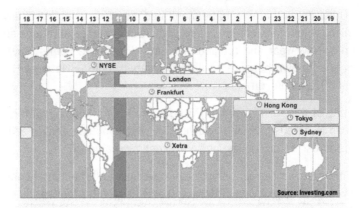

Source: Investing.com

During the Asian session (11 pm to 8 am GMT) market activity is insignificant since the volume is very low, which generally leads to very few and mostly overlapping movements.

With the opening of the European session (7 am to 4 pm GMT), the volume increases as the number of traders increases; but it is not until the American session begins (12 pm to 9 pm GMT) that the highest concentration of activity occurs. During the first half hour or so of the American session it is very difficult to follow the behavior of the market. Upon the opening of the session, all the trades that took place when the market closed, after the end of the previous session, are reflected in the price; this generates a high level of generally random volatility that can skew our strategy. This is why it is best to wait a few minutes until the market digests all that noise and the majority of traders start to position themselves with intent.

It is worth noting that trading sessions experience their highest volume during the hours when they overlap since this is when the largest number of traders are active.

Regular Trading Hours (RTH)

Regular Trading Hours (RTH) refers to the regular trading session hours available for an instrument on a specific exchange or market center. Regular hours vary based on the instrument, exchange, and day of the week.

Electronic Trading Hours (ETH)

Once the RTH are over there is usually a short break of 30 to 60 minutes which the exchanges use for maintenance and for running batch processing jobs to complete the day's trading transactions. Once that is done the ETH session starts and this runs overnight until the following morning when the RTH start again. The ETH session typically starts at around 5.30 pm and ends the following morning at 8.30 am (Central Time U.S.).

Globex

Globex is an electronic trading platform developed by the CME used to trade futures, options and commodity contracts across a wide range of assets that operates 24 hours a day, unrestricted by geographic borders or time zones, so it combines the RTH and ETH sessions.

Fees

Trading is not free. The majority of traders are not fully aware of the impact that trading fees can have on their results.

I'm not sure why but most of us start trading without bearing these fees in mind. If we decide one fine day to look at our trading history we might be in for a major shock.

It is worth noting that, generally speaking, what initially appeared to be a winning strategy can turn into a losing one once we have accounted for the fees.

Without a doubt, it is one of the most destructive elements in trading, mainly for those whose haven't quantified its significance.

My recommendation is to try to trade using longer time frames since the negative effect of fees decreases as the time frame increases.

The fees that apply vary according to the asset and the market in question. The most important ones are listed below.

Transaction, custody and dividend fees

There are all sorts of types of trading fees. Each broker has their own fees but fortunately, due to the competitiveness of the sector, most of them charge similar costs.

A **transaction fee** is a fixed amount or a percentage that is paid each time you enter or exit the market.

A **custody fee** is a cost we pay simply to have our stocks deposited with the broker.

We must also pay a fee to receive the amount that corresponds to us in the form of **dividends**, which is when the company in which we have shares distributes its profit among its shareholders.

Financing costs

This type of fee has to do with keeping trades open at the time of settlement, in order to stay open overnight.

The nature of these costs vary depending on the market. They depend on the value of the position, and they are applied daily.

A **swap** is an interest charge applied in the currency or forex market that is paid or charged at the end of each session for holding an open position for more than one day. Also, some days (usually Wednesdays) these interest charges are tripled to make up for the weekend.

Since swaps are charged depending on the direction taken in the trade (important to check the volume of swaps for the currency pair) there are strategies that try to benefit from this interest charge, known as **carry trades**.

Spread

The Spread, as discussed above, is the difference between the best available buy and sell prices. Of course, this difference is one of the benefits that the broker obtains in exchange for their services.

These can be fixed or variable, depending on the broker. Fixed fees, as the name suggests, remain constant; while variable fees fluctuate and change according to market conditions. This can be dangerous during certain key periods of high volatility, for example before and after the announcement of relevant news or economic data. This is why it is important to stay up to date with the news, to avoid getting caught up in these moments.

If the EUR/USD has a buy price of 1.3105 and a sell price of 1.3100 and we execute an order to enter the market, we would have to pay the cost of 5 pips, which the broker would keep as payment for their service as an intermediary. The curious thing in this case is that when we open the trade, our position is already incurring a loss because we have had to assume that cost. The price would have to fluctuate in our direction by those 5 pips to reach a breakeven point (neutral position, no profit or loss).

You need to be careful with some forex brokers that use very subtle marketing techniques, such as offering very low or even zero spreads but in return charge much higher fees. And vice versa, you will also find brokers that advertise themselves as charging zero fees but offer extremely high spreads. As always, it is our job to be aware of this. Do your job and do your research so you can make the best decisions.

The Auction Process

As we know, due to the functioning of financial markets based on the law of supply and demand, for an order to be executed, it must be paired with another order with the opposite intention. This means that for a sell operation (supply) to be executed, it must be paired with a buy operation (demand) and vice versa.

The market moves thanks to this exchange process between agents. It is vitally important to understand this concept, since practically all the actions that we will explain later in the technical analysis module are based on this principle.

It is no coincidence that we are talking about the auction process right after presenting the types of traders that exist depending on the position they hold: strong or well-informed hands, and weak or uninformed hands.

When well-informed traders decide to build a buy position, it is the uninformed traders who are going to provide them with that liquidity; the counterparty they need to match their market entry and exit orders. As we can see, everything is fits together.

Really, this is exactly the same as any other type of market in which goods are exchanged. If you put your house up for sale, until there is a buyer interested in buying it, no trade can take place. For someone to buy, there must be someone else selling what that person wants. The same thing happens in financial markets. Whether it be stocks, contracts, or units that are being traded, for every buyer there is always a seller on the other side, and that other side is known as the counterparty.

LEARNING PROCESS

To achieve some mastery in the world of trading and investment, a trader must go through a series of stages in which they will gradually discover all the elements that a successful and consistent form of trading requires.

As with any other learning process, the goal is to acquire a new skill or competence. We aim to progress from a point in which we are absolutely unaware of the existence of a particular concept to another in which we master it and apply it skillfully.

Aided by the four-stage learning process defined by psychologist Abraham Maslow, we can take an example of what this process looks like, and what each stage entails, in order to apply it to the world of trading.

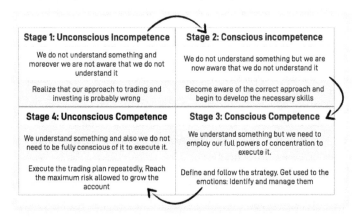

Stage 1: Unconscious Incompetence	Stage 2: Conscious incompetence
We do not understand something and moreover we are not aware that we do not understand it	We do not understand something but we are now aware that we do not understand it
Realize that our approach to trading and investing is probably wrong	Become aware of the correct approach and begin to develop the necessary skills
Stage 4: Unconscious Competence	**Stage 3: Conscious Competence**
We understand something and also we do not need to be fully conscious of it to execute it.	We understand something but we need to employ our full powers of concentration to execute it.
Execute the trading plan repeatedly, Reach the maximum risk allowed to grow the account	Define and follow the strategy. Get used to the emotions: Identify and manage them

Stage 1. Unconscious Incompetence

First contact with trading

This is a state in which we do not understand something and moreover we are not aware that we do not understand it.

At this stage traders are taking their first steps in the financial markets. Most won't really understand what they're getting themselves into. They have completely misguided expectations and their approach to trading is entirely wrong.

The aspiring trader begins to learn in a self-taught way, through books and other free material that they find on the internet. They may take a course, but the chances are they won't be discerning with regards to the quality of their training; so in most cases, unfortunately, they will be receiving poor quality information.

Countless hours surfing the internet, reading about the beauty of trading and what an "easy" path it offers to gaining financial independence. They will join their first Facebook and Telegram groups. And create a Twitter account so they can follow the "pros".

They may begin to learn how to handle social trading platforms. Most will have already opened a demo account and the most daring will have already lost real money on the market.

They basically have no idea about the concept of risk management at this stage. Excessive leverage, martingales, averaging down etc. Their exposure to risk is simply brutal.

And let's not even start on the emotional aspect. The behavior of a person at this stage is the supreme expression of mass psychology described in so many investment books.

The best outcome for the investor at this stage would be to realize that their current approach to trading is wrong and that if they really want to make progress they need to work much harder.

Stage 2. Conscious Incompetence

Laying the foundations of trading

This is the state in which we do not understand something but we are aware of this deficit and we dedicate our own resources, voluntarily or involuntarily (time, money, effort) expanding the information we have about a particular skill and learning about it.

At this stage the trader is already aware of the direction they need to take on their journey toward consistent trading. They begin to recognize common mistakes that they should avoid and to gradually create a solid foundation.

They begin to understand the true workings of the financial market. They start to place importance on risk management and the psychological aspect of trading. They have probably already drafted early versions of their trading plan.

At this point they will already know everything about the trading environment in terms of the participants, types and pairs of orders, types of brokers, the trading platform, etc. They will be aware of fees, fundamental events and in general all the small details that are involved in trading when developed in a slightly more professional way.

They will already have some capacity to distinguish between high quality and poor quality training and hopefully they will have taken several of these courses. Still misguided expectations. The odd bankrupt account because they launched straight into real trading without realizing the possibilities of the system they learned.

The objective at this stage is to become aware from an informed perspective of what trading and investing really means and to pick up the skills and knowledge necessary to master it.

Stage 3. Conscious Competence

Trading with a real account but little exposure to risk

This is the state in which, having practiced a great deal, we perfect the skill and use it, but only while employing our full powers of concentration. We are not able to execute this skill unconsciously.

At this stage the trader may already have their system almost fully defined and they may have drawn up several more versions of their trading plan.

They will have run their first backtests and be in a much more confident position to take on the markets. Countless hours of study and screen time.

They will have achieved good results using their system on a demo account and will be ready to trade in the market with real money. The recommendation is that they only risk small amounts until their trades become consistently profitable.

They still get nervous when opening a position. They get annoyed when hit with a Stop Loss and are ecstatic when they achieve their targets. They are still emotionally dependent on the result. At times they win and at times they lose. They haven't yet achieved any consistency.

The objective is to statistically measure the strategy and be aware that, as Mark Douglas says in "Trading in the Zone", consistency is achieved by exploiting that advantage in the long term. Also, they need to get used to these emotions; identify them and try to manage them.

Stage 4. Unconscious Competence

Trading with a real account

This is the state when we can carry out an activity without necessarily being aware of it while we are doing it. We have practiced it so much that we have internalized our actions.

At this stage the trader continues to accumulate real trades and their experience starts to come into play.

They understand all the aspects of their trading business and they work on exploiting their advantage in the financial markets.

They focus on the action without thinking about the result. They have achieved a high degree of emotional control and accept the result without any sort of reaction.

The trader obtains consistently profitable results.

Some say that trading at this stage becomes boring, since it involves repeating the same thing over and over again, almost without thinking.

The objective at this stage is to reach the maximum risk allowed in your trading plan and to try to increase the money in your account.

PART 4. TECHNICAL ANALYSIS FAST TRACK

This book focuses on Technical Analysis as the main approach to trading and investing, so in this chapter we will delve further into this discipline to try to understand the logic behind its application as well as the tools that we have at our disposal.

Throughout this chapter we will study three of the best approaches to analyzing the market. You should be aware that these topics cover a huge amount of content and in no case is this book intended to be a specific manual for each of them. What you will find here are the key concepts as well as the most useful application in each case. The aim is to pique the interest of the reader enough for them to want to specialize in the one that inspires the most confidence.

Why Technical Analysis?

Price shifts occur when market agents decide that the asset in question is expensive or cheap. To reach this conclusion, each participant relies on a multitude of strategies and reasoning.

It is impossible to know exactly why a market moves up or down, but what we can analyze is the representation of all the interactions between the Agents, and this is evidenced in the price.

This is the underlying logic of Technical Analysis. We do not know the number of participants in a market; nor what tools have they used to obtain their own particular valuations; nor what kinds of different speculative strategies they may be executing; nor if institutional options traders have intervened with the intention of minimizing their risk. The only thing we know is that all this interaction is ultimately represented on the price chart.

This whole compendium of potential situations is ultimately reduced to what is depicted on the price chart, which is ultimately the source of information on which all Technical Analysis approaches are based.

The Origin of Technical Analysis

The Dow theory is considered to be the origin and cornerstone of technical analysis. It was presented by Charles Dow, co-founder along with Edward Jones of what we now know as the Dow Jones Industrial Average (DJIA) index.

This theory is based on 6 basic principles:

1. **The market discounts everything**. This refers to the idea mentioned previously that the price reflects everything.

2. **There are three kinds of market trend**: primary, secondary and minor. The price moves in waves of different sizes in which smaller waves are part of bigger ones.

3. **The main trends have three phases**: an accumulation phase, a public participation phase, and a distribution phase. This has to do with the market cycle and with the law of cause and effect, where for an effect (trend) to develop, a cause (range) must first have occurred.

4. **Markets must confirm each other**. Dow referred to two indices of that era. He claimed that no signal would be significant unless it occurred in both markets at the same time.

5. **Volume must confirm the trend.** Applying the law of Effort vs result, the idea is that trend movements are accompanied by volume, denoting an interest in that direction; and that movements of

a corrective nature are accompanied by low volume, denoting a lack of participation. Both signs would confirm the health of the trend.

6. **A trend is presumed to exist until definitive signals prove that a reversal has occurred**. This involves assessing, using analytical tools, whether the current trend will continue in the same direction or whether there it will reverse.

These principles laid the foundations for the creation of other methodologies that were developed later, hence its significance. Some approaches that we will look at later develop these ideas and provide us with specific tools with which to put these principles into practice.

High-Level Technical Analysis

I have given this section of the book the title "Technical Analysis Fast Track" because we are going to get straight to the point and study those tools which are most suitable.

There are countless methodologies that we can put into practice when analyzing charts, but most of them are based on extremely subjective or illogical principles; so I suggest you take a qualitative leap in your learning process and dedicate your time to mastering those techniques that are most useful for trading in current markets.

During my learning process I studied all the different trading methods that exist out there and little by little I realized and identified which tools make sense and which do not. I want you to be able to take this shortcut which will save you time and money, because it is what I would have done in my early days if I had known about it. Once you understand how markets actually work in today's ecosystem, it doesn't make sense to apply outdated methods that have no real underlying logic. Especially when there are alternatives that do meet these requirements.

Coincidentally, the technical analysis methods that do not meet these expectations are the same ones that offer a low degree of specialization. My intention is to make the reader realize that if it were that easy, everyone would do it. And this isn't the case. The reality is that most people lose money when trading or investing because they apply unproven methods that appeal more to subjectivity than to logic and reasoning. The problem with this lies again with the trader, or rather, with their mind; because our brain sometimes sees what it wants to see. But if we were to apply objectivity to the matter we would realize the irrationality of some of these approaches.

I'm referring to approaches that treat the market as if it were a static entity which somehow, as if by magic, tends to repeat certain patterns over and over again, just because. I am referring to those approaches that appeal to the use of indicators as the main tool to know what is happening in the market when in reality they have little or nothing to do with this task (although they may be useful for others).

Coincidentally, these same approaches are also the oldest, the first to emerge when financial charts began to be studied. The problem is that, as we have already seen, technological advances have prompted a spectacular change in this field, with more and more capital flooding the markets which has completely changed the behavior of all the agents involved.

These older approaches based on no real underlying logic may have had their moment in the sun and were applied with a high degree of success and performance; but as we all know, financial markets have evolved and most of these tools continue to treat the market exactly as they did 80 years ago. It is precisely for this reason that I believe there is no logical reason to apply them.

My reasoning is this; as we saw at the beginning of the book, financial markets are driven by the continuous interaction of buyers and sellers under the law of supply and demand. Taking this principle as basic and universal, those methodologies that try to analyze this interaction between buyers and sellers are one step ahead of the rest. The only way that our analyses can be adjusted to the most objective reality possible of what may be happening in the market is to analyze the signals emitted by those who intervene in the market; and these signals are ultimately reflected, as we all know, in the price and volume.

Based on this, the following methodologies can be classified as high level:

- Price action.

- Price and Volume (Volume Spread Analysis).

- Wyckoff Method.

- Market/Volume Profile.

- Order Flow.

All of these analyze supply and demand in its purest possible form through price and/or volume.

This does not mean that you cannot trade and even earn money using other methodologies. I always say that somewhere on planet there must be someone making money using simple moving averages or trading with some other low-level tool; but my belief is that this is the exception rather than the rule. It makes much more sense that an analysis will be accurate if what we are analyzing is the information on what drives the market: price and volume; rather than other sources of information that appeal to other principles (in some cases almost mystical ones).

Methodologies considered low level include:

- Traditional chartism.

- Fibonacci levels.

- Elliot's theory.

- Wolfe waves.

- Gann fans.

Many may disagree with my view, but I simply want us to maintain a critical mindset. It will be this critical mindset that will lead you little by little to this reasoning. So don't believe anything I tell you. If you like, take the time to study all these approaches and draw your own conclusions.

Later on we will delve into those methodologies that are worth spending more time on, which I have dubbed high-level Technical Analysis.

CHARTS

Charts are the fundamental tool of technical analysis and are mainly used to represent price data.

They are created with the time variable on the horizontal axis and the price variable on the vertical axis. Playing with the time variable allows us to analyze the chart using whatever time frame we choose.

While the price will always show the same information (since this is objective data on the level at which transactions have been executed), the time variable allows us to represent that same information in a different way depending on the time frame used to look at the chart (minutes, hours, days, weeks or months).

Although some very advanced charts created with complex mathe-matical programs exist today, at this stage just having some knowledge of the most basic and common representations of price that can be found on most platforms is enough.

Line Charts

Line charts display price information as a series of data points connected by a solid line.

Each of the points selected to create the final chart represents the closing price of the selected time frame; in other words, it only informs us about one item of information, the closing price. As a result, this type of chart is not widely used for comprehensive price analysis.

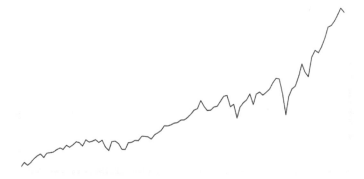

However, the way it graphically represents the information means it is especially useful for carrying out a quick comparative analysis of strength/weakness between assets.

The following chart shows how two assets that belong to the same sector are performing differently. If we wanted to invest in a particular sector of the economy, we could carry out a comparative analysis between the stocks within that sector and select those that have been preforming better than the rest since, in accordance with one of the principles of technical analysis –ceteris paribus–, it is likely to continue to behave in the same way in the future, i.e. better than the rest.

It is also useful for long-term analysts (such as investors) who do not use technical analysis as their main tool and who simply want to see the actual evolution of the asset (closing price), leaving aside all other information that could be considered noise (opening, maximum and minimum prices).

Bar Charts

Also known as OHLC Charts (Open, High, Low, Close) since they provides information about the opening, maximum, minimum and closing prices. In short, these charts show us the total price action for the selected time frame.

This type of chart together with the candlestick chart and unlike the line chart is designed to offer a better relative analysis between the representations of the selected time frame. The information we obtain from the current bar compared to any previous bars tells us a lot about what is likely to happen next. Further on we will look at the methodology that is based on this reading of bars and candlesticks.

Many traders prefer to use bar charts over the candlestick charts, due to the fact that a bar chart offers more neutral information in that it doesn't show price movements in different colors as the candlestick chart does, allowing them to maintain an independent bias. As we can see, the information offered by both charts is the same, so it is up to the trader to deiced which one to use.

Candlestick Charts

Of Japanese origin, these are also known as Japanese candlestick charts. This type of chart deals with the same price information as the bar chart with the only difference that it represents it more visually by including a rectangular box (called the real body) between the opening and closing prices.

A candlestick chart reveals the nature of the particular candle at a glance, without the need to carefully look for the direction of the horizontal lines that show the opening and closing prices on the bar chart. This makes them much easier to interpret.

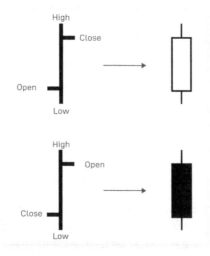

Originally, a bullish candlestick was represented with a white box and a bearish one with a black one. Today, trading platforms allow the user to configure the way they are displayed with colors; green for bullish candlesticks and red for bearish ones is the most common choice, making the analysis even more visual.

Linear and Logarithmic Scales

We can use one of two different scales for these charts. The linear or arithmetic scale shows all the variations of the market in the same way, in absolute terms by units of the same size; while the logarithmic scale does so in relative terms, by percentages.

In other words, the linear scale will visually represent a rise from $5 to $10 in the same way as one from $10 to $15 since in both cases the market has moved 5 units. The logarithmic scale, by contrast, will depict movements of different sizes since it takes into account that from $5 to $10 the increase is 100% and that from $10 to $15 it is 50% (to be 100%, it would have to be from $10 to $20).

The logarithmic chart adapts to the market as the latter moves. As the price increases the distance decreases. A logarithmic scale is generally re-commended over a linear one, especially since market agents measure re-turns in percentage terms rather than in units. It makes more sense to mea-sure gains and losses in percentage terms rather than units.

In terms of different time frames, I recommend using the logarithmic scale when analyzing longer time frames (weeks or months), and either of the two when trading in the shorter term (intraday). In the shorter term there isn't usually a big difference since the charts will be made up of a small number of candlesticks so any scale can be used. For longer time frames, things are different, because the number of candlesticks can be considera-ble.

TECHNICAL ANALYSIS BASICS

The following pages are part of the fundamental content of technical analysis. It is the first thing that is usually taught and although this content alone won't guarantee success in the market, it is important because it lays the foundations on which more complex concepts are developed by other methodologies.

How the Markets Move

Price movements do not always develop in the same way, but rather in waves of different sizes, duration and direction.

Prices do not move between two points in a straight line but move up and down through fluctuations in a pattern of upward and downward waves.

The waves are fractal in nature and interrelate with each other; smaller waves are part of intermediate waves, and these in turn are part of larger waves.

Each upward and downward movement is made up of numerous minor upward and downward waves. When one wave ends, another begins in the opposite direction. By studying and comparing the relationship between waves – their duration, speed and scope–, we will be able to determine the nature of the trend.

Wave analysis provides a clear view of the relative changes between supply and demand and helps us judge the relative strength or weakness of buyers and sellers as the price movement progresses.

Through careful wave analysis, we will gradually develop the ability to determine the end of a wave in one direction and the beginning of another in the opposite direction.

The Price Cycle

The basic market structure only appears in one of two forms:

▶ Trends. These are known as uptrends if they go up, or downtrends if they go down.

▶ Ranges. These can be accumulation ranges if they are at the beginning of the cycle, or distribution ranges if they are in the higher part of the cycle.

As we have already seen, price movements during these phases occur in waves.

During the accumulation phase, professional traders buy all the stock that is available for sale on the market. When they ensure through various maneuvers that there is no more floating supply left, they launch an upward movement. This phase of the trend is about the path of least resistance. The professionals have already verified that they will not encounter too much resistance (supply) that prevents the price from reaching higher levels. This concept is very important because until they verify that the path is clear (absence of sellers), they will not launch the upward movement, and they will perform test maneuvers over and over again. If the supply is overwhelming, the path of least resistance will be downwards and the price at that point can only fall.

During the uptrend, buyers are more aggressive than sellers. At this stage, large, less well-informed traders and the general public also enter the market under whose pressure the price rises. This upward movement will continue until buyers and sellers consider that the price has reached its fair value; buyers will see it as worth their while to close their buy positions; and sellers will see it as worth their while to start taking short positions.

The market has entered the distribution phase. A market ceiling will be forming and large traders are said to have completed the distribution (selling) of the stock that they had previously bought. The market also witnesses the entry of the final greedy buyers as well as informed traders who have entered to sell.

When they verify that the path of least resistance is now downwards, they launch the downtrend phase. If they observe that demand still exists and has no intention of going anywhere, that resistance to lower prices will only leave one viable path: upwards. If the price continues to rise after a pause, this structure is called a re-accumulation phase. The same happens in the case of a downtrend: if the price is in a bearish trend and there is a pause before continuing with the decline, this sideways movement is known as a redistribution phase.

During the downtrend sellers are more aggressive than buyers so only lower prices can be expected.

Being able to determine where the market is in the price cycle is a significant advantage. Knowing the general context helps us avoid entering at the wrong end of the market. This means that if the market is in a bullish phase after accumulation we should avoid going short and if it is in a bearish phase after distribution we should avoid going long. You may not know how to take advantage of the trend movement; but with this premise in mind, you are sure to avoid losses by not trying to trade against the trend.

When the price is in accumulation or uptrend phases, it is said to be in a buying position, and when it is in distribution or downtrend phases, it is said to be in a selling position. When there is no interest, that no campaign has taken place, it is said to be in a neutral position.

A cycle is considered complete when all stages of the cycle have been followed: accumulation, uptrend, distribution, and downtrend. These complete cycles occur in all time frames. This is why it is important to take into account all time frames; because they might each be at different stages. The market must be looked at from this point of view to understand the context and to analyze it accurately. The key is to remember that the smaller graphical structures will always depend on the larger graphical structures.

Once you learn to correctly identify the four phases of price action and adopt a completely impartial point of view, independent of any news, rumors, opinions and your own prejudices; you will be closer to taking advantage of your trading system.

Trends

Prices change and the waves that result from those price changes generate trends. The price of a security moves through a series of waves in the direction of the trend (impulses), which are separated by a series of waves in the opposite direction (corrections).

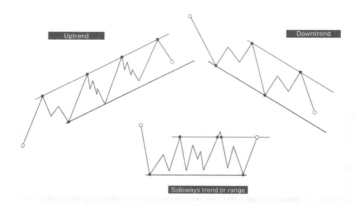

The trend is simply the line of least resistance and therefore the trader's job is to identify it and analyze its evolution to decide what type of strategy to adopt at any given time.

When a market is climbing and encounters resistance (selling), it either overcomes that resistance or the price will reverse; the same happens when the price is falling and encounters resistance; it either overcomes all the buying or the price will reverse. Those turning points are critical moments and provide excellent zones in which to trade.

We can distinguish between three types of trends, depending on the direction of the movement: uptrend, downtrend and sideways trend. The most objective description of an uptrend is when the price follows a series of growing impulses and corrections, where the peaks and troughs are increasingly higher. Similarly, we can identify a downtrend when the peaks and troughs are ever lower, leaving a series of decreasing impulses and corrections. Finally, a sideways trend occurs when highs and lows keep fluctuating within a price range.

Trends are divided by their duration into three different categories; long, medium and short term. Since there are no hard and fast rules for classifying them according to the time frame, they can be categorized by how they fit in relation to the one above. In other words, a short-term trend will be observed within a medium-term trend, which in turn will be seen within a long-term trend.

Ranges

The market spends most of its time in this type of situation, therefore ranges are extremely important.

Sideways trends or ranges are zones in which the previous movement has stopped and there is a relative balance between supply and demand. It is in ranges where accumulation or distribution campaigns take place in preparation for a subsequent uptrend or downtrend. It is this force of accumulation or distribution that is the catalyst for what will develop in the subsequent movement.

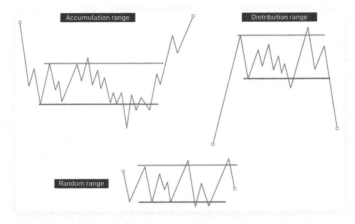

Trading inside the range offers optimal trading opportunities with a very high risk/reward potential; however, the best trades are those in which the trader is able to successfully position themselves within the range to take advantage of the subsequent trend movement.

While no new information is generated that could significantly change the valuations made by the market agents, in range trading the lower part of the range is seen as an area where the price is cheap, which will result in the appearance of buyers; while the upper part is seen as an area where the price is expensive, which will lead to selling to participants. Both actions will cause the market to move up and down between these zones.

In trend trading, since the price is already moving, part of its progress will have been lost. By taking advantage of the opportunities within the range, there is the possibility of capturing a bigger movement.

To be correctly positioned at the start of the trend, you must be able to analyze price action and volume as the range develops. Fortunately, the Wyckoff method offers a unique set of guidelines for traders to successfully accomplish this task. The identification of events and the analysis of phases are essential tools for the correct reading of the range.

If you don't see a clearly defined trend, the price is most likely in a range phase. There are one of three basic interests behind this neutral or sideways trend: either traders are accumulating, in preparation for an upward movement; they are distributing, in preparation for a downward movement; or the price is fluctuating up and down because there is no definitive interest.

Random fluctuations should be ignored as there is probably no professional interest in that market. It is important to understand that there isn't always professional interest behind every range; and that therefore, if there is little interest in a security, the price simply fluctuates because it is in equilibrium and movements in one direction are neutralized by movements in the opposite direction; but no major trader is taking advantage of these fluctuations to position itself in anticipation of a subsequent trend move.

According to the law of cause and effect, the price must spend some time within the range in preparation before a subsequent move. And this movement will be directly proportional to the time spent in the range. This means that ranges with a short duration will generate shorter movements and ranges that last longer will generate movements over a longer period of time.

A range is defined by two points connected by a channel. As long as the price stays within the range, it will undergo no major movement The key is at the edges. When these are broken, this can open up excellent trading opportunities.

You need to understand that the definitive breakout from the range and the start of the trend cannot occur until a clear imbalance between supply and demand has been generated. At that point, the market must be in the control of well-informed professionals and these must have verified that the direction in which they will move the price is the path of least resistance.

This means that if they have accumulated with the aim of pushing prices higher, they will first verify that there will be no resistance (selling) to stop that rise. When they verify that the path is clear, they will initiate the movement. Likewise, if they have been distributing (selling) with the intention of lowering prices, they need to make sure that floating demand (interest in buying) is relatively low.

Drawing Trend Lines

Lines are used to delimit the ranges and they define the angle at which the trend is moving. They are a superb visual aid for analysis, useful for assessing the health of the movement; both to identify price exhaustion, and to evaluate a possible reversal in the market.

In general, they help us to anticipate what the support and resistance levels of the price will be. Moreover, when the price approaches or touches these lines this suggests we should look for additional signals that might indicate a reversal, which would open up several trading opportunities.

The more times the price touches a line, the more significant the level becomes for analysis. You have to be careful not to draw lines indiscriminately, especially over every minor movement. Knowing how to correctly draw lines requires good judgment or it can lead to confusion in your reasoning.

When the price penetrates a line we need to stay alert and be prepared to act. Depending on the position where the breakout occurs, as well as the action itself, this can suggest different scenarios. A deep understanding of price action and volume is necessary to determine the most likely scenarios.

Before looking at the different ways of drawing lines and how these can depict the situation of the market, it is important to bear in mind that any method of drawing lines simply informs us about the dynamics that the price is currently following, which we should only use to influence our trading approach and never as a decision-making tool in isolation.

Visually identifying how the price follows certain lines (which are subjective) simply puts us in a position to see that the price, for whatever reason, is following this dynamic; and that based on the principles of technical analysis, it is most likely that it will continue to behave in the same way in the future. But no more than that. It should not be used as a tool by itself to make buying or selling decisions.

This information should be used as merely another input within our trading checklist and for forecasting different scenarios. For example, if we identify an uptrend, we will want to trade long, and only consider short trading if the price breaks that upward dynamic. This is an example of the effective use of identifying market dynamics and drawing lines.

Another interesting thing to keep in mind is that line drawing does not have to be exact, it does not have to connect points precisely on the chart. This goes against everything we have been taught about drawing charts, but let's apply a bit logic to the issue. As I said, drawing lines is useful to show the dynamic of the price. This should be very visual to the point that we hardly even need to draw the lines to identify this dynamic. With this as a basis, how important is it that the line is anchored a few more points up or down? It really isn't, because this won't change the basic reading of what we are trying to identify.

Having said all that, let's now look at the most basic lines that can be drawn on a chart:

Support and resistance

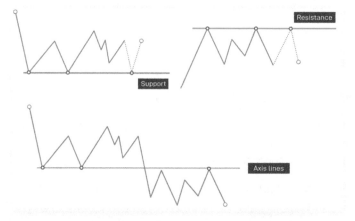

A horizontal line identifies an old zone of imbalance between supply and demand. When it connects at least two price lows, this can be considered a support. This is a zone in which buyers appeared in the past to outperform sellers by stopping the price decline and buyers are expected to reappear when it is visited again in the future.

A horizontal line connecting at least two highs identifies a resistance zone, in which selling outstripped buying, which halted a rise in price; that is why sellers are expected to reappear when this level is reached again in future.

When a line serves as both support and resistance, it is known as an axis line. Prices tend to revolve around these axis lines. These price levels constantly change roles; a broken resistance becomes a support, and a broken support becomes a resistance.

Trend lines

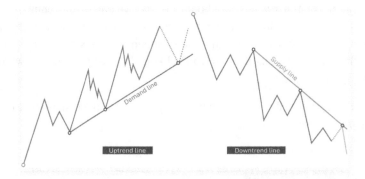

After identifying the nature of the trend, the next step is to establish a guideline to take advantage of the movement. This involves a simple connection between two or more price points.

In a downtrend, the trend line is drawn by connecting two decreasing peaks. This line is called the supply line since it is assumed that sellers will appear when the price reaches this level again in future.

In an uptrend, the trend line is drawn by connecting at least two increasing lows. This line is called the demand line since it marks the point where buyers will supposedly reappear.

We can continuously readjust trend lines in order to identify the one that best reflects the price action and which has therefore been touched the most times. The more times the line has been followed, the more strongly we will be able to interpret it when it is touched again in the future.

Keep in mind that a line with too much of a gradient will be broken too soon, meaning it hasn't been drawn correctly.

As long as the price remains within the established levels, the movement is said to be healthy and you should consider holding or adding positions in favor of that direction.

When the price approaches a trend line there is a threat of a breakout and this may mean that the trend is reaching exhaustion, suggesting a change in the pace of the trend or a definitive trend reversal.

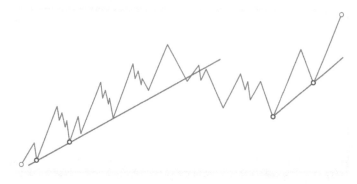

A trend line break by itself is not a conclusive symptom of anything, as it could be a true or false breakout. What is significant is how the line is broken, the conditions under which it happens, and the subsequent price reaction.

After a movement of a certain distance, the price may reach a point of resistance causing the trend to change its pace and plateau. During this pause (sideways movement or range) the force that originally drove the trend may be renewed or even strengthened, resulting in a continuation of the trend with greater momentum than before.

Under these conditions, the trend lines must be redrawn to conform to the new established angle. For this reason, just because the trend line is broken doesn't mean you should believe the trend will reverse.

Channels

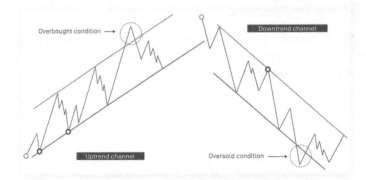

The ideal channel will have multiple touch points and should capture the majority of the price within its limits.

When the uptrend line or demand line is pulled towards the opposite extreme, anchoring itself in parallel at the peak that is located between the two troughs used for its creation, the overbought line is created; and together they define an ascending channel. This channel indicates a rising price.

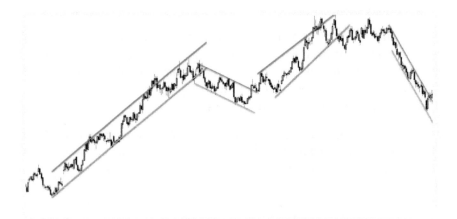

Traders should be aware of overbought conditions. These conditions are created when the price exceeds the upper part of the ascending channel. If the acceleration is too fast, the price reaches a point where it is highly sensitive to long hedging (profit taking) and in general to the withdrawal of more experienced buyers; which suggests a weakening of the uptrend. This generally guides the price towards downward corrective action.

Human beings seem to be attracted to extremes. In financial markets this trend is manifested in the form of greed. Prices are pushed higher and higher until the public fill their boots with stocks that are generally overvalued. When this happens, an overbought condition is said to exist.

When the downtrend line or supply line is pulled towards the opposite extreme, anchoring itself in parallel at the trough that is located between the two peaks used for its creation, the oversold line is created; and together they define a descending channel. This channel indicates a falling market.

Traders should be aware of oversold conditions. These conditions are created when the price falls below the lowest point of the ascending channel. If the downtrend moves too fast, the price reaches a point where it is highly sensitive to short hedging (profit taking) and to a general withdrawal of more experienced traders who were selling; which suggests a weakening downtrend. This generally guides the price towards upward corrective action.

In a bullish market there is another extreme that takes control: fear. As the price falls, traders become concerned. The lower it falls, the more fearful they are. The participants reach such a level of fear that they can't take it anymore and they sell their positions. This panic selling in creates this oversold condition.

These periods of excessive buying or selling that lead to a stop in price movements can occur in any time frame.

Reverse trend lines

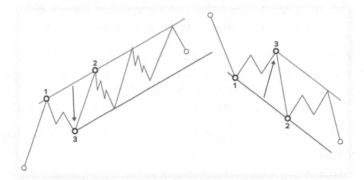

In fast-moving conditions where a clear trend has yet to be established, a reverse use of lines is a good way of trying to structure the price movement, at least initially.

It involves creating the supply line first in an upward trend and using this to generate a demand line; and to first create the demand line in a downtrend to then generate the supply line from it.

At the start of a bullish advance, if the price has made two major upward impulses without any significant bearish correction, you can estimate at which point to expect the price correction by first creating the supply line and dragging it down to create the uptrend line; and in the same way, first drawing the demand line to create the downtrend line from it.

As I said, this way of drawing lines is only valid for trends that have just emerged and the dynamics of which have not yet been defined. What we are trying to achieve through the reverse use of lines is to hypothesize about where the price might react if that is what the structural dynamic of the market will be.

Converging lines

There will be times when you find that the overbought and oversold lines created based on their trend lines do not work effectively. The price may never reach these lines since it will probably be following a different dynamic.

The way to fix this deficiency is to create these lines independently, regardless of the trend line.

The means creating the overbought line by connecting two peaks and the oversold line by connecting two troughs. The objective is to try to find the structural logic behind the movements to take advantage of this, regardless of whether the same angle of progress is followed on either side.

Visually they are seen as patterns of exhaustion. In the case of uptrends, the fact that the price isn't able to reach the original overbought line is a symptom of weakness and alerts us to a possible downward turn. Similarly, if the price no longer falls as far as the original oversold line in a downtrend this indicates a symptom of underlying strength and alerts us to a possible upward turn.

PRICE ACTION

Price Action deals with the pure analysis of the information provided by price data on bar or candlestick charts.

This methodology offers two analysis options:

- **General, through the analysis of market movements**. This method attempts to analyze the anatomy of the current movement with respect to the previous one, in general terms; that is, by grouping candles. This form of analysis gives us a broader view of what is happening in the general context of the market.

- **Specific, through the analysis of candlestick patterns**. This focuses on comparing the shape of the current candlestick with previous ones. This offers us more accurate and useful information for the short term.

The objective of price action analysis is to assess how the price has performed both in general and specifically and to try to determine the market sentiment and where it is likely to go in the future.

This methodology does not involve any indicators. Price action ultimately represents all the reasoning, expectations and decision-making that has been executed by the agents who are trading that particular asset; therefore, all the relevant information that needs to be evaluated is deemed to be already included in the price.

Price action is a universal methodology since its principles can be applied to any asset and in any time frame.

Candlestick Patterns

Candlesticks are graphic tools that send out signals about the continuous interaction between buyers and sellers.

One of the most important elements to take into account to correctly read the candlesticks is the contact in which they appear; because the same kind of candlestick at a different point can be read in a completely different way.

For example, a bullish candlestick with a large body and wide range identified at the beginning of an uptrend denotes bullish intent and is likely to be followed by higher prices; but that same candle found when the uptrend has already been going for some time could be a climax that suggests that the movement is already exhausted and could be followed by a reversal.

Another fact that should be taken into account throughout the study of this subject is that all the information is analyzed and used in relative terms; that is, comparing certain candlesticks to others that have previously appeared. When we talk about a candlestick being big, small, wide, narrow, etc. we always do it comparatively speaking since otherwise it would not make any sense.

With this in mind, let's now look at what key information we need to look for when analyzing candlesticks:

Direction. This tells us who is in control.

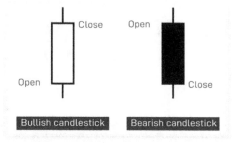

- Bullish candlestick: if the closing price is above the opening price. Buyers are dominant.

- Bearish candlestick: if the closing price is below the opening price. Sellers are in control.

Sentiment. This is about classifying the candlestick depending on the location of its closing price compared to that of the previous candlestick.

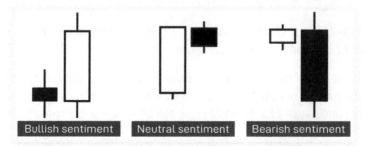

- **Bullish.** When the closing price is above the high of the previous candlestick, this indicates a bullish sentiment.

- **Neutral.** When the closing price is within the range of the previous candlestick, this indicates a neutral sentiment. It may suggest some sort of pause, consolidation, or lack of interest. This is generally the case at least, but if the closing price is within the range of the previous candlestick and has a huge wick at either end, this would suggest a radically different sentiment.

- **Bearish.** When the closing price is below the low of the previous candlestick, this indicates a bearish sentiment.

Closing price. The closing price allows us to determine the sentiment of the candlestick in question. It is useful to divide the candlestick's range into three equal parts to get a specific picture of the level of conviction traders have shown in their interaction.

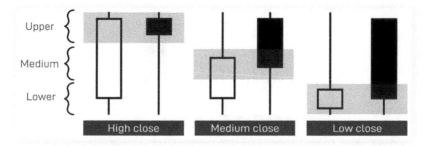

- **High.** A closing price within the upper third of the candlestick indicates a very bullish sentiment, with buyers showing a high level of conviction.

- Medium. A closing price within the middle third of the candlestick indicates a neutral sentiment. It suggest that neither buyers nor sellers have taken effective control over the other.

- Low. A closing price in the lower third of the candlestick suggests a bearish sentiment where sellers have shown themselves to be more aggressive.

Size. Body length, the difference between the opening and closing price. This shows the extent of dominance of whoever is in control.

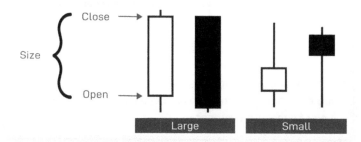

- Large. The body covers at least 2/3 of the total range. This shows the intentionality and aggressiveness of those trading in that direction. They are often referred to as high-quality buyers or sellers.

- Small. The body covers 1/3 of the range of the candle. Represents lack of interest and conviction. Referred to as low-quality buyers or sellers.

Spread. This is the total distance between the candlestick's high and low price. It is a representation of volatility and/or participation.

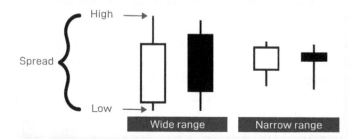

- Wide: Under normal conditions, this suggests an interest on the part of traders in moving in that direction, provided that the body is large. You should be aware that a wide range around the time significant news is broadcast is usually treated as noise and you shouldn't assume there is any intention behind the movement in question.

- Narrow: If it appears in normal conditions (in regular hours when all traders are present) it is assumed that participation has been low, which can be attributed to a lack of interest in the movement.

Wicks. These indicate dominance in shorter time frames.

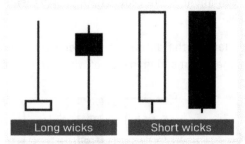

Long wicks   Short wicks

- Long. A long wick suggests the appearance of an action of intent in some lower time frame, which can be an early warning of the beginning of a major movement.

- Short. A candlestick with a minimal or no wick shows there is total control by the traders. A candlestick whose low is the opening price and whose high is the closing price suggests the total and absolute control of the buyers. By contrast, a candlestick whose high is the opening price and whose low is the closing price informs us that the sellers are in total control.

The direction, size, range and wicks provide the key clues that we need to analyze to try to interpret correctly and as objectively as possible the message behind them about who is most likely to have control of the market (buyers or sellers) and where the price is most likely to go next (up or down).

This key information allows us to distinguish in a practical manner the two most important types of candlestick that we need to able to identify in order to predict these last two aspects (control and future movement):

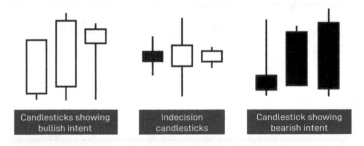

Candlesticks showing bullish intent   Indecision candlesticks   Candlestick showing bearish intent

Candlesticks showing intent

This type of candlestick represents a movement in one direction of the other. Buyers or sellers have gained control by trading more aggressively than the other side.

It is a candlestick with a large body and a wide range whose closing price will be in the final third. It may or may not have a wick, but if it does, this should be on the opposite side to the direction of the candlestick.

Depending on the direction, it may be bullish or bearish:

- **Candlestick showing Bullish intent** (strength). Clear conviction on the part of the buyers. This is generally represented by a bullish candlestick with a wide body and range and a closing price in the upper third; although bullish intent could also be indicated by the appearance of a long wick at the bottom of the candlestick.

- **Candlestick showing Bearish** intent (weakness). Aggressive sellers. Depicted by a bearish candle, with a wide body and range and a closing price in the lower third. If there is a wick, it should be at the top of the candle.

Indecision candlestick

This type of candlestick represents a lack of interest or a balance between buyers and sellers. These candlesticks usually have narrow bodies and ranges and closing prices in the middle third, although they may also appear with a wide range and small body; in other words, with very long wicks at each end.

Candlesticks and reversal patterns

A huge number of different configurations of candlestick patterns and graphical representations can be found in price action manuals which are mainly used as market entry triggers. Doji, Pinbar, Engulfing, Piercing and Dark Cloud are just some of these.

In essence, what traders are looking and hoping for in all these candlestick patterns and configurations is a shift in the control of the market; a change of sentiment in favor of one or other side (buyers or sellers). The vast majority of these patterns, or at least the most important ones, ultimately only include one, two or three candlesticks that end with the appearance of candlestick showing intent. That is why I have paid particular attention to showing you how to identify one of these sorts of candlesticks.

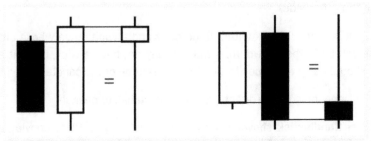

The appearance of candlesticks showing intent ultimately confirms a change of control among market participants in the very short term.

At this point, it is worth going back to the concept of fractality that was brought up several pages ago. As already mentioned, fractality refers to the fact that the market behaves in the same way regardless of the time frame. And the appearance of these patterns is especially linked to this idea. As I have already said, a candlestick that clearly shows intent can be represented in different ways depending on the time frame in which the chart is displayed.

Two of the reversal patterns most used by all price action traders are the Engulfing and Hammer patterns. An engulfing candlestick is one whose range completely encompasses the range of the previous candlestick; while a hammer candlestick is one that shows the strength of one side or the other through the appearance of a very long wick at one of its ends.

Applying a little logic to these behaviors will lead us to the conclusion that they are actually the same action and that the only difference is the time frame we are looking at. An engulfing pattern is nothing more than a hammer candlestick in a longer time frame; and a hammer candlestick, if we were to use a shorter time frame would appear as an engulfing pattern.

The last two charts show a real-life example of this. The upper image shows a bullish engulfing pattern on a 4-hour chart on a support zone; which would look like a hammer candlestick with a bullish sentiment on the 8-hour chart.

For a better understanding of the concept the following chart is an example of what actually happens inside the candlestick (in shorter time frames) and how that interaction finally produces the graphical representation of the candlestick with a long wick at the bottom.

As we have said, this wick, which is the same as an engulfing pattern, indicates the change in control and how a downtrend has been turned into an uptrend, ultimately indicating the bullish sentiment. This is a perfect example of the fractality of the market.

Pivots, Movements and Trends

Given the subjectivity involved in technical analysis, anything we can do to make our analysis more objective can help us enormously. Our minds often make us see things that haven't actually happened, so incorporating fixed and objective rules into the way we interpret price action can help more accurately read charts.

With this in mind, we are going to define the following concepts objectively so that there is no possible subjective interpretation. This is simply to ensure that we always evaluate the same actions in the same way.

The concepts of pivots, movements and trends are the basic and fundamental tools on which the analysis of market action is based.

Pivots and liquidity zones

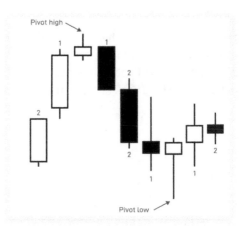

The most basic component of price action is the pivot. A pivot is simply a price formation that creates a turning point or pivot in the market. The pivot is created with at least two candlesticks to the left and to the right of the one that reaches the pivot point.

Other authors also accept minor pivots formed by only one candlestick to the left and to the right instead of two. As always, there is no one better configuration, it is up to the trader to determine which one they want to work with. The only objective and certain thing is that the more candlesticks make up the pivot, the greater strength it will have.

The power of pivots lies in the use they have for the participants. As well as for correctly analyzing the trend, they are generally used to identify trading opportunities and for position management since they create zones where orders pending execution are located (limit orders).

Limit orders are used to enter and exit the market, but they can be of a different nature depending on the position you have at that time: if you are out of the market you can use them to enter long or short; and if you are in the market you can use them to exit it by taking profits or losses.

A large number of these orders tend to be located in the vast majority of pivots with these four interests behind them depending on the valuations made by the agents. And the greater the strength of the pivot (the more candlesticks there are to the left and to the right), the greater the liquidity located at the pivot point. This is why the greater the number of candlesticks used to create the pivot, the greater its strength because there will be more liquidity at this point.

The logic is that participants see it as a support and resistance level at which the price has reversed previously, which leads them to believe that in the future when it reaches that same zone it will pivot again. This information is interpreted differently by different traders, which is why there are all kinds of limit orders pending execution. Some want to anticipate the pivot, others seek to enter for momentum, others set up their Stop Loss at that point assuming that if it exceeds this zone, support or resistance will have been effectively broken and it would confirm that their analysis has been wrong, etc. As I say, the reasons are manifold.

The only objective fact is that at these points areas known as **liquidity zones** (since limit orders are identified as liquidity) are created that are extremely useful and should be taken into account, both to analyze the trend, and because we can expect an imbalance between supply and demand to appear in them that offers us a trading opportunity.

To summarize, the importance of these liquidity zonas lies in the auction process presented in the fundamental concepts section which stated that all agents must have their counterparty in order to be able to trade: that for each buyer there must be another seller with whom to execute the transaction. And this concept is also closely linked to the idea of informed and uninformed traders. Ultimately, the informed trader who is positioned on the correct side of the market will provide liquidity to the uninformed trader who has failed to correctly identify the signs or who has made incorrect valuations.

Large traders need to enter these liquidity zones since only there will they find all the orders they need to build their position. Otherwise, were they to enter the market in a low liquidity zone, they would cause slippage that would negatively impact the average price obtained.

You should bear in mind that the further back in time a liquidity zone is, the less important it will be; fewer traders will have orders placed there. A recommended option for identifying the best pivot points is to only take into account the liquidity zones that belong to the prevailing context of the current market. In other words, if we are in an uptrend, we should only look at pivots that have formed during that uptrend. If the price has just completed a full cycle and an uptrend is then followed by another downtrend, any bullish pivot point in the downtrend will be less significant, especially if they are very far back in time.

Another situation that may arise is the appearance of several pivot points together. In this case, traders will usually have placed their orders in the pivot furthest back in time. This should be the one that we primarily take into account both for trading zone functions and to manage the position itself.

And finally, bear in mind that the longer the time frame in which the pivot was created, the greater the strength of the liquidity zone.

The critical factor when analyzing what is happening after the price reaches that liquidity zone is to observe how the market reacts immediately after this action. Once the price interacts with that zone, only two things can happen; orders are absorbed and the price continues in the same direction, or a reversal occurs. Drawing conclusions from that action and reaction is our job as traders.

A very important thing to keep in mind is that the more times a liquidity zone is visited, the more likely it is that a real breakout will occur from it; in other words, the chances that the price will continue in the same direction will increase. The reasoning is obvious: each time the area is visited, liquidity is consumed, and therefore there is less and less liquidity available there. The power of the passive position of traders decreases because they have progressively less liquidity. Then, finally, an aggressive action on the part of the opposite side will be able to definitively absorb the orders located there and continue the movement in that direction. This recommendation is very useful for trading in ranges that we will see later on.

Based on everything I have mentioned, liquidity zones provide us with an excellent location in which to manage our position and obtain profits.

Movements

The shifts that are generated between pivot points are called movements. These movements may be impulsive or corrective in nature depending on the direction in which they move with respect to the current trend. If the movement is in the direction of the current trend it will be impulsive in nature and if it is against the current trend, it will be corrective.

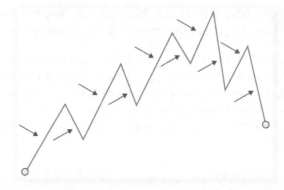

As I have already explained, pivot points generate liquidity zones, which can be seen at the end of each of movement. We already know that these locations are areas of interest in which there is a great deal of liquidity, providing us with ideal places to make trading decisions.

It is worth pointing out that the end of a movement always generates a liquidity zone; but not all liquidity zones generate a new movement.

As this real chart shows, the first downward movement observed on the left side ends at the second liquidity zone and not at the first. This is because in order for us to identify the end of a movement we need to see a complete pivot with two candlesticks to the left and to the right (or whatever configuration you have decided to follow). And in the case of the movement we have just analyzed, we can see that a new pivot point has not been generated in that area because there aren't two lower candlesticks on its left side.

Ends of movements

These patterns were introduced by JH Grandgerard, founder of the Ten-denciasFX academy. They implied a major contribution to the trading community in general and to price action students in particular, and one that is very much appreciated.

JH told us that movements will generally end in one of the following four ways:

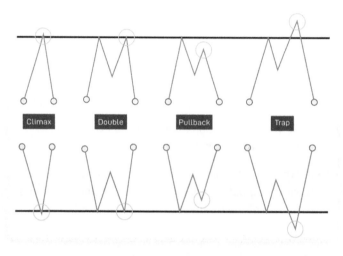

- **Climax**: The movement after the last impulse completely and po-werfully reverses the previous impulse.

- **Double** top/bottom. The movement responsible for reaching a new high/low stays at the same level as the previous high/low and then reverses.

- **Pullback**. The movement responsible for reaching a new high/low fails to reach the previous high/low before reversing.

- Bear/Bull **Trap**. The movement responsible for reaching a new high/low slightly exceeds (by up to 20%) the previous high/low before reversing.

The most interesting thing about all this is that thanks to the fractal behavior of the market these four forms can be seen in all market move-ments regardless of their degree and importance. This means that, generally speaking, both individual movements and trends will end in many cases in one of these four ways.

Trends

A trend is created as the result of two successive movements in the same direction. Trends vary in nature and we can categorize them as normal, slow and fast:

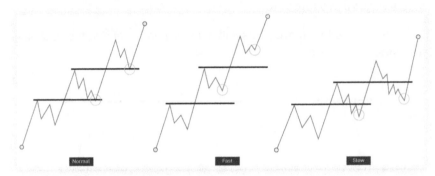

- **Normal**. When corrections generate a new pivot point at the level where the previous impulse ended.

- **Fast**. When corrections do not reach the level where the previous impulse ended before pivoting and developing a new movement in the direction of the trend.

- **Slow**. When corrections fall below the level where the previous impulse ended generating the new impulse.

This categorization can be useful for assessing the strength or weakness of the trend in order to implement one strategy or another (for or against the trend).

Trend Analysis

Using speed, depth and projection tools we try to assess the strength or weakness of the current trend to estimate when it is likely to end.

This will put us in a position to know when is a good time to look for an entry to join the trend (signs that indicate the trend is strong) and when it is better to stay out of the market (signs that show the movement is weak) to avoid entering on the wrong side or even to consider the possibility of trading against the trend.

Speed

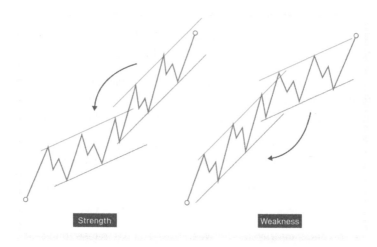

Speed refers to the angle at which the price is moving; therefore, if the price is currently moving faster than in the past, the trend is strong. If, on the other hand, it is moving slower than in the past, it suggests weakness.

Depth

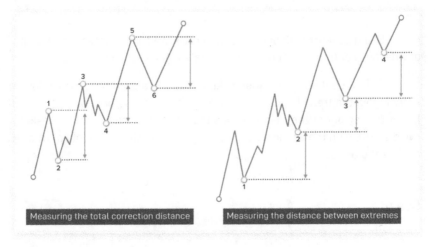

Measuring the total correction distance

Measuring the distance between extremes

A depth analysis assesses the distance that the trend corrections travel to determine if the weakness has increased or decreased.

As with projection analysis, we can assess depth using two measurements: the total distance of the correction from its origin to its end; and the distance that the price travels from the previous low to the new low.

- The distance traveled by the correction between 3 and 4 is less than the distance traveled between 1 and 2 = a strong trend.

- The distance traveled by the correction between 5 and 6 is greater than the distance traveled between 3 and 4 = a weak trend.

- The distance traveled between lows 2 and 3 is less than that traveled between lows 1 and 2 = a weak trend.

- The distance traveled between lows 3 and 4 is greater than that traveled between lows 2 and 3 = a strong trend.

Projection

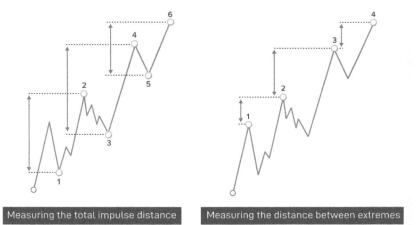

Measuring the total impulse distance | Measuring the distance between extremes

This tool is used to evaluate the distance traveled by an impulse wave and compare it to the previous ones to determine if the strength has increased or decreased.

For a trend to stay alive, each impulse must surpass the previous impulse. If an impulse is unable to make further progress in the direction of the trend, this signals that the movement may be nearing its end.

- The distance traveled by the impulse between 3 and 4 is greater than the distance traveled between 1 and 2 = a strong trend.

- The distance traveled by the impulse between 5 and 6 is greater than the distance traveled between 3 and 4 = a weak trend.

- The distance traveled between highs 2 and 3 is greater than that traveled between highs 1 and 2 = a strong trend.

- The distance traveled between highs 3 and 4 is less than that traveled between high 2 and 3 = a weak trend.

Continuation and Change of Trend

Continuing with the idea of maximizing the objectiveness of our analysis, we can assume that we are seeing a change in the nature of the trend when the pivot point that originated the last high/low (reference pivot point) is broken.

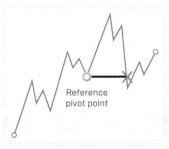

This change in nature simply informs us about the dynamics of the market and offers us a contextual framework. After its appearance, we should then observe one of these two possibilities:

Continuation of the trend

The first possibility of this breakout of the reference pivot point is that it is simply a consolidation prior to the continuation of the current trend.

This is what we look for if we are following the basic strategy of trading with the trend. It is in that area of the reference pivot point where we will be waiting to find our entry trigger.

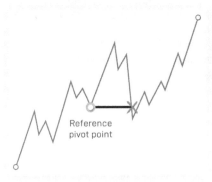

The reference pivot point breakout could give rise to new momentum in the direction of the preceding trend. Initially, this is the most likely possibility based on the previously mentioned hypothesis on which technical analysis is based, namely that the market is most likely to continue to behave as it has done up to now. And therefore, after the reference pivot point breakout, we should assume there will be a continuation of the trend rather than a reversal.

Change of trend

The second possibility is that a transition is about to take place in which the market goes from the trend in one direction to the trend in the opposite direction.

However, just because the pivot point has been broken does not mean we should assume that it signifies the birth of a new trend in the opposite direction. This signal is essential if that transition is to occur, but this alone is not enough; we would need to see something else to confirm that transition to a new trend in the opposite direction.

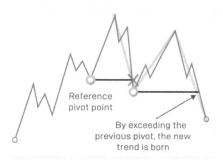

Reference pivot point

By exceeding the previous pivot, the new trend is born

The problem arises when the price is not able to hit that new high after the reference pivot point has been broken. If instead of doing so the price starts to hesitate and finally hits a lower high, this is an early indication that we could be facing the start of a new downtrend.

Therefore, we will only objectively deem it to be the start of a new trend when, after the previous reference pivot point breakout, the price manages to hit a new high/low in that new direction, at which point the price will already have shown two movements in the same direction.

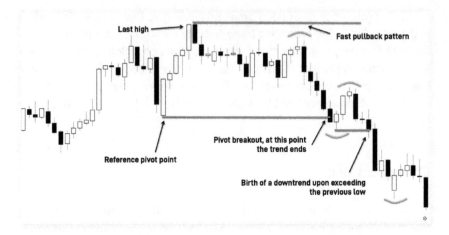

The end of a trend and the birth of the next one can develop in two ways, through fast or slow patterns.

- **Fast patterns.** These are the same patterns mentioned previously with regard to the end of the movements, but this time extrapolated to a higher level, applied in order to identify the end of the trend.

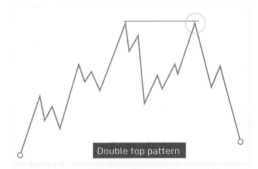

Double top pattern

- **Slow patterns.** More complex accumulation and distribution processes in which more time is taken to prepare the subsequent movement. This falls within the scope of the Wyckoff method that we will see later on.

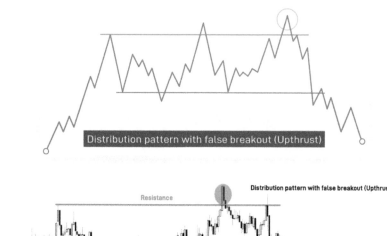

Distribution pattern with false breakout (Upthrust)

Distribution pattern with false breakout (Upthrust)

Resistance

Support

Reference pivot point

Types of Strategies

The first thing that we must be clear about before looking to trade is the current context of the market. Otherwise we cannot select the type of trade that is best suited to that moment. As we have already seen, markets can only be in one of two states: in range and in trend.

There are several options and each trader must search and select the one that best suits their profile. Ideally, you would specialize in one of these and not move on to the other until you have completely mastered the first. After some time has passed and having gained some experience, you will be in a position to handle all types of strategies and take advantage of any market environment to your benefit.

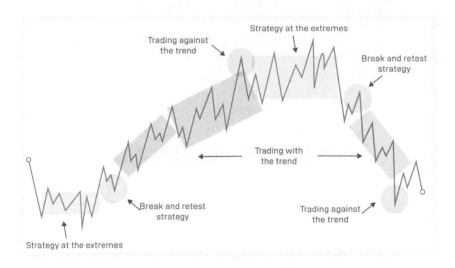

Trend context

The strategies that fall within this category can be classified according to the direction of the trade based on the direction of the current trend. If you want to trade in the same direction as the trend, this is said to be a trading with the trend or a trend following strategy, whereas if you wish to trade in the opposite direction to the current trend, you would be trading against the trend or following a trend reversal strategy.

We are going to analyze in depth the pros and cons of each of these:

Trading with the trend

This is one of the most applied strategies in the world of trading and investment. It is based "simply" on identifying the beginning of the trend and trading with it under the premise that the market will continue to move in that direction until the trend is exhausted.

I have put "simply" in quotation marks because identifying the trend is not always an easy task. First, we need to follow some objective rules, and second, decide in what time frame we are going to apply the strategy. Let's say you have decided to trade with the trend; but with which trend? The weekly, daily, hourly chart?

Many traders say that this type of strategy is the one that offers the greatest return and has the greatest probability of success; but this makes no sense unless they can back it up with a statistical study to confirm it, (and even if they did, we would need to see how this study has been carried out). As we will see later in the section on risk management, the Risk/Reward ratio and the percentage of successful trades will determine the strategy's true success rate. The takeaway here is that we should not make any claims without comprehensive knowledge because what may initially appear to be influenced by our perception, may not actually be the case.

In this context, we can assume that any corrections, which are in themselves minor trends, will be likely to fail, thus offering opportunities for trading with the trend.

The following chart shows two examples of trend trading at the appropriate locations. The first occurs in the zone of the pivot point of the previous high, a trading zone within the context of a normal trend. The second entry is at a point where the trend shows a certain amount of strength since the reversal is generated on a newly created pivot point which hasn't reached the pivot point of the previous impulse. These are the areas win which we can look for the end of the movement using one of the four patterns and/or the appearance of our entry trigger.

Incorporating other basic concepts of technical analysis, the ideal trading situation would be to observe said behavior in confluence with the trend line that informs us about the dynamics that the market is following. The more elements of this type converge, the more confidence we will have in the trade.

As well analyzing the speed, depth and projection of the trend to determine its strength, we can take into account other signals:

- Most of the candlesticks in the direction of the trend (impulse) show intent that denotes interest and with very little overlap between them.

- Most of the candlesticks in the opposite direction (corrections) are indecision candlesticks, they overlap with each other and suggest a lack of participation.

- We see normal and fast trend types.

- No significant trend lines are broken and minor ones that are broken result in sideways corrections.

- There is no movement that breaks the channel line creating an overbought or oversold situation that could suggest a trend climax.

The trend trading zones are around previous pivot points (axis lines) or around generated pivot points.

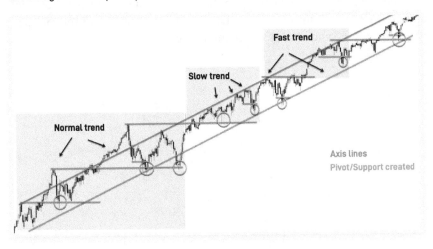

Trading against the trend

Trading against the trend, as we have already commented, is a strategy of trading in opposite direction to that of the trend in progress.

These trades tend to be riskier since, as we saw in the principles of technical analysis, the market is most likely to continue behaving in the way it has been doing up to now. And under this basic premise, we know that it is more likely that the trend will continue its course rather than reverse.

If we see that the trend has only recently started, looking for reversal trades against the trend doesn't appear to be the most sensible thing to do. This doesn't mean that you cannot be successful with a reversal trading strategy, but this wouldn't be the norm in the long run. In this context, it would seem more reasonable to look for trades that go with the trend.

But since everything comes to an end, the intelligent application of this type of trading is based on identifying early signs of possible exhaustion of the trend to start to assess the possibility of entering in the opposite direction.

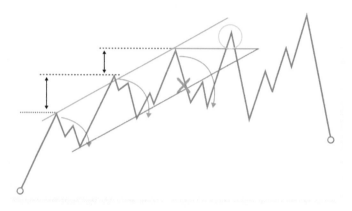

One way to identify this possible exhaustion is by applying the trend health analysis previously described: slowing down, ever larger corrections and ever smaller impulses. It would also be interesting to see at this point slow trends in which the corrections fall below the highs of the previous impulses.

Another way to measure the strength of the current trend is to identify its structural dynamics based on drawing trend lines and only decide to trade against the trend if said dynamics are broken, which would indicate a change in the market context.

The simplest thing to do in this case is to wait for the trend line to be broken, revealing the price dynamic. Al Brooks, one of the gurus of price action trading tells us that the most important rule of thumb is that you should only consider trading against trend when there has been a significant break in the trend line. And even then, you should still be looking to trade with the trend because after the first impulse against the trend, the market will almost always come back to test the last high/low. At this point, the market will follow one of the end of trend patterns (Climax, Double Top/Bottom, Pullback, or Bull/Bear Trap).

One tip to keep in mind is that the stronger the move that breaks the trend line, the more likely the reversal will be successful.

Another place in which to look for potential trades is when the price reaches a zone of excess that suggests overbought or oversold conditions. This involves waiting for a climax on the channel line in search of a mean reversion. This type of trade implies entering the market earlier than those we have previously looked at and therefore could entail a greater risk.

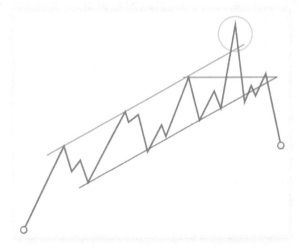

We would have greater confidence in this trade if said climax were also reaching a zone of previous liquidity. We must bear in mind that at that moment the price dynamic has not yet been broken, and it may not be broken even having reached that condition. The prevailing context continues to be a trend in the opposite direction, so, with this dynamic not yet broken, it is most likely that the trend will continue its course. Therefore, when trading with this type of early entry, we should not expect a large movement to take place. It may on occasion be the start of a total reversal of the trend but in most cases this won't happen; so it is best to take profits at the opposite end of the channel.

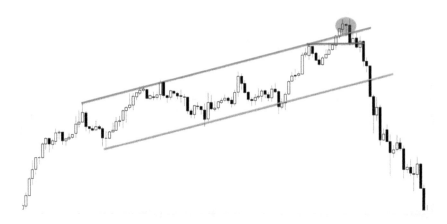

In addition to the breaking of the trend line and the strength of this breakout movement, we can take into account other signals that will give us greater confidence in the reversal:

- The movement is made up of candlesticks showing strong intent.

- The movement travels a long distance.

- The movement was born after a failed breakout of the channel line.

- The movement breaks the reference pivot point of the previous trend.

- The movement that comes back to test the last high/low lacks momentum; evidenced by many overlapping indecision candlesticks.

The trading zones are still around previous price pivot points.

Range context

The market spends most of its time in a range, which means this environment offers participants the most opportunities for executing trades.

We are going to see what two types of strategies we can apply in this type of context where the market is in equilibrium or in range:

Break and retest strategy

Strategy at the extremes

Strategy at the extremes

In a trading range, participants find themselves comfortably trading, exchanging their contracts and building their positions. The information available on the asset in question means that most of them have very similar valuations, which generates a state of efficiency or equilibrium, as demonstrated by the continuous fluctuations in price.

As long as this state of equilibrium is maintained, the market will reach the extremes of the range, levels that are seen as unfair, and the most avid participants will appear on the scene to try to profit from this inefficiency. They buy at support levels and sell at resistance levels looking for that mean reversion movement.

The key in this situation is to decide when we are actually in a range so we can start trading. One of the signs is a reference pivot point breakout in the preceding trend. Another may be simply fluctuations that, although they generate ambiguous highs and lows, do not have the ability to advance significantly out of range. We should at least wait for the price to generate two rebound points from the support level.

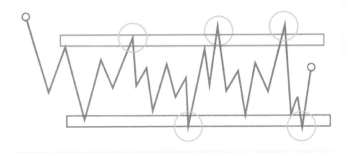

At that point, it is worth locating the trading zones at both extremes and wait for the price in one of the generated pivot points to guarantee better success, waiting for a reversal pattern that signals the entry trigger in the opposite direction.

With regard to the anatomy of ranges, it is advisable to try to trade in those that have enough distance between their extremes, avoiding narrow ranges made up of overlapping candles and congested movements.

Break and retest strategy

When new information appears, the valuations of agents change and the market enters a new state. An inefficient state where one of the two sides (buyers or sellers) stops trading in the belief that value and price are converging in that price zone.

This inefficiency is represented as a breakout in which the price leaves the trading range within which it was fluctuating. It is precisely at this moment where many traders decide to enter the market hoping that this imbalance will be the definitive one and will make the price move to more extreme levels.

Many traders like to enter the market when there is a breakout from support/resistance levels, previous highs/lows or trend lines, taking advantage of the market momentum, which is also known as momentum trading.

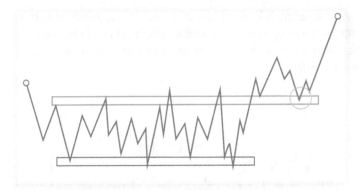

I always say that these breakout situations are not trading opportunities. The reason why is very simple; it is impossible to know whether we are seeing a real or a false breakout. The only way to be able to intuit what is more likely (real or false breakout) is to see how the price reacts after this event.

Keep in mind that the vast majority of breakouts are maneuvers designed by large professional traders to build up liquidity that end up becoming failed breakouts and create reverse trading opportunities. Entering the market at every sign of a breakout is not the smart thing to do. To overcome this problem, I advise that you don't trade at the breakout point and instead, wait for a test on the zone to take place in order to assess with greater confidence whether the breakout is false or not.

The trading zones here are once again the earlier pivot points you will find if there is one further back than the rest, or the previous zone of imbalance where several fluctuation points probably converge. An entry trigger on that area would offer us the opportunity we are waiting for to enter the market.

Entry Triggers

Nothing is set in stone when it comes to entry triggers. There is no universal rule nor anyone in a position to say that one way is better than another. Many traders wait for a candlestick showing intent to appear (the option I prefer to use as an entry trigger), but there are other options; from waiting for the breakout of a minor trend line, to entering with limit orders hoping for the future reversal of the movement. The options are endless and it is up to the trader to decide which one best suits their personality and trading style.

The appearance of the entry trigger as a determining factor for sending market entry orders is relatively important; but just as important (or even more so) is to have a well-identified zone in which to wait for said entry trigger.

As mentioned at the beginning of this topic, the same market actions can offer contradictory information depending on where they are located. Therefore, it is vitally important to have carried out a correct analysis of the context and to be in the appropriate location prior to the appearance of an entry trigger.

Once we are in the correct location, we can use different configurations as a definitive signal to enter the market. Below are examples of some of the most used entry triggers:

Candlesticks showing intent or reversal patterns

Once you are in the right location and want to enter the market, the appearance of a candlestick showing intent or a reversal pattern are the most commonly used indicators that denote interest from the participants to push the price in that direction in the short term. This can be taken as a definitive signal to open the position.

If we are in an uptrend, the first thing to do is identify the trading levels. Within these, we then need to wait for the price to develop one of the end of movement patterns associated with a correction (climax, pullback, double bottom or bear trap) and then right in the trading zone of the patterns we need to wait for the appearance of our candlestick showing intent or reversal pattern as the definitive signal to enter the market.

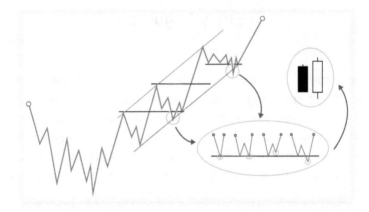

With the appearance of the entry trigger, we can then use any order to enter the market. My personal preference is to use a stop order at the breakout end of the candlestick. This ensures that in addition to the signal of intent evidenced by the candlestick or the reversal pattern, we also require that the participants continue to push the market in that direction, continue to demonstrate aggressiveness.

Bear in mind that the price, having generated the entry trigger and with the entry order placed, might not reach the desired level, it may pivot and move in the opposite direction, in a demonstration that it is not ready to start a new movement yet. Using this type of order ensures that we will only enter the market if there is a certain continuity in the movement. If we enter with some other type of order (market or limited order) we would incur losses in the event the price emits a false signal and pivots.

Continuing with an example of position management, one way to protect the position would be to place the Stop Loss at the opposite end of the entry order. If we are really facing the imminent start of a new movement, the price will move rapidly in the direction of our position. Anything other than that means we won't be interested in keeping the position open as it could be a false signal and lead to bigger losses.

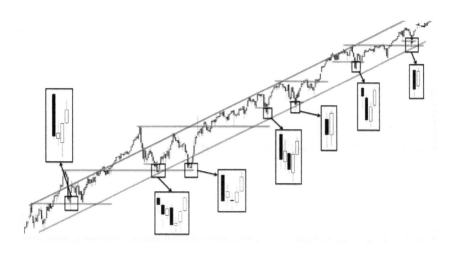

Indecision candlestick

An example of an early entry would be to place our entry order at the breakout of the last indecision candle that appears, assuming that this indecision is due to a lack of interest on the part of the agents to move in that direction.

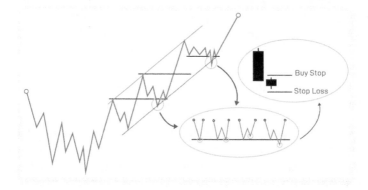

Although it is true that it can probably offer us better ratios since we would be in a position to place a very tight Stop Loss, it is a rather risky method. Although we are in the right location, the market environment is one of complete uncertainty and by taking action with this type of trigger we are making the assumption that the price will go in the direction we hope. And obviously there is no guarantee of anything.

The market could execute our entry order with some kind of wick and then reach our level of protection. And it could keep doing this over and over again. We would be better off, and feel more confident, waiting for the appearance of that candlestick showing intent that suggests that we could be facing the imminent onset of the imbalance movement; even though the location of our orders is further away and we would obtain a worse risk/reward ratio.

After a minor consolidation breakout

Another widely used approach to enter the market is to wait for the breakout of the correction trend line. In this case, what we need to do is identify the dynamics of the movement that is heading towards our trading level and draw its trend line. Now we simply have to wait for it to be broken to then enter the market.

With this break, what we are waiting for is the appearance of that pivot point that will change the market environment once again, transitioning from a correction to an impulse; in the hope that this new impulse movement in turn generates a greater degree of transition in which the market moves from a state of pause or consolidation (the correction movement), to another state of trend continuity (the impulse movement).

Ideally, we would want this breakout from the trend line to take place with candlesticks showing strong intent, which as we know is evidence of the aggressiveness and imbalance in favor of one side of the participants. At that point we will probably already see some of the four ends of movement patterns (climax, pullback, double top/bottom or bull/bear trap); which, added to the breaking of the trend line, offers us a later entry but with greater confirmation of a reversal in the movement.

We already know what options we have to subsequently place an order. The most conservative option is again to enter with stop orders at the breakout of the candlestick that meets our characteristics and breaks the trend line.

To recap, this entry and the one previously seen with the candlestick showing intent or reversal pattern could be part of the same entry, with the only added filter that we would be waiting for the trend line or the consolidation pattern that is forming to break. Sometimes that show of intent will also break the trend line, and sometimes it won't. From a trading approach point of view it can be a useful factor to take into account.

In this chart we see an example of a trade with all the previously mentioned signals; in the trading zone (previous pivot), a corrective movement develops that ends with a trap pattern   and then shows signs of strength with a Bullish candlestick that manages to break the trend line of said corrective movement. It is a very representative example of everything we have seen, and although it demonstrates an ideal trade, we can sometimes see something like this in a real-life situation.

These last few charts showing different entry triggers are all in the context of trading with the trend. I have used this context because it is much easier for us grasp this particular situation, and to understand the concept of an uptrend better than that of a downtrend. But it goes without saying that these examples of triggers (there are obviously many more) can be used in any trading context (with the trend, against the trend, at the extremes of the range and at breakouts). The important thing is to ensure we have properly identified our trading level or zone and to wait there for the appearance of our entry trigger.

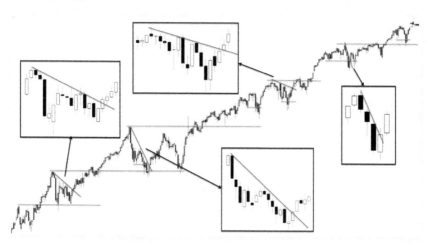

PRICE AND VOLUME

When we talk about price and volume analysis, or Volume Spread Analysis (VSA) as it is known within the English-speaking community, we must mention the father of this approach: Tom Williams.

Tom Williams was a syndicate trader who specialized in the teachings of Richard Wyckoff and went on to develop his own method of reading the market based on the actions of the big players or smart money as he called it.

He realized that in order to objectively read what was happening and perceive the true market sentiment, it was necessary to study and understand the relationship between all the data on price (especially the range of the candlestick and the closing price) and volume.

Using the different tools that this reading of the market offers us, we can identify the involvement or absence of the major traders: when they are entering or leaving the market, as well as the degree of interest and participation that they show in the movements. Understanding and internalizing all these concepts undoubtedly enables the trader to carry out better decision-making.

VSA Basics

VSA methodology was designed to find imbalances between supply and demand on any asset and time frame.

As we have already mentioned, to carry out a market analysis using this methodology we need information on both the price and the volume being traded.

It is worth remembering that as with the price action analysis methodology, any study must be carried out in comparative terms, that is, in relation to what was previously seen on the chart. To correctly interpret any market action, it must be compared with the previous behavior of the price.

VSA, in addition to price, also takes into account the variable of volume, which makes it more complex than a purely price action approach. Note that in no case does more complex necessarily mean better since sometimes the simplest approach can offer better results. There is no doubt, however, that the data on volume provides us with objectively very valuable information for analysis.

But what is volume? Well, volume is simply the number of transactions that have taken place at a given time. It is the number of stocks, contracts or units that have been traded between market participants.

Volume informs us about the activity that has taken place in a particular time frame. Based on this, it is universally accepted that a high volume suggests a high participation, a lot of interest in trading; while a low volume informs us of a low participation and therefore, of little interest.

It is important at this point to ask who has the capacity to produce high volumes. As you have probably guessed, these particular stocks can only come from the big traders, the smart money that Tom Williams was referring to.

By connecting all these concepts we can draw the following conclusion, which is one of the first and most important lessons in price and volume analysis: high volumes are an indicator that major traders are taking action. The question we must then ask ourselves is why are there major traders interested in participating in that zone, what are their intentions? Why? What do they expect the price to do? To answer these questions we have to analyze the volume along with the price action. It's about seeing what the price does with that volume.

These are questions that Volume Spread Analysis tries to answer by correctly identifying market sentiment in general (the location where such actions appear) and certain behaviors in particular (signs of strength and weakness).

The Law of Effort vs Result

An analysis based on the law of effort vs result looks at the price action and volume in order to determine if there is harmony or divergence in order to interpret whether the interest in that particular action is genuine or false.

In financial markets, effort is represented by volume while the result is represented by price. This means that the price action should reflect the volume action. Without effort there cannot be a result. It is about evaluating the dominance of buyers or sellers through the convergence or divergence of price and volume.

A significant increase in volume indicates the presence of professional money aimed at generating a movement (continuation or reversal).

If the effort is in harmony with the result, it is a sign of the strength of the movement and suggests its continuation. If the effort is in divergence with the result it is a sign of the weakness of the movement and suggests a reversal.

You should also be aware that the price movement will be in direct proportion to the amount of effort spent. If the two are in harmony, a major effort will cause a movement with a longer duration; while a minor effort will be reflected in a movement of shorter duration. Meanwhile if there is an indication of divergence, the result tends to be in direct proportion to that divergence. A smaller divergence tends to produce a smaller result and a larger divergence, a larger result.

We will now look in more detail at the actions to which we can apply this law of effort vs result:

In the development of a candlestick

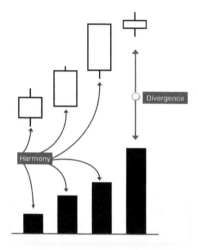

This is the simplest evaluation. It involves analyzing price action and volume based on a single individual candlestick.

Candlesticks are the definitive representation of a battle between buyers and sellers in a certain period of time. The final result of this interaction between supply and demand transmits a signal to us. Our job as traders who analyze price action and volume is to know how to correctly interpret that signal. In this case in isolation.

What we are looking for is an alignment between the traded price ranges and volume. For a signal of harmony, we would expect to see wide ranges at high volumes and narrow ranges at low volumes. The opposite would indicate a divergence.

Because this is the minimum thing we should assess, the candlestick-by-candlestick analysis is especially useful for us to identify the entry trigger and to see isolated key actions such as climaxes.

In the subsequent shift

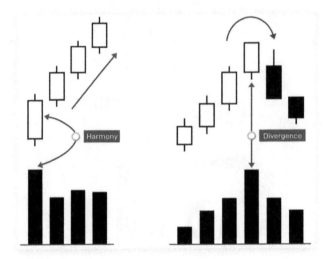

This involves analyzing the price action and the volume on a larger scale; on the subsequent price shift.

We want to evaluate if that volume generates a movement in the direction of the original candlestick or if, by contrast, after observing that increase in volume, the price moves in the opposite direction. Therefore, we would detect harmony between effort vs result if that candlestick plus that volume cause the movement to continue in the same direction; and divergence if the market pivots.

Normally, at the beginning of each impulse there is a relatively high volume that supports it; whereas this volume is not seen at the beginning of a correction. It is worth bearing this in mind when analyzing the nature of a movement.

• If we want to treat a movement as an impulse, we will expect to see that high volume at its origin, which would indicate an institutional presence supporting said movement and that the probability is a continuation in that direction.

• If we see that a movement is generated without a large volume at its origin, objectively it would appear to be a movement without any institutional participation and this suggests to us that this movement is a correction or, in the case of an impulse, it would denote divergence.

The key here is to remember that the market will only move if there are large institutions interested in pushing it in that direction.

In the development of movements

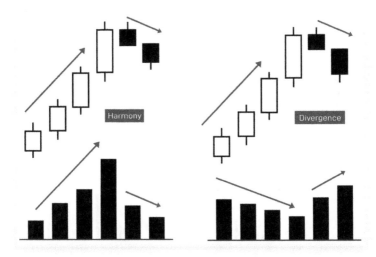

Here we increase the scope of our analysis to cover the price action and volume in terms of complete movements.

As a general rule, impulses will be accompanied by an increase in volume as price moves in the direction of the least resistance; and movements of a corrective nature will be accompanied by less volume.

Therefore, a movement is in harmony when as an impulse it is accompanied by increasing volume and as a correction, by decreasing volume. Similarly, we can detect a divergence if we see an impulse accompanied with a smaller volume relative to what was previously seen, or in the case of a correction if the volume is relatively higher (it would be necessary to evaluate at that point if it really is a correction).

By Waves

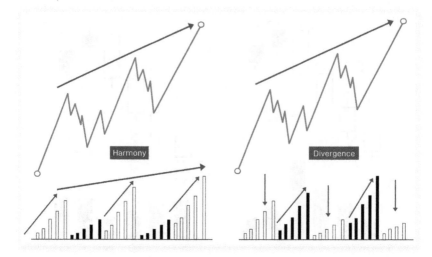

This tool (originally created by David Weis) measures the volume that has been traded in each wave (upwards and downwards). All in all, it allows us to assess market conditions and more accurately compare bullish and bearish pressure between movements.

A key fact to keep in mind when analyzing waves is that not all volume traded in a bullish wave will be purchases and that not all volume traded in a bearish wave will be sales. Just like with any other factor, it requires analysis and interpretation. The analysis of effort vs result is exactly the same. It is about comparing the current volume wave with previous ones; both with the one going in the same direction and the one going in the opposite direction.

There is harmony if in an upward movement the bullish impulses are accompanied by bullish waves with a greater volume than the bearish corrections. Harmony also exists if the price hits new highs and each bullish impulse does so with an increase in the volume of the waves. By contrast, divergence exists if the price moves upwards but the bullish waves are ever diminishing; or if in this upward movement the bearish waves demonstrate greater strength.

Upon reaching key levels

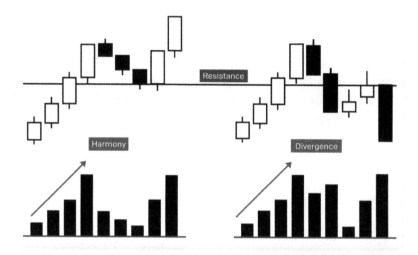

This is yet another way evaluating this law of effort vs result; this time, in terms of breakouts and trading zones.

It is quite simple: if the price approaches a level with volume and performs a real breakout, we can say that there is harmony between effort and result in that breakout movement. That volume had the intention of increasing and has absorbed all the orders that were located there.

If, on the contrary, the price approaches a level with volume and performs a false breakout, we can say that there is divergence. All that trading volume has been participating in the opposite direction to the breakout.

The key is to see if the price holds on the other side of the level or not. It may take some time before continuing in the direction of the breakout with a new impulse; as long as it does not lose the level, in principle the breakout should be treated as if it were real.

This can be applied to any type of level. Whether horizontal (supports and resistances), sloping (trend lines, channel lines, inverted lines, converging or diverging lines), dynamic levels (moving averages, VWAP, bands); as well as any other level established by a specific methodology.

Signs of Strength and Weakness

Signs of strength and weakness are actions carried out by large traders that inform us about their interest and positioning. Given their importance, they can contextualize the market sentiment, so we need to be aware of the appearance of these sorts of behaviors and be able to identify them as quickly as possible.

Once these large agents have made their assessments on the price of assets, they will wait for them to reach overbought or oversold positions, opening up an attractive opportunity, at which point they will appear with conviction in the market.

Because these major players have the ability to influence the market through their actions, it is essential that we, as retail traders, are aware of the appearance of these signals in order to position ourselves in their same direction and obtain a return alongside them.

The VSA methodology describes several actions which it names differently, even when the behavior is similar, based on the whether the positioning of the smart money is bullish or bearish. To simplify, we will look at only the main signals of the methodology. These are the most important ones which we should be continuously looking out for on the chart.

Climaxes (Buying climax and Selling climax)

A climax is a powerful signal of an intentional positioning in the market. After a trend movement, the irrationality of the participants (uninformed) will cause a parabolic movement in the price that will reach extreme positions in the market:

- When the current trend movement is bullish, the expected event is a Buying Climax during which the market enters an overbought condition.

- When the market is in a downtrend it will reach an oversold condition as a result of a Selling Climax.

At this point, the market will have reached a level which is no longer of interest and informed traders will abandon their positions (held during the trend movement) and even start to position themselves on the opposite side waiting for a price reversal.

The theory tells us that this action appears with high or ultra-high volume, on a wide-range bar or candlestick and a closing price at the extremes. Although this definition may be correct, it is not entirely complete since the market can represent the same action in different ways:

- On a set of bars with a relatively narrow range and a high and constant volume for all of them.

- On a two-candlestick pattern with high volume (engulfing).

- On a single candlestick with high volume and a large wick at the top (pin bar).

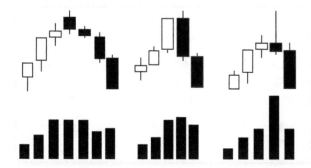

As we saw in the price action section, thanks to the fractality of the market, all these representations in the end denote the same thing: that the large traders have been extremely active; the only difference being the time frame that is being used.

The key to correctly reading this event will be if, after its appearance, the price has no continuity and instead causes a reversal in the market, indicating a clear divergence under the law of effort vs result.

One of the principles that I always keep in mind and that governs my chart analysis is that every market action must be confirmed or rejected by the price action itself. This means that all technical analysis approaches that are based on the study of supply and demand are unable to indicate in real time what is really happening. The market sentiment can only be confirmed by how it reacts to this key action.

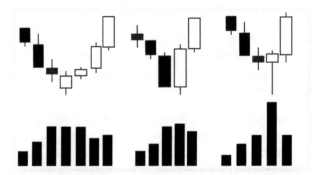

In other words, at the point when a Buying Climax is potentially taking place, we cannot be sure that this is indeed the case. Only after seeing how the price reacts to this appearance of volume can we consider the possibility that we are seeing a Buying Climax. And only when the market stops rising and turns downwards are we in a position to confirm that the action is definitely a Buying Climax.

What advantage can we obtain by correctly identifying a climax? Since it is an action in which the previous trend movement stops and it suggests there is institutional involvement, we can draw two clear conclusions:

- We should start to consider no longer trading with the previous trend. At least until we can confirm whether the new structure it creates is a continuation or a change of direction.

- It offers us a clear opportunity to take profits from our open positions.

Climaxes are not in themselves locations in which we should trade. Opening positions at this point is not recommended because the risk is too high. If we enter the market at this point we would be betting on a change in the direction, but it is not something we can be sure of in real time. We need to see how the price reacts subsequently to confirm whether we're talking about a climax. At the very least, we should wait for the appearance of a test candlestick (No Demand and No Supply) that suggests a lack of interest for continuing in that direction. In this case we would then have two signals that would indicate the underlying strength or weakness.

Although we cannot use it to enter the market, a climax can be very useful as a signal to leave it. We know this action informs us about institutional participation, so if we have already held our position for a long time, this action indicates that large traders may be closing their positions; that the market is already at a fair price and this has made them change their valuations.

False breakout (Upthrust and Shakeout)

Traditional VSA offers a specific representation of what a false breakout is or should be. It is generally defined as a wide-range candle (or bar) that creates a new extreme (peak for Upthrust and trough for Shakeout) and whose closing price is on the opposite side, also accompanied by a high volume.

What is actually of interest is the action rather than the candlestick.

- In other words, in the Upthrust example, it is when the price hits a new high, is rejected and closes at the candlestick's lower end; and in the case of the Shakeout it would be the other way around, the price hits a new low and closes at the higher end of the candlestick.

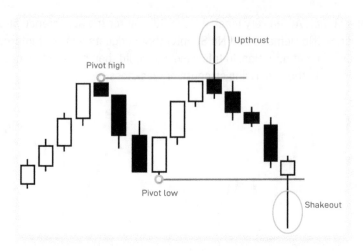

What is important is not how the false breakout is represented but the implications it has. It matters little whether the action is executed over one, two or more candlesticks, or whether the range of the candlestick is higher or lower, or whether the volume is high or low. All of this is interpretable and we would reach the same conclusion regardless of how it is ultimately represented. What is relevant about this particular action is the result: that the price has tried to break some type of previous price level and has been rejected; there has been no interest in continuing in that direction and it is most likely that this movement has been used by the large traders to position themselves on the opposite side.

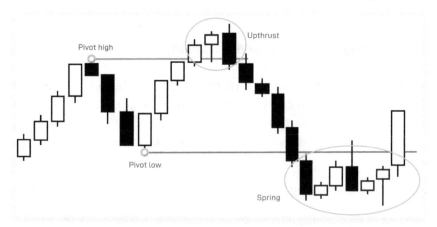

As I say, this action can be depicted in a multitude of ways, either through a single candlestick (as shown in the first chart), in a candlestick pattern (as we see in the Upthrust shown on this chart) and even in a longer-term action (as we see in the Spring shown on this chart).

Some traders even treat the appearance of a hammer candlestick as an Upthrust even if it has only broken the high of a few previous candlesticks, and hasn't even broken a single pivot point in that time frame (because it would be a pivot point in smaller time frames). More interesting than whether said action can be treated as an Upthrust because it complies with these characteristics, is whether these actions break previous highs based on the logic of liquidity zones. What offers a guarantee in these actions is not the visual representation of the candlestick but what underlies these. And this is the search for liquidity, the strong inrush of smart money causing a reversal of the movement in a very short period of time.

In terms of volume, if these two events appear with a high volume we can say that the sudden shift is due to the fact that large traders have appeared to stop and reverse the movement; while if it does so with a low volume we can say that the shift is due to the fact that these large traders had no interest in continuing in that direction. Therefore we must be very circumspect in our volume analysis because there is a high degree of interpretation involved depending on how the action finally develops, although what will vary is the result, and this is what is important.

A very high volume in the false breakout suggests that there has been a lot of interest in that area and it is likely that the price will return to it later to check whether or not there is still a presence there. This action is performed through certain tests, which are described further on.

Price Action methodology and VSA are inextricably linked. If you recall, we used price action to establish limits that we identified as pivot points which represented liquidity zones. Well, these pivot points and liquidity zones are the minor highs and lows where we will wait for these false breakouts to occur.

Upthrusts and Shakeouts are false breakouts of those liquidity zones in which a huge number of pending orders are located. When a shakeout occurs, what happens is a false breakout where large traders take on all those pending orders in order to initiate the desired trend. This is the way financial markets move: by seeking liquidity. If large traders were not able to find the counterparty they need to match their orders, it would be impossible for the market to shift. Therefore, they need to create the feeling that it is a genuine breakout move, attracting more traders, activating automatic momentum strategies and absorbing all those orders.

To feel confident that we are dealing with an Upthrust it needs to have broken some previous high and appear in the appropriate location, such as:

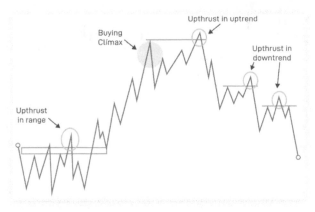

- In a range, in the upper part, in a resistance zone.

- In an uptrend as long as a Buying Climax has already appeared among the last few candlesticks.

- In a downtrend close to the channel line and in an overbought condition.

Meanwhile, to feel confident we are dealing with a Shakeout it needs to have broken a previous low in the appropriate locations:

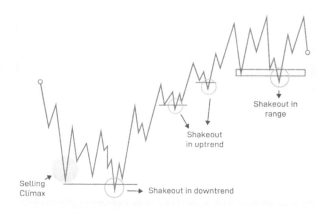

- In a downtrend as long as a Selling Climax has already appeared among the last few candlesticks.

- In an uptrend close to the channel line and in an overbought condition.

- In a range, in the lower part, in a support zone.

Up to now we have used the term Shakeout to refer to this break in a downtrend but it can also be called a Spring. Essentially it is the same behavior: a break of previous lows; although it is true that the Shakeout represents a more violent event both in terms of the price action (rapid V-shape reversal) and volume (very high).

Test (No Demand and No Supply)

This type of action is known as a test. In this case, what is being tested is the intention of large traders to continue in that direction. The test can be considered successful if a candlestick appears that suggests a lack of participation of smart money. And without this participation the market will not be able to go very far.

- A No Demand candlestick is a bullish candlestick with a narrow range and lower volume than the previous two candles.

- A No Supply candlestick is a bearish candlestick with a narrow range and lower volume than the previous two candles.

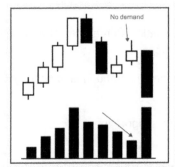 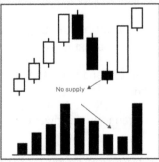

Since volume is the variable that we analyze to determine the interest of participants, a No Demand pattern that appears with a low volume suggests that there is no interest from large traders at the higher prices, especially if we have previously seen a significant sign of weakness, such as a Buying Climax or an Upthrust.

These types of candlesticks are the same indecision candlesticks that we saw for Price Action, the only difference being that we are also reading the volume to confirm that sign of indecision. This would therefore seem a better option if you want to use this type of candlestick as an entry trigger since it offers greater confirmation than that provided only by price action.

Generally these test candlesticks will appear within the set of candlesticks just after the event denoting major strength or weakness. Although this is the ideal approach, we should not be too strict in its application. If instead of the next 5 candlesticks it appears within the next 10, the test can still be considered reliable.

As the market enters a zone where there was previously a high volume, there can be one of two results:

- **Valid test**. The volume is now low, which clearly indicates a lack of interest and suggests that the market is now primed for a shift in the trend towards the path of least resistance.

- **Failed test**. The volume is still high (relatively), which would indicate that there are still traders willing to keep pushing the price. The best thing to do in this case is wait or for repeated tests to appear that confirm that there is no stock available; or that the market is continuing in the direction of its latest movement.

As a result of the above, these tests can be a good moment to enter the market. If the test is valid, we can "bet" in favor of the force that is applying the most pressure and that in theory has greater control of the market.

The correct context in which we are going to look for the No Demand signal is after having identified the appearance of the large traders previously positioning themselves to sell in the aforementioned signs of weakness:

- In a range, as an Upthrust test in the resistance zone.

- In an uptrend, provided that we have previously seen some significant sign of weakness, such as a Buying Climax and/or an Upthrust.

- The best place to take a short position is when you see a No Demand bar in a downtrend following the occurrence of an Upthrust that breaks some previous high.

Meanwhile, we should look for No Supply candlesticks after observing signs that the smart money is positioning itself to buy:

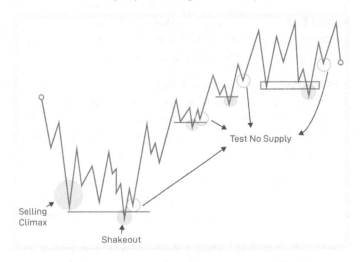

In a downtrend only if we have previously seen a Selling Climax and/ or a Shakeout.

- In an uptrend after the appearance of a Shakeout. This is the context of greatest strength.

- In a range, in a support zone as a Shakeout test.

Test candlesticks need to be confirmed. After their appearance on the chart we need to see a sign of intentionality in the price that suggests that the path of least resistance is definitely in that direction and that a new impulse is likely to start imminently.

• After seeing a No Demand, a signal of bullish intent that closes above the No Demand high.

• After seeing a No Supply, a signal of bearish intent that closes below the No Supply low.

The biggest problem with test candlesticks is that if you are waiting for them to appear before entering the market, you will sometimes be left out because they do not always appear. This is due to momentum. If the market really is ready to move, it won't need to perform any kind of test and will initiate the impulse imminently. In fact, if you analyze all the real charts we have seen up to now, you will be hard pressed to find a candlestick with these characteristics. You just need to be aware of this.

As we can see, the trading method is practically the same as we saw previously with the Price Action methodology, the difference being that VSA includes a reading of volume and offers a more objective interpretation of what may actually be happening in the market.

While price action looks at the nature of movements to help predict when the current trend is likely to end, VSA looks at the volume at the extremes and gives us a more objective perspective of when this is most likely to happen. For example, thanks to the price action we may believe we are at early stage of a trend and are looking to trade with it; but a volume peak might appear that suggests that it is a climax in which the underlying sentiment is in the opposite direction. And we already know the importance of this type of action. Would we continue to trade in the same direction? Possibly not.

If we have identified a potential Buying Climax that suggests an underlying weakness and a selling position, we may have significant doubts about a future potential Shakeout and perhaps the most sensible thing to do is to look for new signs of weakness such as an Upthrust.

If we do not take into account the volume analysis, we may see it as a simple correction of the trend that will then develop new momentum because the underlying context is bullish. Which would lead us to open a buy position and most likely would end in a loss.

There is no approach better than the other, it all depends on the characteristics of the trader. Price action offers greater simplicity while VSA is more complex since it incorporates the volume variable into the analysis. Volume analysis provides us with a greater understanding and can allow us to more objectively read the situation.

WYCKOFF METHOD

The Wyckoff method is a technical analysis approach based on the study of the relationship between supply and demand. It was developed by Richard Wyckoff around 1930 and his approach is simple: when well-informed traders want to buy or sell, they execute processes that leave their imprint on the chart through price and volume. The Wyckoff method is based on identifying this intervention by professionals to try to elucidate who is most likely to have control of the market and to then trade alongside them.

Wyckoff worked for many years as a broker and thanks to his particular understanding he observed that it was possible to judge the future course of the market through its very actions, since price action reflected the plans and intentions of those who dominated it. The fact that Wyckoff worked as a broker and drew these conclusions is especially relevant; since it is something that he was able to verify happened over and over again. He was able to confirm how prices moved and what kind of maneuvers were executed by the major traders so they could take control of the market (absorb all the available liquidity). Although today the context and the markets have changed, the principles are still valid due to the underlying logic of the approach: the analysis of the continuous interaction between the participants.

Wyckoff built on the early work of Charles Dow and contributed enormously to the principles of technical analysis. Principles that have endured over time and have become a reference for traders and investors; the most important of which are the three fundamental laws and the processes of accumulation and distribution.

The Wyckoff method was one of the first technical analysis approaches and is considered the origin of Volume Spread Analysis. Tom Williams studied the teachings of Richard Wyckoff in depth and adopted some of the main ideas of his methodology to develop Volume Spread Analysis. The main difference between price and volume analysis and the Wyckoff method is that the latter includes the time variable in its analyses, as seen in the phases of the structures; which provides us with a much better definition of the context and a roadmap, as we will see below.

In this section we will address the fundamental principles of this approach, providing the reader with an initial overview of the Wyckoff Method. If you want to delve deeper into this subject, I would recommend reading my second book "La Metodología Wyckoff en Profundidad" (The Wyckoff Method in Depth) which breaks down the elements of the method in detail.

The 3 Fundamental Laws

The 3 fundamental laws offer us a unique theoretical conceptual framework since they are based on a real underlying logic, which puts it far ahead of any other form of technical analysis.

The contents of this section are the cornerstone of the method which is the only one that can inform us about what is really happening in the market. It is the only one that explain what's going on in a logical way.

The 3 fundamental laws are described below:

The Law of Supply and Demand

This is the true driver of the market. The market moves thanks to an auction process in which the market participants –buyers and sellers– trade.

This law is sometimes invoked to argue that price moves because there are more buyers than sellers and vice versa, but this is a mistake. As we have already mentioned, there are always the same number of buyers and sellers in the market because for someone to be able to buy there must be someone able to sell. No matter how much someone is interested in buying, if there is no seller willing to act as the counterparty, it is impossible for the transaction to take place.

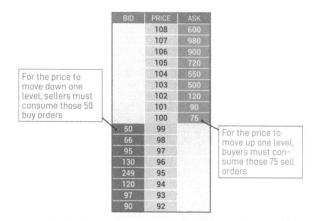

BID	PRICE	ASK
	108	600
	107	980
	106	900
	105	720
	104	550
	103	500
	102	120
	101	90
	100	75
50	99	
66	98	
95	97	
130	96	
249	95	
120	94	
97	93	
90	92	

For the price to move down one level, sellers must consume those 50 buy orders

For the price to move up one level, buyers must consume those 75 sell orders

The key to really analyzing why prices are moving up or down lies in the attitude (aggressive or passive) that traders adopt when it comes to participating in the market. For the price to move towards one side or the other, the participants must show more conviction in the pressure they apply than the opposite side. This aggressive attitude is what makes the market move.

A lack of interest, the absence of one of the two sides can facilitate the movement of the price in the opposite direction, but ultimately the aggressiveness of the other side is still needed to push the price. In other words, an absence of supply can facilitate the price rise, but if there are no aggressive buyers willing to consume the orders pending execution that are located in the ASK column, the price will not be able to move higher.

This is the law of supply and demand. Based on its principles, all sorts of methodologies, tools and software have been developed to try to analyze this interaction between buyers and sellers.

The Law of Cause and Effect

This is based on the idea that something cannot happen out of the blue; that for the price to develop a trend movement (effect) it must first have built up a cause.

Although the market can generate causes rapidly (such as the four patterns described in the price action section), in most cases these will appear on the chart displaying much slower patterns; these are the processes of accumulation and distribution.

An important aspect of this law is that the effect generated by the cause will always be in direct proportion to that cause. Consequently, a major cause will produce a greater effect, and a minor cause will result in a lesser effect. It is logical to assume that the longer the market spends in a range developing a campaign, the greater the distance the subsequent trend will travel.

Wyckoff traders know that it is in these lateral conditions where trends are born and that is why we are continuously in search of the beginning of new structures to begin to analyze the price action and volume in order to position ourselves as soon as possible with the trend. A trend will end and a cause will begin. A cause will end and a trend will begin. The Wyckoff method is centered around the interpretation of these conditions.

These ranges can be observed in any asset and time frame. Open a chart now and watch the behavior of the market. You will notice that before any trend movement there is a sideways one. This is repeated over and over again. As you can see, the focus here is on the objective behavior of the market, not something with no logic or foundation.

The Law of Effort vs Result

This is about analyzing the price and the volume in comparative terms to conclude whether the actions of the market denote harmony or divergence.

The law of effort vs result has already been described in depth with its different variants and interpretations in the section on VSA. So as not to repeat and duplicate the same content, I recommend you go back to it for another look if necessary.

As I have already indicated, the law of effort vs result was introduced by Richard Wyckoff and subsequently adopted by Tom Williams as the basis of VSA. Because it is one of the cornerstones of VSA it is the only aspect of the Wyckoff method that has already been examined in depth. You can study the remaining specific content of the method in the book "La Metodología Wyckoff en Profundidad" (The Wyckoff Method in Depth).

The following table contains a summary of all the elements we have looked at regarding the analysis of harmony and divergence between price action and volume:

Suggestion	In the development of a candlestick	In the subsequent shift	In the development of movements	By waves	Upon reaching key levels
Harmony	High volume that develops a wide range	High volume in a bullish candlestick that drives the price up	High volume in an impulse	Rising wave in an impulse	High volume that breaks the level
	Low volume that develops a narrow range	High volume in a bearish candlestick that drives the price down	low volume in a correction	Declining wave in a correction	Low volume that doesn't break the level
Divergence	High volume that develops a narrow range	High volume in a bullish candlestick that doesn't drive the price up	Low volume in an impulse	Declining wave in an impulse	High volume that doesn't break the level
	Low volume that develops a wide range	High volume in a bearish candlestick that doesn't drive the price down	High volume in a correction	Rising wave in a correction	Low volume that breaks the level

Accumulation and Distribution Processes

Accumulation and distribution structures will help us identify the involvement of professionals as well as the general sentiment of the market up to the current moment, allowing us to come up with genuinely objective scenarios.

These processes are seen on the chart as ranges or sideways trends. While these develop, the major traders prepare their campaign and position themselves on the right side of the market; they are generating the cause of the subsequent movement.

One of the major advantages of correctly interpreting accumulation and distribution processes is that it puts us in a position to identify **the context of the market**. From the context we can deduce which side has the most control, which is the path of least resistance and where the price is likely to go.

The context can be read in different ways depending on the location of the price. For example, if we are in Phase E, in an uptrend and with an accumulation process in our favor, the context is one of strength and we should only think about buying. This means we can avoid entering on the wrong side of the market and in the direction of least resistance (in this example, upwards).

Another use of the context is to favor the development of smaller structures within larger ones. This is a very powerful idea that the most advanced Wyckoff traders execute in their analyses in which they incorporate the use of multiple time frames.

The accumulation process

An accumulation range is a sideways price movement in which large traders carry out an absorption maneuver to accumulate stock in order to be able to sell it at higher prices in the future and make a profit on the difference.

It is in these range conditions that we see the law of cause and effect at work. In the case of the accumulation range, the purchase of the asset (cause) will have the effect of a subsequent uptrend movement; and the extent of this movement will be in direct proportion to the time the price has spent constructing that cause.

Preparing a major move takes considerable time. A large trader cannot buy everything they want in one go because if they execute an order for the entire amount, they would obtain a lower price due to the slippage generated by their own order. In order to carry out this task, large traders must launch a campaign and build their position little by little. These actions leave their footprint on the chart and this is represented in the form of accumulation structures.

For strong hands or informed traders to start buying, the market needs to have reached a point of extreme fear from weak hands or uninformed traders, who will provide the liquidity; a situation in which the price will also be undervalued and will represent an interesting opportunity.

When there is no more interest in continuing to sell, a turning point occurs. Control of the security is held by informed traders and they will only close their positions at much higher prices. A slight increase in demand would now cause a sharp upward movement in prices, starting the uptrend.

The distribution process

A distribution range is a sideways price movement in which informed traders close out their buy positions and launch a campaign to go short.

In this context the market will most likely have reached an overbought situation where uninformed traders will have pushed prices up, guided by extreme excitement. A situation that will create opportunities for those with the right vision and with lower valuations of the price. These informed traders will try to maintain a large (short) position in order close it at a lower price and earn a return on it.

Once the range runs out of steam, the professional traders will not initiate the downtrend movement until they can verify that the path of the least resistance is indeed in that direction. They do this through tests to evaluate the interest of the buyers. They will analyze what interest exists in the upward movements and depending on the participation supporting it (this can be deduced by the volume traded in that movement) they will assess whether there is demand available or if, on the contrary, there are no more buyers. An absence of volume at this point would suggest a lack of interest in reaching higher prices.

When there are no more buyers willing to continue buying, a turning point occurs. Control of the asset is held by informed traders and they will only close their positions at lower prices. A slight increase now in supply would cause a sharp downward movement in prices, starting the downtrend.

Events and Phases of the Structures

Events and Phases are elements unique to the Wyckoff method and help us to follow the development of the structures. This enables us to anticipate what the price will do after the appearance of any of these structures, providing us with a **roadmap** we can follow at all times.

The price can develop different types of structures depending on the conditions of the market at the time. This is why we need an approach that confers some flexibility to price movements but at the same time is governed by certain fixed elements that offer as much objectivity as possible to the reading.

These fixed aspects of the method are the events and phases that make up the development of the structures. Two basic accumulation and distribution structures are described below which provide a very general idea of the dynamics in which the price moves under the premises of the Wyckoff method.

These could be considered examples of ideal structures, but the important thing is to bear in mind that the market will not always display them in the same way, and it is here that we must allow for the market's flexibility.

List of Events

Just like VSA with its three key actions (climax, false breakout, test), the Wyckoff method is made up of a series of events (including those just mentioned) that we can expect to happen step by step, providing us with a roadmap to guide us at all times on what will occur next.

The events are the same for both accumulations and distributions. The only thing that changes in some cases is the nomenclature, but the underlying logic behind them is the same.

1. **Preliminary stop**. This is the first attempt to stop the current trend movement that will always fail. It's an early warning that the trend may be coming to an end. A significant increase in volume will be seen at this point.

2. **Climax**. This is the culmination of the preceding trend. Having traveled a great distance, the price will hit an extreme that will lead to the appearance of large traders. It is generally accompanied by a large volume although this is not always the case; sometimes this end of the trend will appear through an action with little volume, denoting the exhaustion of the movement.

3. **Reaction**. This is the first big signal that suggests a change in market sentiment. The market goes from being under the control of one of the two forces to a market in equilibrium.

4. **Test**. This event can be read differently depending on where it takes place. In general terms, it tries to assess the commitment of traders, or lack of, at a certain moment and direction.

5. **False breakout**. Key moment in the analysis of the structure. This is the last liquidity-seeking action that large traders use which serves a triple purpose before initiating the trend in the direction of least resistance.

6. **Breakout**. This is the greatest test of a professional trader's commitment. If they have done a good job of absorption previously, the price will break the structure relatively easily and continue to move beyond it.

7. **Confirmation**. If the analysis is correct, a break test will occur which will confirm that professional traders have positioned themselves in that direction and continue to support the movement.

List of Phases

Phase analysis is a contribution from Dr Hank Pruden, one of the most renowned Wyckoff traders. It helps us to structure the accumulation and distribution processes, which together with the events, puts us in a position in which we know what to expect.

The phases are based on the fact that all campaigns (accumulations and distributions) require a certain time until they are complete. During this time the price develops the structures that we have already mentioned. The power of phase analysis lies in the fact that the development of these structures generally follows repetitive patterns, so if we are able to correctly identify what is happening (accumulation or distribution), we will be in a better position to successfully predict scenarios.

- **Phase A**: Stop of the previous trend The main function of this phase is to stop the previous trend movement and return the market to a state of equilibrium between the forces of supply and demand (the participants). We move from a trend context to a range context. This phase is particularly important because its very nature provides us with an excellent place to take profits if we have an open position. It is made up of the stop, climax, reaction and test events.

- **Phase B**. Construction of the cause. After the Secondary Test, Phase B begins which serves to build the cause in preparation of the subsequent effect. During this phase, the market is in equilibrium and it is here that the major traders take advantage to absorb most of the stock they require before the end of the campaign. This is generally the longest phase. In it, various tests can be carried out at the extremes of the structure.

- **Phase C**. Test. Phase C begins with the start of the false breakout event and ends with its testing. In this phase, the large traders check the level of interest of the other participants at certain price levels.

- **Phase D**. Trend within the range. This phase starts after the end of the breakout test and continues until the confirmation event is fully developed. With no opposition in sight, the path of least resistance is clear. The market is in disequilibrium and this can be seen on the chart through the development of the breakout event.

- **Phase E**. Trend outside the range. This phase begins after the confirmation event. A successful break test with no traders appearing in the opposite direction provides definitive confirmation that one side has absolute control of the market and we should therefore only look to trade in that direction. This Phase is made up of a succession of impulse movements and reactions outside the range.

Basic accumulation structure

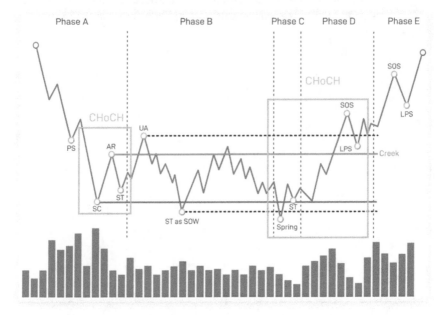

Creek. Resistance level for accumulation or re-accumulation structures. It is set by the high generated by the Automatic Rally and by any highs that may develop during Phase B.

CHoCH. Change of Character. This indicates the environment in which the price will soon move. The first CHoCH is established in Phase A where the price moves from a downward trend environment to a consolidation environment. The second CHoCH occurs from the low of Phase C to the high of the SOS in which the price moves from a consolidation environment to an upward trend environment.

Phase A. Stop of the previous bearish trend.

- **PS**. Preliminary Support. This is the first attempt to stop the downward movement that will always fail.

- **SC**. Selling Climax. Climax action that stops the downward movement.

- **AR**. Automatic Rally. Bullish reaction. An upward movement that establishes the high in the range.

- **ST**. Secondary Test. Test of the level of supply in relation to the climax action. Establishes the end of Phase A and the start of Phase B.

Phase B. Construction of the cause.

- **UA**. Upthrust Action. Temporary break of the resistance level and re-entry into range. This is a test at the peak generated by the AR.

- **ST as SOW**. Secondary Test as Sign Of Weakness. Sign of weakness in the form of a test. Temporary break of the support level and re-entry into the range. This is a test at the low generated by the SC.

Phase C. Test.

- **SP**. Spring. Bearish false breakout. This is a test in the form of a breakout below the lows of Phases A and B. There are three different types of Springs.

- **Spring Test**. Downward movement towards the lows of the range in order to check the commitment of sellers.

- **LPS**. Last Point of Support. Last support level of the supply. Test in the form of a bearish movement that fails to reach the low of the range.

- **TSO**. Terminal Shakeout or Shakeout. Definitive false breakout. Abrupt movement breaking the lows that penetrates deep through the support level and a fast recovery.

Phase D. Bullish trend within the range.

- **SOS**. Sign of Strength. Bullish movement generated after the Phase C Test event that manages to reach the top of the range. Also called JAC. (Jump Across the Creek).

- **LPS**. Last Point of Support. Last support level of the supply. These are the rising lows that we find in the upward movement towards the resistance level.

- **BU**. Back Up. This is the last big reaction before the bull market starts. Also called BUEC (Back Up to the Edge of the Creek).

Phase E. Bullish trend outside the range Succession of SOS and LPS generating a dynamic of rising highs and lows.

Basic distribution structure

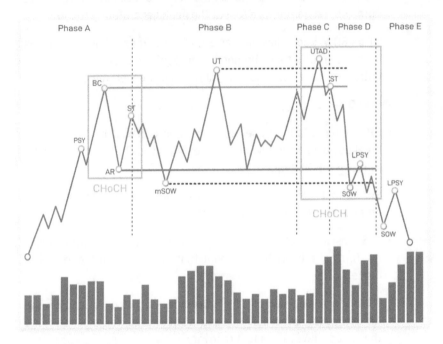

ICE. Support level for distribution or redistribution structures. It is established by the low generated by the Automatic Reaction and by any lows that may develop during Phase B.

CHoCH. Change of Character. This indicates the environment in which the price will soon move. The first CHoCH is established in Phase A where the price moves from an upward trend environment to a consolidation environment. The second CHoCH occurs from the high of Phase C to the low of the SOS in which the price moves from a consolidation environment to a downward trend environment.

Phase A. Stop of the previous bullish trend.

- **PSY**. Preliminary Supply. Preliminary resistance. This is the first attempt to stop the climb that will always fail.

- **BC**. Buying Climax. Climax action that stops the upward movement.

- **AR**. Automatic Reaction. Bearish reaction. Bearish movement that establishes the low of the range.

- **ST**. Secondary Test. Test of the level of demand in relation to the climax action. Establishes the end of Phase A and the start of Phase B.

Phase B. Construction of the cause.

- **UT**. Upthrust. Same as a UA event in the accumulation process. Temporary break of the resistance level and re-entry into range. This is a test at the peak generated by the BC.

- **mSOW**. minor Sign of Weakness. Same as an ST as SOW event in the accumulation process. Temporary break of the support level and re-entry into the range. This is a test at the low generated by the AR.

Phase C. Test.

- **UTAD**. Upthrust After Distribution. Bullish false breakout. This is a test in the form of a breakout above the highs of Phases A and B.

- **UTAD test**. An upward movement that climbs to check the level of commitment of the buyers after the UTAD.

Phase D. Bearish trend within the range.

- **MSOW**. Major Sign of Weakness. Bearish movement that starts after the UTAD that manages to reach the bottom of the range generating a change of character.

- **LPSY**. Last Point of Supply. Last support level of the demand. These are the diminishing highs that we find in the downward movement towards the support level.

Phase E. Bearish trend outside the range. Succession of SOW and LPSY generating a dynamic of diminishing highs and lows.

Trading Zones

The Method provides us with the exact zones in which we are going to act, as well as examples of triggers to enter the market, making the task of where to look for trades as easy as possible. The method calls these primary positions.

Direction	Phase C			Phase D		Phase E
	In the false breakout	In the false breakout test	In the last point of support	In the trend movement within the range	In the breakout test	In the trend movement outside the range
Buy	Spring # 3	Spring Test #1 #2	Last point of support	• Sign of strength bar • Minor reaccumulation structure • Minor spring	Last point of support "No Supply Test candlestick"	• Sign of strength bar • Minor reaccumulation structure • Ordinary Shakeout
Sell	Upthrust with no volume	Upthrust test	Last point of supply	• Sign of weakness bar • Minor redistribution structure • Minor Upthrust	Last point of supply "No Demand Test candlestick"	• Sign of weakness bar • Minor redistribution structure • Ordinary Upthrust

This table provides a summary of the trading positions as well as the different actions that we can use as triggers to enter the market. My book "La Metodología Wyckoff en Profundidad" (The Wyckoff Method in Depth) provides an in-depth analysis of each of these.

In terms of the advantages and disadvantages of each of the different trading positions, the key is to be aware that the more developed the structure, the more confidence we will have in any trades we make, but the lower the potential profit will be for that very reason. In other words, the sooner we obtain the signals, the greater the potential for a longer movement but the less reliable these signals will be.

Entry in Phase C

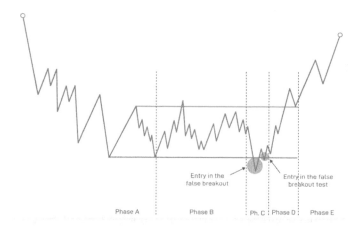

Entry in the false breakout

Entry in the false breakout test

Phase A   Phase B   Ph. C   Phase D   Phase E

This is the position that offers the best Risk/Reward ratio since we are at one extreme of the structure and the potential movement is relatively broad.

The downside of entering at this location is that it is less precise because the range has not had much time to develop in comparison to the other two trading positions.

Entry in Phase D

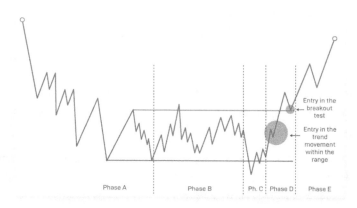

Entry in the breakout test

Entry in the trend movement within the range

Phase A   Phase B   Ph. C   Phase D   Phase E

If the false breakout + test are successful, we should now see a show of intent that will take the price in the opposite direction. This is the context with which we will work and look for trades in that direction.

Entry in Phase E

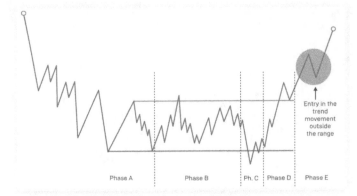

Entry in the trend movement outside the range

Phase A   Phase B   Ph. C   Phase D   Phase E

After confirming that we are looking at a real breakout and the imminent start of a trend movement outside of the range, we must now focus on looking for trading opportunities in favor of the preceding accumulation/distribution.

These types of trades are the "safest" since we are positioned in line with the latest accumulation or distribution. However, the disadvantage is that the potential duration of the movement is lower although everything will depend on the volume of the cause that has been built during the structure.

Wyckoff Vs VSA

As I mentioned at the start of this topic, the biggest difference lies in the use of time as an extra variable, and by extension, the context and road-map that the method offers us.

Just as VSA is a more comprehensive approach than Price Action, the Wyckoff method is a more comprehensive approach than VSA; although, as in the other case, it is also more complex.

For example, both approaches focus on trading when there is a false breakout. As we have already said, by its very nature, the false breakout is the key event in the market. Because of its implications, it is the most significant action when it comes to analyzing the interaction between supply and demand.

Price and volume analysts expect this type of action to take place in a liquidity zone without taking into account anything other than the prerequisites of the behavior itself; which is basically that a previous climax has taken place.

One of the great advantages of the Wyckoff method is that it only trades those false breakouts within the range that have a high probability of being the ones that unbalance the market and cause the trend movement.

The Wyckoff method incorporates a phase analysis which provides a blueprint for the development of these structures. As we have seen, the false breakout in Phase C that is going to act as a turning point and therefore is going to guide us on which direction to go in. One of the characteristics of phase analysis is that Phase B will generally last longer than Phase A and C. This makes sense since it is during this phase that most of the absorption process (accumulation or distribution) takes place. Therefore, if a false breakout occurs to which this filter does not apply, the VSA trader may enter the market looking for a major movement; whereas the Wyckoff trader, with this principle of proportionality in mind, will not.

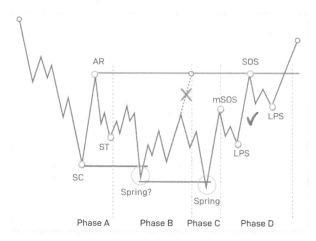

Once the price is already in Phase E going with the trend movement, the two approaches start to converge because regardless of which analysis we use at this stage we will be aware of the underlying context and we should only be looking to trade in one direction.

Simplified Wyckoff Strategy

Based on the principles we have seen, we can put together a strategy that has a high probability of success. We simply need to wait for the market to be in trend and in an accumulation or distribution process to trade only those false breakouts moving in that direction. In other words:

- Trade Springs in an uptrend and with an accumulation below.

- Trade Upthrusts in a downtrend and with a distribution above.

When should we stop looking for long trades in favor of the accumulation that we have identified? When we see a distribution process against or a confirmed downtrend. At that point, we should start looking for short trades.

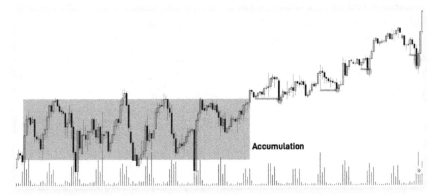

Accumulation

This type of strategy will ensure we never trade on the wrong side of the market: we shouldn't look for Springs in a downtrend nor Upthrusts in an uptrend. Although the Wyckoff method involves positioning yourself soon as possible in the market to take advantage of the maximum distance of the movement, many traders simply wait for the range to fully develop and look to obtain a shorter movement that is more reliable.

Distribution

Meanwhile, we shouldn't look for Upthrusts in favor of a distribution as soon as we identify an accumulation structure or a confirmed uptrend, at which point we should start looking for Springs.

An undoubted advantage of VSA is that it simplifies everything while still taking into account the most important events: the climax, the false breakout and the test; adopting this sort of "simplified Wyckoff" strategy as its own.

VOLUME PROFILE AND ORDER FLOW

The Market/Volume Profile and Order Flow approaches are much more complex tools and I would only recommend their study to traders with advanced knowledge in the application of methodologies that analyze the interaction between supply and demand as explained above.

If you are successful in your journey towards becoming a trader, you may want to delve into these further down the line. To do this, I recommend that you study my latest book "Wyckoff 2.0: Structures, Volume Profile and Order Flow". In it I describe a new way of trading on the markets which combines the development of Wyckoff structures together with the objectivity of the Volume Profile approach. It is a much more comprehensive book and only suitable for the most advanced traders.

Volume Profile is an indicator that is derived from another source of information. It is simply a tool that obtains the data of the traded volume and displays it for each price level. While volume is traditionally represented vertically and is subject to the time variable, Volume Profile is represented horizontally and is linked to the price variable.

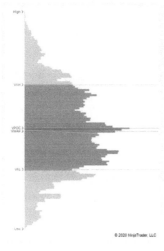

Volume profiles are visually displayed on the chart as a horizontal histogram whose values are distributed according to the traded volume of each price level. Depending on the number of contracts that are exchanged at each price level, the shape of the distribution will vary. The more transactions, the greater the length of the horizontal line; while a short horizontal line represents fewer trades.

Thanks to the Volume Profile we can identify the areas of interest on the chart. Interest is simply measured by the activity that has been generated in a particular area; and that activity is identified by the volume traded. This tool can therefore help us to identify the areas of greatest and least interest and we can use it evaluate the price that interacts with these areas in order to determine if there is acceptance or rejection at those prices.

The biggest advantage of this tool is that it provides us with completely objective information that fits perfectly within the context provided by the principles of the Wyckoff method.

Volume Profile is incredibly useful for the following:

- **Identifying structures**. Very useful when the extremes of the structures analyzed using the Wyckoff method are not very clear.

- **Determining the market bias** through the analysis of trading zones and trading levels.

- **Analyzing the health of the trend** based on the positioning and shape of the volume profiles.

- **Calibrating the management of the position**, allowing us to improve our entry, Stop Loss and Take Profit.

- **Trading principles using value areas**. The best strategies for trading with Volume Profile.

However, Volume Profile is undoubtedly most useful for pinpointing areas in which to trade most profitably. Following the principles of the Wyckoff Method and its structures, we can take advantage of these high trading areas to set up our Take Profit positions.

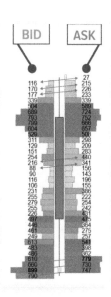

Order Flow is a tool used to analyze the flow of trading orders and the way contract-to-contract trading takes place. It is the equivalent of using a magnifying glass to see what is going on inside the candlestick; to see how the orders are being matched. As you can see in the diagram, the numbers represent the contracts exchanged at each price level. It is the Order Flow trader's job to interpret all this information.

Having studied in depth the way the orders are matched, you will come to the conclusion that it is all tremendously subjective and that its use is only recommended at certain times: when the price reaches the trading zones in which we are waiting for the imbalances that will trigger our entry in the market.

Because the vast majority of key actions that we are trying to identify through Order Flow analysis have to do with **imbalances** between supply and demand. What we are looking for here is a high volume of trades (high number of traded contracts) in one of the columns and at the same time a low volume of trades in the opposite column). What this suggests is that one side of the market has a greater intention to push the price, which can be useful when we try to enter the market.

Based on these imbalances and depending on where they occur, order flow analysis allows us to identify actions such as **absorption** and **initiative**; and together provide us with **reversal and continuation patterns**.

Order Flow is without doubt one of the most advanced analysis tools available to the general public. My latest book presents these key concepts in detail, so I encourage you to study them if you are interested and only after you have gained a certain amount of experience.

PART 5. RISK MANAGEMENT

Money management and all it encompasses is an extremely complex issue, and the subject of study for many experts over the years. From an institutional point of view it requires the use of mathematical formulas and statistical measures. However, this section offers a basic presentation of the most important concepts that we need to take into account, as retail traders, in order to manage our money in the best possible way.

At this point, it goes without saying that losing trades, and therefore financial losses, will occur. They are part of the trading business and we can't do anything to avoid them. This is due to the random element and uncertain environment of the market. We may have identified an anomaly and have the tools to exploit it, but our strategy will not be foolproof. Since this loss is inevitable, all we can do is handle this situation as effectively as possible, and for this we need to apply risk management to our trading.

The fundamental rule and the first objective that we must pursue, and on which everything that has to do with risk management revolves, is the importance of the preservation of capital. Moving forward, every decision we make should be geared towards this objective. In doing this, we will avoid falling into bad practices that will eventually fritter away our money. If we succeed in preserving capital in the first place, our second objective should be to grow our account while maintaining a controlled risk.

Our objective is to ensure that we can continue trading after a bad trade, a bad day, or a series of losses. In short, **to preserve capital** over making money. Losses are more important than gains. Cutting losses is the key to success. More important than how much you earn on winning trades is how little you lose on losing trades.

In order to preserve your capital and be able to ow your account, you need a winning strategy. Money management in itself will not produce a winning system. It is possible, but it's not ideal. What we are interested in is a strategy that offers some form of advantage, not one that is random and is simply turned into a winning strategy thanks to the magic of money management. These types of practices will also ensure we don't bankrupt the account in the long run.

The basic tool for capital protection is the Stop Loss. This can help us protect our funds and limit losses when we find ourselves on the back of losing trades.

CAPITAL MANAGEMENT

Capital management is one of the fundamental pillars of financial investment. It has to do with quantity, with the risk that we are going to allow for in a particular trade and therefore, the amount of money we want to risk.

Clearly, in the first instance, we need to have enough capital. An account with sufficient funds for sound money management. The funds we decide to allocate will depend on the type of market we are trading in, the cost of its points and the required margins.

This is vital because even with a good trading strategy we can bankrupt the account if we do not properly control risk. Our goal is to stay in the market for the long term, and for this we must be prepared to suffer a series of losing trades.

To ensure we are in the strongest possible position to manage our capital, we are going to analyze all the concepts detailed below from a statistical mindset, based on the numbers. This is, without doubt, the best way to obtain objective conclusions on how to manage our capital.

Position Size

Since we do not know what the result of the next trade will be, and with the basic premise of preserving capital in mind, we must calculate the optimal size of each position so we risk just the right amount, to maximize the potential profit while keeping the risk under control.

Particularly important is the premise that we do not know what the result of the next trade will be. Therefore, the amount we risk should not depend on whether the previous trade was a winning or losing one. Each trade is independent. Only the capital we have at that moment should be taken into account when taking any decisions.

The size of the position can be decided in two ways:

- **First determining the size of the position** (shares, contracts, units). The Stop Loss will then be set at the corresponding distance in line with the previously set loss. And it will vary depending on this monetary amount.

  The larger the position size, the smaller the Stop Loss (the closer to the entry level it will be); and the smaller the size, the wider the Stop Loss.

- **First determining at what price level we will position the Stop Loss**. In which case it is the position size that will vary.

  The closer to the entry level the Stop Loss is, the larger the position size; and the further away it is, the smaller the position size.

  From a technical analysis perspective, this is the recommended way to apply capital management, since technical analysis helps us to identify those zones where we will place our orders.

Therefore, the fundamental elements for determining how much we are going to risk per trade, knowing that we will use the method of first determining the price where we will position the Stop Loss are:

- Knowing the value of the fluctuation units of that market.

- The distance at which we will position our Entry and Stop Loss levels.

- The percentage of the account that we are going to risk.

With this information we can then calculate the position size. There are a multitude of tools available on the internet that facilitate the task of calculating the position size. These are some of the easiest to use for both forex and futures and stocks:

https://www.dailyforex.com/forex-widget/position-size-calculator

https://evilspeculator.com/futuresRcalc

https://chartyourtrade.com/position-size-calculator

Throughout this chapter we will see different ways of applying risk management, but this one that we have just seen, defining it based on a percentage of the capital that we have in the account, is the simplest and most recommended.

Risk/Reward Ratio

This is the ratio of the estimated profit against the possible loss. To calculate it we need to measure the distance between the entry level and the Stop Loss level. This distance represents the R. Then we need to measure the distance between the entry level and the Take Profit level and calculate how many times that R is repeated.

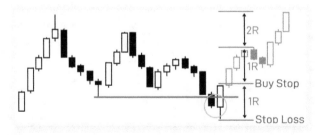

If it is repeated twice —in other words, the distance between the entry and the profit is twice the distance between the entry and the Stop Loss—, the Risk/Reward Ratio of the trade will be 2.

Understanding this ratio is very important. It will allow us to know what percentage of trades we can lose, while still having liquidity. Regardless of whether or not we can obtain statistics on which to base our trades (given the issues this implies in discretionary trading), understanding this concept is vital, since it gives us an objective perspective of what might happen in the long term; it is what is known as a mathematical expectation.

Mathematical Expectation

A mathematical expectation is defined as the average profit per trade. For a system to generate profitability in a sustained manner, a sine qua non condition is that the system has an average profit per trade greater than zero and therefore a positive mathematical expectation. Therefore, its value must be positive and the higher it is, the better.

The mathematical expectation formula is as follows:

(% Wins * Average Profit) - (% Losses * Average Loss)

Mathematical expectation is linked to the concepts of the Risk/Reward ratio and win percentage. The following table is an interesting representation of the possible combinations it offers us. This very useful information gives us perspective and objectivity when evaluating a strategy.

% wins	% losses	0.2	0.4	0.6	0.8	1	1.2	1.4	1.6	1.8	2	2.2	2.4	2.6	2.8	3	3.2	3.4	3.6	3.8	4	4.2	4.4	4.6	4.8	5
5	95	-0.94	-0.93	-0.92	-0.91	-0.90	-0.89	-0.88	-0.87	-0.86	-0.85	-0.84	-0.83	-0.82	-0.81	-0.80	-0.79	-0.78	-0.77	-0.76	-0.75	-0.74	-0.73	-0.72	-0.71	-0.70
10	90	-0.88	-0.86	-0.84	-0.82	-0.80	-0.78	-0.76	-0.74	-0.72	-0.70	-0.68	-0.66	-0.64	-0.62	-0.60	-0.58	-0.56	-0.54	-0.52	-0.50	-0.48	-0.46	-0.44	-0.42	-0.40
15	85	-0.82	-0.79	-0.76	-0.73	-0.70	-0.67	-0.64	-0.61	-0.58	-0.55	-0.52	-0.49	-0.46	-0.43	-0.40	-0.37	-0.34	-0.31	-0.28	-0.25	-0.22	-0.19	-0.16	-0.13	-0.10
20	80	-0.76	-0.72	-0.68	-0.64	-0.60	-0.56	-0.52	-0.48	-0.44	-0.40	-0.36	-0.32	-0.28	-0.24	-0.20	-0.16	-0.12	-0.08	-0.04	0.00	0.04	0.08	0.12	0.16	0.20
25	75	-0.7	-0.65	-0.60	-0.55	-0.50	-0.45	-0.40	-0.35	-0.30	-0.25	-0.20	-0.15	-0.10	-0.05	0.00	0.05	0.10	0.15	0.20	0.25	0.30	0.35	0.40	0.45	0.50
30	70	-0.64	-0.58	-0.52	-0.46	-0.40	-0.34	-0.28	-0.22	-0.16	-0.10	-0.04	0.02	0.08	0.14	0.20	0.26	0.32	0.38	0.44	0.50	0.56	0.62	0.68	0.74	0.80
35	65	-0.58	-0.51	-0.44	-0.37	-0.30	-0.23	-0.16	-0.09	-0.02	0.05	0.12	0.19	0.26	0.33	0.40	0.47	0.54	0.61	0.68	0.75	0.82	0.89	0.96	1.03	1.10
40	60	-0.52	-0.44	-0.36	-0.28	-0.20	-0.12	-0.04	0.04	0.12	0.20	0.28	0.36	0.44	0.52	0.60	0.68	0.76	0.84	0.92	1.00	1.08	1.16	1.24	1.32	1.40
45	55	-0.46	-0.37	-0.28	-0.19	-0.10	-0.01	0.08	0.17	0.26	0.35	0.44	0.53	0.62	0.71	0.80	0.89	0.98	1.07	1.16	1.25	1.34	1.43	1.52	1.61	1.70
50	50	-0.4	-0.3	-0.20	-0.10	0.00	0.10	0.20	0.30	0.40	0.50	0.60	0.70	0.80	0.90	1.00	1.10	1.20	1.30	1.40	1.50	1.60	1.70	1.80	1.90	2.00
55	45	-0.34	-0.23	-0.12	-0.01	0.10	0.21	0.32	0.43	0.54	0.65	0.76	0.87	0.98	1.09	1.20	1.31	1.42	1.53	1.64	1.75	1.86	1.97	2.08	2.19	2.30
60	40	-0.28	-0.16	-0.04	0.08	0.20	0.32	0.44	0.56	0.68	0.80	0.92	1.04	1.16	1.28	1.40	1.52	1.64	1.76	1.88	2.00	2.12	2.24	2.36	2.48	2.60
65	35	-0.22	-0.09	0.04	0.17	0.30	0.43	0.56	0.69	0.82	0.95	1.08	1.21	1.34	1.47	1.60	1.73	1.86	1.99	2.12	2.25	2.38	2.51	2.64	2.77	2.90
70	30	-0.16	-0.02	0.12	0.26	0.40	0.54	0.68	0.82	0.96	1.10	1.24	1.38	1.52	1.66	1.80	1.94	2.08	2.22	2.36	2.50	2.64	2.78	2.92	3.06	3.20
75	25	-0.1	0.05	0.20	0.35	0.50	0.65	0.80	0.95	1.10	1.25	1.40	1.55	1.70	1.85	2.00	2.15	2.30	2.45	2.60	2.75	2.90	3.05	3.20	3.35	3.50
80	20	-0.04	0.12	0.28	0.44	0.60	0.76	0.92	1.08	1.24	1.40	1.56	1.72	1.88	2.04	2.20	2.36	2.52	2.68	2.84	3.00	3.16	3.32	3.48	3.64	3.80
85	15	0.02	0.19	0.36	0.53	0.70	0.87	1.04	1.21	1.38	1.55	1.72	1.89	2.06	2.23	2.40	2.57	2.74	2.91	3.08	3.25	3.42	3.59	3.76	3.93	4.10
90	10	0.08	0.26	0.44	0.62	0.80	0.98	1.16	1.34	1.52	1.70	1.88	2.06	2.24	2.42	2.60	2.78	2.96	3.14	3.32	3.50	3.68	3.86	4.04	4.22	4.40
95	5	0.14	0.33	0.52	0.71	0.90	1.09	1.28	1.47	1.66	1.85	2.04	2.23	2.42	2.61	2.80	2.99	3.18	3.37	3.56	3.75	3.94	4.13	4.32	4.51	4.70

There are traders who discard trades because their ratio is lower than one, in the belief that this could lead to ruin in the long term. Here we see a perfect example of the usefulness of this concept. Basically, the key idea to understand is that, as the table shows, we can be profitable in the long term using different configurations:

- Low Risk/Reward ratio and High Win Percentage

- High Risk/Reward ratio and Low Win Percentage

As we can see, even with a high percentage of losses we can still remain profitable. This is something that many traders do not understand; but with a loss percentage of 80% and a Ratio greater than 4 (with every losing trade we subtract 1, but with a winning trade we add 4) we would have a strategy involving a positive mathematical expectation that would provide us with long-term profits. While on the other hand, a high success rate is irrelevant unless we know the ratio used by the strategy. For example, a strategy that wins 70% of the time but that wins very little each time would be a losing strategy with a ratio of 0.4. In this case, every time we win we add 0.4 but every time we lose we subtract 1.

So what ratio should we use? Do we discard trades if they do not offer us a particular ratio? As always, for discretionary trading there is one configuration that is better than the other and everything will depend on the profile of the trader and the strategy in question. Generally, trend-following strategies tend to have lower win rates but a higher ratio; while other strategies such as mean reversion tend to have a higher win rate but a lower ratio.

My personal point of view, as a technical analyst, is that trades should not be discarded based solely on this ratio. The reason for this is that the market is a living entity and does not always move in the same way. Its conditions change and the trading zones on which we base our decisions can vary. If the market offers us an opportunity, it seems to me that the most sensible thing to do is to take it. Sometimes it will have a high ratio and sometimes a low one. The idea is that we must adapt and try not to pigeonhole the market in any way.

Drawdown

A drawdown is a peak-to-trough decline of the capital curve when we suffer a losing streak. The biggest drop in the curve is known as the Maximum Drawdown. The drawdown is considered to have been exceeded when the curve reaches the previous high before the drop.

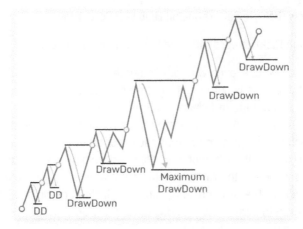

Understanding this concept is important in order to reinforce the idea that risk management is a vital element in any trading system. As well as the distance of the percentage drop, another important factor when analyzing the Drawdown is its duration.

In the event that we incur losses, the gains that we must subsequently achieve to recover those losses and return to the initial state increase proportionally. In other words, say we lose 10% of the capital in the account; if we subsequently gain 10% we would still not reach the level we were at before the drop.

The following table shows what percentage profit we need in order to recover from a particular loss:

% loss	% profit
1 %	1,01 %
3 %	3,09 %
5 %	5,26 %
10 %	11,1 %
15 %	17,6 %
20 %	25 %
25 %	33,3 %
30 %	42,9 %
40 %	66,7 %
50 %	100 %
60 %	150 %
70 %	233,3 %
80 %	400 %
90 %	900 %
100 %	Bankruptcy

If we lose 10% of the capital in the account, we need to obtain a return of 11.1% to reach the baseline, the breakeven point of the account. But of course, this becomes more difficult as the loss percentage increases. For example, to recover from a 50% loss we would need to double the amount in the account, in other words make 100% of the capital that we had at that point. No easy task.

From this concept we move on to the following one, which has to do with the number of losing trades that we can allow ourselves during a losing streak. Thanks to both concepts, we can objectively understand why it is important not to take on an excessive risk per trade.

No. trades	Capital	Loss	Remaining	Loss in %
1	10000	100	9900	-1,0
2	9900	99	9801	-2,0
3	9801	98	9703	-3,0
4	9703	97	9606	-3,9
5	9606	96	9510	-4,9
6	9510	95	9415	-5,9
7	9415	94	9321	-6,8
8	9321	93	9227	-7,7
9	9227	92	9135	-8,6
10	9135	91	9044	-9,6
11	9044	90	8953	-10,5
12	8953	90	8864	-11,4
13	8864	89	8775	-12,2
14	8775	88	8687	-13,1
15	8687	87	8601	-14,0
16	8601	86	8515	-14,9
17	8515	85	8429	-15,7
18	8429	84	8345	-16,5
19	8345	83	8262	-17,4
20	8262	83	8179	-18,2
21	8179	82	8097	-19,0
22	8097	81	8016	-19,8
23	8016	80	7936	-20,6
24	7936	79	7857	-21,4

As we have seen, recovering from a loss of 50% of our capital would mean having to double the account. Almost certainly impossible, since suffering that level of loss implies that you are likely following a trading strategy that really isn't exploiting an advantage, in other words a losing strategy in the long term.

So, let's say that a maximum loss that a system can suffer which is potentially recoverable would be one with a Drawdown of 20 or up to 30%.

Now, how can we reach those drawdown levels depending on the risk we assume per trade? This is what we will see in the following tables:

No. trades	Capital	Loss	Remaining	Loss in %
1	10000	200	9800	-2,0
2	9800	196	9604	-4,0
3	9604	192	9412	-5,9
4	9412	188	9224	-7,8
5	9224	184	9039	-9,6
6	9039	181	8858	-11,4
7	8858	177	8681	-13,2
8	8681	174	8508	-14,9
9	8508	170	8337	-16,6
10	8337	167	8171	-18,3
11	8171	163	8007	-19,9
12	8007	160	7847	-21,5
13	7847	157	7690	-23,1

No. trades	Capital	Loss	Remaining	Loss in %
1	10000	500	9500	-5,0
2	9500	475	9025	-9,8
3	9025	451	8574	-14,3
4	8574	429	8145	-18,5
5	8145	407	7738	-22,6

By risking 1% of our capital per trade we can allow ourselves a losing streak of 23 trades and reach a Drawdown of 20.6% at that point. Easy to understand, right? But what if we risk 2%? Well, in that case we would have already reached this percentage after only 12 trades. And what if we risk 5% per trade? Well, with only 5 losing trades we would have already exceeded the established limit. Herein lies the importance of maintaining a low risk per trade percentage.

What should be clear is that 5 losing trades in a row is highly probable; and if we don't manage risk the properly, we may find ourselves in a situation from which it is very hard to recover. Optimal risk management requires a statistical mindset and the use of objective data to verify these concepts.

Incidentally, the numbers are even worse when you consider that to all the above we would also have to add all the trading expenses and various fees involved.

Trading Limits

Many traders apply limits as another risk management measure in their operations. Some try to establish a maximum number of open trades within a certain time frame (day, week, month) while others simultaneously put limits on the risk they take on.

They are usually motivated to take these types of measures on emotional grounds. If they have a bad day for whatever reason, they may take these types of measures to avoid significant damage to the account, resulting in a break from trading for that day, week or month.

Although this may be a good option to protect our account, personally I don't apply it when I trade for the very basic reason that, as I have already mentioned, each trade is independent of the previous one, and a winning one can appear at any moment.

Imagine if you are involved in short-term trading and have set a limit of three consecutive losses. In other words, if you suffer three losses, you will stop trading for that day, in the belief that your analysis isn't quite working out; but if, according to my trading plan, the market then offers me an opportunity, why wouldn't I take the next trade? What if that is the one that might enable me to win and end the day positively?

This is certainly a controversial idea. Of course, you could enter the market again and suffer a new loss, which would reinforce your idea that the trading limit was well established; or, you could take it, end up with a profit, and scrap this management measure forever.

Another reason why I decide not to set limits is because of the analysis strategy I use. Being a discretionary method based on the analysis of the interaction between supply and demand, imbalances to one side or the other can occur at any time, generating good opportunities in both directions. Specifically, my reading of the market based on price action, VSA and Wyckoff enables me to take long and short trades in short periods of time. A particular action might initially influence us in a certain direction but the result of the action could then ultimately lead to the opposite sentiment, resulting in an entry in the market in the opposite direction. The idea I'm trying to get across is that I might suffer a couple of losing trades in the same direction due to a misreading of the market, but subsequently an event might occur that throws the market off balance and makes the scenario clearer, offering me a new opportunity with greater guarantees than the previous ones; and if

I happened to have reached my trading limit, I wouldn't take that position, a position that could turn out to be a winning one.

Trading limits are a good option if we have developed a strategy based on quantitative analysis and we have verified that this risk management measure effectively allows us to obtain better system performance in the long run, better than if we didn't implement it. It can also be very useful in the early stages, when the trader does not yet have a great deal of experience and is susceptible to trading without any emotional control.

A trading limit that can be very useful under any circumstance in establishing a point at which to stop the strategy, assuming that the advantage you were trying to exploit (if there really was such an advantage), has moved elsewhere or disappeared.

For this purpose, and based on what we have already seen, win percentages and what we need to recover from a Drawdown, an appropriate limit at which we could stop operating that strategy and reevaluate the whole system entirely might be 30%. If we are applying proper risk management, a 30% drawdown is significant enough to indicate that something out of the ordinary may be happening. At that point we would then try to find a flaw in the system and in the event we weren't able to improve it, we would probably be better off discarding the strategy altogether.

TYPES OF MONEY MANAGEMENT

Let's continue with the theory, because there are several methods we can use when it comes to money management. We will only look at the three most well-known and most commonly used. One of them, the Martingale method, will be presented only as an example of what should NOT be done. A lot of people confuse the world of trading and investment with gambling, and nothing could be further from the truth.

This section includes several tables to support all the ideas that are presented. To ensure the results can be correctly interpreted and compared, the examples are based on the premise of a Risk/Reward Ratio of 1; that is, each time we lose we subtract 1 and each time we win we add 1. This will make it a lot easier to understand all the concepts.

Martingale

This management method has its origin in casinos, and in particular, in roulette. Its premise is very simple: double the position size after every losing trade, in an attempt to try to recoup losses as soon as possible.

When implementing this type of money management, the trader focuses in particular on the streaks of the system; somehow managing to make a system perform well, despite it not exploiting any advantage and being based on no logic whatsoever. But as we have already seen, this is artificial. This is the kind of management that might turn a losing strategy into a winning one. The problem is that not all that glitters is gold.

Systems that apply this type of management usually display a capital curve in which the most important characteristic is the steep troughs and the rapid V-shaped recoveries. The appearance after these shocks is as if nothing had ever happened. In fact, if you eliminate those troughs from the line, its progression would be practically linear. This would make it the Holy Grail of trading.

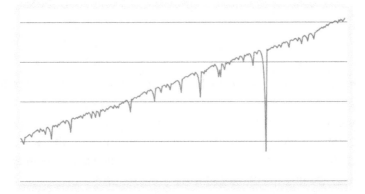

Proponents of the Martingale argue that it is impossible to suffer an infinite number of losing trades. Statistically, this may be the case, but this isn't the issue. The biggest problem is that by the time a winning trade appears, you may no longer have enough capital to take a big enough position and you may end up bankrupting the account.

Unless you have infinite capital (and when I say infinite I mean truly infinite), suffering a losing streak of 10 trades, and even more, is very possible; and at times like that your account may be seriously diminished and unable to attempt another trade. Bear in mind that this system implies doubling the amount you are risking in the event of a loss.

Trade	Capital	% risk	Loss	Equity
1	10000	0,2	-20	9980
2	9980	0,4	-40	9940
3	9940	0,8	-80	9861
4	9861	1,6	-158	9703
5	9703	3,2	-310	9392
6	9392	6,4	-601	8791
7	8791	12,8	-1125	7666
8	7666	25,6	-1962	5703
9	5703	51,2	-2920	2783
10	2783	102,4	-2850	-67

As we can see in the table, even if you start with a very low risk of 0.2% of the account's capital, a losing streak of 7 trades would already force you to risk no less than 25.6% of all of your capital in the next trade, which is sheer madness. And of course after 10 losses you are out.

It should be noted that in this example, the system is calculating the risk of the next trade in relative terms. In other words, the risk doubles based on the equity of the account, on the available capital. An even more aggressive version would be to calculate the size of the next trade in absolute terms; that is, based on the amount lost and without taking into account the capital available, which would further accelerate the losses.

Less extreme variants of the Martingale system have arisen in which the risk is not directly doubled; rather, it is progressively increased at a fixed rate. In the following table we can see an example of this starting, as in the previous example, with a very low risk of 0.2%.

Trade	Capital	% risk	Loss	Equity
1	10000	0,2	-20	9980
2	9980	0,4	-40	9940
3	9940	0,6	-60	9880
4	9880	0,8	-79	9801
5	9801	1	-98	9703
6	9703	1,2	-116	9587
7	9587	1,4	-134	9453
8	9453	1,6	-151	9301
9	9301	1,8	-167	9134
10	9134	2	-183	8951

What is debatable here is whether risk is being properly optimized. In effect this is the task of money management, to optimize risk. In other words, you start by risking a relatively very small amount, which could lead you to obtaining less profitability in the event that winning trades start to appear. As we can see, the martingale system focuses more on losing trades than winning trades.

Trade	Capital	% risk	Loss	Equity
1	10000	1	-100	9900
2	9900	1,2	-119	9781
3	9781	1,4	-137	9644
4	9644	1,6	-154	9490
5	9490	1,8	-171	9319
6	9319	2	-186	9133
7	9133	2,2	-201	8932
8	8932	2,4	-214	8717
9	8717	2,6	-227	8491
10	8491	2,8	-238	8253

To try to solve this problem we might want to start trading with a higher percentage, let's say 1%. Well, we would find ourselves in the same situation, with the focus still on the losing trades rather than the winning trades. Just as losing streaks appear, so do winning streaks. An important aspect to point out is that every time a winning trade appears, the risk level is reset and a new series begins. We could be on a winning streak and be dedicating only 1% to it when perhaps we have the capacity to risk 2% of the account, meaning we miss out on winning a considerable amount.

Trade	Capital	% risk	Earnings	Equity
1	10000	1	100	10100
2	10100	1	101	10201
3	10201	1	102	10303
4	10303	1	103	10406
5	10406	1	104	10510
6	10510	1	105	10615
7	10615	1	106	10721
8	10721	1	107	10829
9	10829	1	108	10937
10	10937	1	109	11046

Moreover, with this type of risk management, based on a softer version of the martingale approach, the appearance of a winning trade would not compensate the previous losses.

Understanding the drawbacks of this method can help you to identify whether the strategy in question is based on this management model. There are many brokers and platforms that offer the possibility of investing in other traders, in the strategies they carry out, as professional managers do. Many of the best strategies that we can see on these platforms carry out this type of management strategy. Learning to identify them will help you to avoid incurring an unacceptable risk, such as the one we incur when exposed to the martingale system.

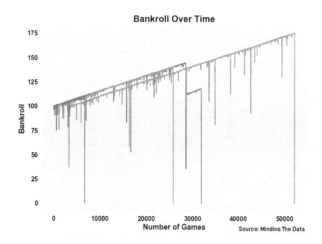

Bankroll Over Time

Source: Minding The Data

The feasibility of this strategy and its long-term results based on a sufficient number of events (trades) has been the subject of several studies, and the account always ends up in the red. We need to approach trading in the most professional way possible, and this strategy is very far removed from what professional managers do.

Exponential Model

The exponential system is a model in which risk is adjusted based on the amount available in the account. In other words, the amount being risked remains proportional to the equity, as it rises and falls. Therefore, the risk is increased when we obtain profits because the capital in the account increases; and it decreases when we suffer losses because of the reduction in capital.

Unlike the martingale system, in which the risk is increased as losing trades occur, in this model the opposite happens: each time a loss occurs, the size of the position decreases, as the risk is adjusted in each individual trade. For this reason it is considered an anti-martingale model.

Another big difference with the martingale strategy is that this type of money management takes into account winning streaks. This means it minimizes losses during a losing streak, while it maximizes profits in the event of a winning streak.

Trade	Capital	% risk	Loss	Equity
1	10000	2	-200	9800
2	9800	2	-196	9604
3	9604	2	-192	9412
4	9412	2	-188	9224
5	9224	2	-184	9039
6	9039	2	-181	8858
7	8858	2	-177	8681
8	8681	2	-174	8508
9	8508	2	-170	8337
10	8337	2	-167	8171

As the size of the trade remains proportional to equity, it is mathematically impossible to completely bankrupt the account, although as we have already commented in the section on trading limits, we should actively manage the account and be in a position to close it before reaching this situation.

Trade	Capital	% risk	Earnings	Equity
1	10000	2	200	10200
2	10200	2	204	10404
3	10404	2	208	10612
4	10612	2	212	10824
5	10824	2	216	11041
6	11041	2	221	11262
7	11262	2	225	11487
8	11487	2	230	11717
9	11717	2	234	11951
10	11951	2	239	12190

When the capital in our account is relatively low, this proportional risk management is also reflected in the reduced impact of streaks on our yield curve. But be careful, because as capital increases, trades will have an increasing capacity to influence the equity curve.

In short, the exponential model is one of the most widely used, thanks to its simplicity and because it manages to allocate risk in a relatively optimal manner.

Linear Model

The linear model does not take into account the money in the account and always risks the same amount in monetary terms. In this case, we do not risk a percentage of what we have, instead we risk a fixed amount, which therefore means that the percentage dedicated to each trade varies.

The biggest advantage of this management model is its simplicity. It is easier to understand, as the position size doesn't change.

The linear approach is different from the exponential system. Here the risk is determined only once in the first trade, depending on the capital. Once the amount to be risked per trade has been set, it is maintained constantly in the future.

Trade	Capital	% risk	Loss	Equity
1	10000	2,00	-200	9800
2	9800	2,04	-200	9600
3	9600	2,08	-200	9400
4	9400	2,13	-200	9200
5	9200	2,17	-200	9000
6	9000	2,22	-200	8800
7	8800	2,27	-200	8600
8	8600	2,33	-200	8400
9	8400	2,38	-200	8200
10	8200	2,44	-200	8000

In this example we see how the linear model would behave when undergoing a losing streak. Keeping the amount being risked constant, it represents a higher risk percentage each time, since the amount in the account is ever decreasing.

In this table we see the inverse effect; by maintaining a constant amount being risked during a winning streak, the percentage that each trade represents in relation to the capital in the account reduces each time.

Trade	Capital	% risk	Earnings	Equity
1	10000	2,00	200	10200
2	10200	1,96	200	10400
3	10400	1,92	200	10600
4	10600	1,89	200	10800
5	10800	1,85	200	11000
6	11000	1,82	200	11200
7	11200	1,79	200	11400
8	11400	1,75	200	11600
9	11600	1,72	200	11800
10	11800	1,69	200	12000

This model is primarily used for withdrawal accounts; accounts in which profits are periodically withdrawn. The account is reset to the initial capital during each period. In this way we avoid having a large amount of money deposited with the broker.

The great disadvantage, of course, is that unlike the exponential model, this model isn't able to take advantage of the principle of compound interest.

MANAGING THE TRADE

Although this section isn't directly related to risk management, there is an indirect link: our management of the position once it is opened can have some influence on the final result.

The importance of position management increases as the time frame of the trade is reduced. While it is true that getting the moment of entry right (timing) is key to improving the performance of any trade, when it comes to shorter-term operations, this timing becomes critical. As traders, our objective is to enter the market at the precise moment in which an imbalance is about to be generated that will push the price in the direction of our position.

We have previously studied the types of orders that we can use to enter and exit the market. Now we are going to look in more detail at some advanced features and uses that we can implement in our management.

Advanced Use of Stop Loss

As previously mentioned, Stop Loss is our lifeline. It is our basic tool for properly implementing risk management. The basic idea is that we should place our Stop Loss at that point which, if it is reached, results in the invalidation of the scenario we have set out.

Obviously this point will depend on the trading strategy being employed. As a rule of thumb, I usually place the Stop Loss at the opposite end of the candlestick   or pattern of candlesticks that has provided me with the entry trigger. With these types of signals, what we are identifying is an imbalance in the shortest term and therefore, if we are correct in our analysis, the impulse movement that we are hoping for should begin. If anything else occurs, we are no longer interested in staying in the market, because the message we receive is that the market is not yet ready to move in that direction; and therefore, the market may need to move in some other way before going in the direction we were initially looking for. In this case, we are no longer interested in staying in.

Trailing Stop

The Trailing Stop or Dynamic Stop is a tool which helps us to optimize the placement of the Stop Loss. It is simply a matter of changing the location of the Stop Loss as the price moves in our direction, in order to protect part of the accumulated profits in a winning trade.

Although this would ideally be an automatic process, this type of tool can also be implemented manually. A very simple example would be, having entered the market, to move the Stop Loss to the end of the last candlestick that denotes intent in favor of that direction. And unless a new candlestick showing intent were to be generated that meets our characteristics, we would not move the Stop Loss.

Instead of leaving the initial location fixed until either the Take Profit or the Stop Loss is reached, what this allows us to do is to somewhat reduce the risk to which we are exposed.

Another widely used manual option is to wait for the creation of new pivot points in favor of the current movement. In this case we would need to move the Stop Loss to the other side of the last pivot point in favor of our direction just when the price reaches the opposite extreme. In a bullish example, as soon as the current movement reaches the previous high, we would move the Stop Loss to below the last pivot point.

But you must be careful with this because as you can see, this common placement of the Trailing Stop feeds the liquidity that is expected to exist at the pivot points, with the resulting problem that the price may move towards this area, generate a false breakout and continue to move in the same direction as before. This is why false breakouts work so well in liquidity zones, because there are always a large number of limit orders pending execution. To solve this problem, we can place the Trailing Stop on the second pivot point closest to the price, instead of on the one that is closest, since there is a very good chance that this price will be reached.

A Trailing Stop is most effectively used automatically. This involves adding a conditional order to the Stop Loss so that it progressively follows the price, as it moves in our direction. The idea is that we establish the initial distance at which we will place said order in monetary units or as a percentage and this will be responsible for continuously modifying the location of said Stop Loss to ensure it always maintains the same distance with respect to the current price.

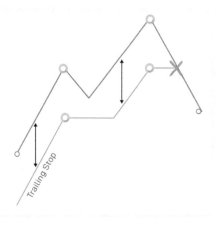

The Trailing Stop only moves in our direction. If we are in a long position, once it has moved higher, it cannot go down again.

Trailing Stops are very configurable, but basically there are two types:

- Those that are activated directly at the point of entering the market.

- Those that are activated after a certain level of profit is reached, in which case there is no Trailing Stop until a certain amount of profit is obtained.

Some traders will regularly use indicators such as moving averages or more advanced tools that analyze volatility, such as the ATR indicator. Automatically setting the ideal distance for the Trailing Stops is not easy. There is no ideal distance, due to the constantly changing nature of markets and stock movement. For this reason an indicator such as the ATR can be especially useful in this application.

The Trailing Stop, by its very nature, is especially useful for trend-following trades or those looking for a long run.

It may also be of interest to use Trailing Stops as a tool to take profits. Instead of using a classic Take Profit order, we can simply use a Trailing Stop to ensure that the price will move as far as possible in our direction and that we are not restricting our potential earnings by using a Take Profit too early.

Breakeven

This term describes the action of relocating the Stop Loss level by moving it to the level of the entry price. With this we can protect the position so that if the price reaches this level, we exit the market without losses or gains.

Bear in mind that in order for us to exit the market with a net result of 0 we must make sure that we factor in all the different fees we have to pay. As a result, it is common practice is to place the Stop Loss slightly beyond the entry level. Many traders refer to this type of management as Breakeven +1. This means that in order to counteract the negative effect of fees, we put the Stop Loss slightly in our favor.

The key question here is, when is it the right time to put the Stop Loss at Breakeven? As always, this will depend on the trader and their strategy.

I like to execute a discretionary strategy, like those proposed in the technical analysis section, whenever the price moves towards a liquidity zone in which there is no way of knowing how it will react once it reaches that zone. The other situation in which I use Breakeven to manage my position is when a certain imbalance or event occurs in the market that suggests a change in sentiment that goes against my position. For this reason it is important that you are proactive when managing your position.

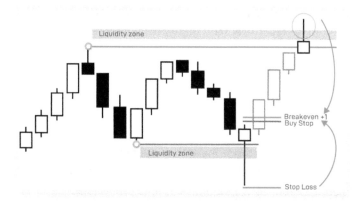

We need to be aware of what is happening in the market to take action as quickly as possible in case an unexpected event or new piece of information simply appears, changing the valuations of agents and causing an imbalance that is not in our favor.

If you are employing an automatic strategy, one way to implement Breakeven could be using Risk/Reward ratios. For example, when the price reaches a Ratio of 1:1 (the same distance in favor as that established between the entry price and the location of the Stop Loss), we place the Stop Loss at Breakeven.

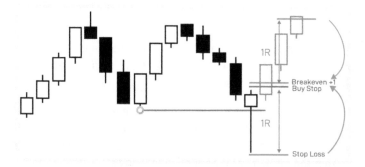

The options are very diverse and everything will depend on the logic of the trading strategy that is being used as well as the knowledge of the trader.

Management Methods

As we will continue to see, position management encompasses a large number of concepts. There are a wide range of options and there is no single trading management method; nor one that is better than another.

Once we have determined the position size, and decided the type of management that we are going to implement, another factor to consider is our type of position management. This is about how we are going to distribute the amount that we have allocated to that position.

All or nothing

This is the simplest method. The trader defines the entry, Stop Loss and Take Profit points; they enter with the full position amount and allow it to develop until it reaches the stop loss or take profit level.

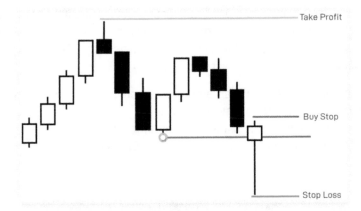

The main advantage of this style is that the trader in no case has to manipulate the position, avoiding the possibility of making bad decisions, guided by feelings such as fear or greed.

But this is a double-edged sword because it is also its biggest disadvantage. By not being aware of what is happening in the market, we may indirectly assume a greater risk, because we will not act even if our analysis suggests that the market sentiment could change.

Generally, this type of management is used for robot-executed automatic trading strategies, as well as in situations where the trader is unable to be in front of a screen.

Active management

This type of management is mainly related to the way in which we take profits.

Many traders (myself included) feel comfortable taking partial profits. This simply means, once the market has advanced in our position and we have obtained certain latent profits, closing part of the position and securing these profits.

As well as taking a partial profit, the trader in this case will protect the position at the Breakeven level. Psychologically it is very reassuring to know that for the rest of the position you will no longer be able to incur any losses and that also, whatever happens, you will close the position in the black, thanks to the profits that you have already secured.

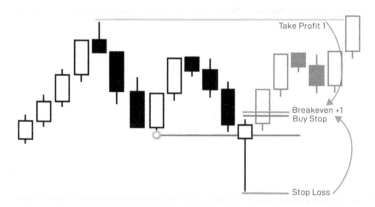

As we can see, and this is another example highlighting how diverse the possibilities are, you can include the Breakeven or not. Nothing is written in stone in this regard. But if you are in front of a screen and you are able to more actively manage your trading, I highly recommend you do so.

The market is an environment full of uncertainty and it is constantly changing in its very nature, so we need to be able to analyze and interpret the information offered to us very quickly in order to make decisions that improve our risk management.

Taking partial profits is usually referred to as making a TP1 (Take Profit 1). How should you distribute the TP1/TP2? Well again there is no absolute truth here. I usually set up a TP1 with half the position. In other words, I close 50% of the position size when the market reaches a liquidity zone, leaving the remaining 50% to run until another profit-taking point (or Stop Loss) is reached.

At this stage let's go back over the most interesting zones where we should be looking to take profits:

- Using **Price Action** we have the liquidity zones.

- Using **VSA** we will try to identify climax actions.

- Using **Wyckoff** we will wait to see the Phase A that indicates the end of the previous trend.

- And using **Volume Profile** we will identify areas with a high trading volume, which are basically old accumulation/distribution structures.

The chart above shows how we have set up the first TP in the most immediate liquidity zone which also coincides with the upper part of the accumulation structure; and we have set up the second take profit when the price reaches that old high volume trading area that corresponds to the distribution structure. Specifically we have established it in the VPOC (Volume Point of Control), which is the level with the highest volume of trading of the entire profile. We could even retain a final marginal part of the position until we see a climax action or Phase A of the Wyckoff Method, denoting that the movement has stopped. The possibilities are endless.

You can decide how you to distribute the percentage of your position to close at each Take Profit point. First, you must decide if you will establish two or more take profits, and secondly, the percentage you want to assign to each of them.

The nature of the trade also influences how you will manage this distribution. If, for example, you are involved in a trend-following trade which you hope will go on a long run, you may want to set a TP1 and a TP2 but also let a final part continue to run using a small amount (5 or 10%) in case the market surprises you and reaches levels that you did not expect, generating a greater profit.

The main advantage of this approach is that it ensures that a winning position doesn't turn into a losing position. It also provides peace of mind.

The disadvantage is that you will obtain less profit if the trade reaches the final target. It is not the same thing to set a Take Profit with the entire position than to reach the same end point with a smaller amount, having previously closed a part of that position.

Averaging

This involves entering the market at different prices, each better than the previous one. In other words, if for example we want to buy, we will do so at a lower price each time, thus obtaining a better average price. In the event that we want to build a short position, it means selling at a higher price each time.

This management model is generally misunderstood and there are many who approach it badly, using it without any method. They get trapped in a position (because they didn't use a Stop Loss) and guided by the hope that sooner or later the market will recover. They decide to enter again to improve their average price. But why should it recover? What if it keeps going against you? At what point will you stop averaging? It is a practice that does not seem to make much sense unless the working hypothesis, the investment idea, is maintained.

A much more effective way to use this management method is to divide the entire position into different packages, by making different entries until it is complete, but always subject to the context and the strategy of the trade.

Let's say you want to buy an asset but that it isn't at the optimal point for you to enter; that even though it is in a trading zone, it is feasible that it may go down even further, given the proportionality of its movements or for some other reason. But of course, at the same time you are afraid that the market will leave you behind, that it will initiate the movement you have forecast and that it will not visit that trading zone which offers you the best chance of entry. Well, one way to solve this would be to enter at that first trading level, assuming it offers the entry trigger with a part of your position; and leave another part aside in case the scenario in which it reaches the trading zone at the lower prices finally comes to pass, re-entering there when it offers us a new entry signal.

This chart shows an example of this. Let's say we find ourselves in the first trading zone, in a pivot generated after an accumulation structure. In that position we know that it could provide an entry into a long position and go higher continuing with the uptrend; but it could also visit the second trading zone, the Creek zone, the zone of resistance of the structure that would now become the support level. Since we have two possible trading zones, we could assign 50% of the position size to each of them. Our biggest problem would be if our entry trigger doesn't appear in the second trading zone, and instead the price re-enters the range again, meaning all that movement was just a false breakout. In that case, we should have previously established the maximum zone or level where we would allow the price to re-enter. At that point we would close the position without hesitation.

My opinion here is that averaging for the sake of averaging is not very sensible. However, if we follow a method and if it is part of our trading plan, well that's another story.

Pyramiding

In contrast to what the averaging method proposes, the pyramid approach implies initially entering with part of the position and subsequently re-entering at worse prices than before. In other words, if we are looking to buy, we would open a first position with part of the total size and later we would complete the position by entering again at higher prices, worsening the average price initially obtained.

This approach turns the previous one on its head. Let's suppose that we are in the reverse situation; that we are in the final possible trading zone waiting for the entry trigger indicated by our trading approach, but for whatever reason we are not as filled with confidence as we would like. If the signal finally appears, we could enter the market with part of the total position and, unless the price goes in our favor, not enter it again. To do this, we would have previously identified the trading zones and planned our possible scenarios. For our second entry we would wait for the price to position itself in favor of a new trading zone, or one previously identified. At that point, we would execute our entry signal again. At that moment we would have used the entire position.

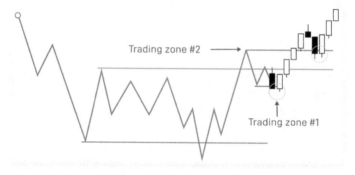

The main advantage of this approach is that it reduces risk in the event of a losing trade. If we enter in the last zone and the price reaches our Stop Loss level, the loss will not be for the entire position. It will only be for that first part.

However, the main disadvantage is that you will obtain lower profits if the trade eventually turns out to be a winner.

You should know that if you study other resources they will present this concept to you in a different way. Normally, pyramiding is often referred to simply as increasing your position as the price moves in your favor, and nothing more. That if we are going long, we would continue buying as the price rises a certain number of points or percentage. This point of view in particular (buying for the sake of it) doesn't seem very sound to me, so I have tried to refine the concept by presenting this position management model in which, yes, we increase the position, but following a certain logic, as long as the market keeps offering opportunities in our favor.

Tips On Position Management

This final section on position management will discuss some interesting tips that may be useful.

Classify trades according to their quality

As time passes and you gain experience, you will realize that there are trades that offer you better guarantees than others.

If you have the ability to identify this sentiment in real time, one way to improve the Risk/Reward Ratio is to allocate a larger or smaller position size depending on the confidence you have in the trade in question.

One way to put this idea into practice is to define some minimum parameters that must be met in all trades before evaluating the trading approach (our trading plan); and later, depending on the extra signals we identify, we can increase or decrease the size. If we identify a signal of underlying strength but one that is not substantial enough, or one that could be more substantial, denoting greater intent in that direction, a good option is to reduce the size of the position. If, on the other hand, we observe a show of strength in the appropriate trading zone, with the right context and in line with our main directional long term bias then we could decide to increase the risk just for that trade.

The idea is to classify trades based on the quality of the signal they offer us. This measure is aimed especially at traders who already have some experience in the markets and who have the ability to almost objectively identify the information that the market is offering.

To carry out this task, it is essential to keep a trading diary and periodically review it. We will deal with both points later.

What to do when the trade goes wrong

Let's say that having opened a position we see that the market doesn't move as we had hoped, that it starts to fluctuate up and down without any clear direction. This is another signal that might make us think the market isn't yet ready to initiate the movement we expected.

In this case, you might want to think about reducing your risk exposure before the Stop Loss closes everything. You will never know to what extent you are making a good decision, but if for whatever reason you don't feel comfortable with the trade you have open, you can close a percentage of it. This may be a good way to remain emotionally calm. Bear in mind that you can always re-enter later, if the market sends out more signals.

Nature of the trade

We often think that the position we are about to open is the one that will make us rich. We start looking at longer time frames, with the aim of turning that trade that was the result of a short-term analysis into one that is going to look for major long-term movement. Of course, 90% of the time this will not happen. And the worst thing is that it could be a good trade (but not good enough for that purpose) but we lose out on obtaining more profits from it by not properly managing the time frame.

The trade should always be managed in accordance with the trading time frame. Don't expect trades that were born in the short term to become major trends; although it is true that on occasion this could happen, usually it is not the case..

Anticipating the entry

This is a very common beginner's mistake. We are in the trading zone awaiting our entry trigger, which let's assume is a candlestick showing intent. Then we see a candlestick that at first glance seems to have the characteristics we are looking for, but before the candlestick ends and closes according to its time frame, we decide to enter in an attempt to anticipate the entry. And surprise surprise, just before the candlestick closes, a minor imbalance occurs in the opposite direction indicating exactly the opposite sentiment we were looking for.

Be very careful with this because it is something that happens frequently. The closing price of a candlestick is one of the most important pieces of information, telling us about the commitment and quality of the traders who have entered in that direction. Don't try to anticipate entry in this way because you will expose yourself to unnecessary risk.

Bad entry

Sometimes you might enter the market in the wrong manner. Perhaps in the way described in the above example when trying to anticipate your entry. What do we do then? Close the trade immediately. Abandoning the position is the most advisable measure.

You have not followed your trading plan, it is not a trade that offers any guarantees or confidence, so there is no point staying in it hoping that the market will go in our favor. When it comes to the market, we must put our feelings aside and act as coldly as possible. And in this situation there can be no excuses.

Key moments

In time you will see that in each market there are particular moments that must be taken into account. For example, if a fundamental event concerning certain economic news that could affect our position is about to be broadcast, the most sensible thing is to manage the position to protect ourselves from potential volatility. In reality, in this scenario, the most advisable thing to do is to leave the market immediately, especially if you are intraday trading.

You should also avoid trading during the opening and closing of markets. Again, these are periods which generate a great deal of volatility that could reduce our position. In this regard, you should also take into account the overnight risk of holding the position while the market is closed.

PORTFOLIO MANAGEMENT

This section is aimed more at the investor than at the trader. Portfolio management has to do with the allocation of assets, with how investments are divided between different markets.

The breakdown of a portfolio, as with practically everything to do with the world of investment, is something very personal and is subject to the investor's profile, their tolerance for risk and the time horizon, among other aspects.

The investor's age is one of the most influential factors on how capital is allocated to create the portfolio. Investors with a longer time horizon usually prefer the majority of their portfolio to be made up of equity assets that are higher risk in search of a higher potential return; while those who are older feel more comfortable creating a portfolio which is more heavily weighted in favor of less volatile and risky assets such as fixed income instruments.

Diversification

Creating a portfolio and deciding allocating investments to different markets in order to reduce risk is known as diversification. Everyone knows the saying "don't put all your eggs in one basket".

The objective of diversification is to protect the investor by allocating capital across assets, in the hope that if one investment loses money, the other investments will offset those losses, or at least not add to them.

The rationale for diversification lies in checking the level of correlation that exists between assets. This is statistically measured by the correlation coefficient and involves verifying how one variable behaves in relation to another; in other words, how one market moves in relation to another.

The spectrum of the correlation coefficient ranges from +1 to -1. A positive correlation (+1) tells us that these assets generally move in the same direction; while a negative correlation (-1) informs us that these assets move in the opposite way; that is, if one asset goes down, the other goes up. In the event that these variables are not related and the movements of one asset have nothing to do with the movements of the other, we would be looking at uncorrelated assets (0). The ideal correlation is zero, so the closer to 0, the better. This means that the portfolio will move regardless of what happens in the market.

Name	Ticker	BND	VOO	TQQQ	VNQ	GLD	SLV	USO	UUP	ETHE
Bonds	BND	1,00	0,17	0,18	0,21	0,29	0,15	0,04	-0,11	0,05
S&P500	VOO	0,17	1,00	0,92	0,85	0,12	0,26	0,39	0,07	0,24
NASDAQ	TQQQ	0,18	0,92	1,00	0,69	0,16	0,28	0,33	0,06	0,24
Real State	VNQ	0,21	0,85	0,69	1,00	0,14	0,27	0,31	0,03	0,23
Gold	GLD	0,29	0,12	0,16	0,14	1,00	0,78	-0,02	-0,42	0,16
Silver	SLV	0,15	0,26	0,28	0,27	0,78	1,00	0,16	-0,31	0,21
Oil	USO	0,04	0,39	0,33	0,31	-0,02	0,16	1,00	0,10	0,12
Dollar	UUP	-0,11	0,07	0,06	0,03	-0,42	-0,31	0,10	1,00	-0,01
Ethereum	ETHE	0,05	0,24	0,24	0,23	0,16	0,21	0,12	-0,01	1,00

06/26/2019 - 09/09/2021 based on daily returns

Source: Portfoliovisualizer.com

Historically, the different markets have not all risen or fallen at the same time; in fact, there have been times when a particular market has performed poorly and another uncorrelated market has improved. This is the basic idea behind diversification.

Diversification in no case guarantees that we will avoid losses, but it can ensure that these, at the portfolio level, are reduced considerably.

09/09/2010 - 09/09/2021 based on daily returns

Name	Ticker	BND	VOO	TQQQ	VNQ	GLD	SLV	USO	UUP
Bonds	BND	1,00	-0,07	-0,05	0,11	0,28	0,14	-0,06	-0,10
S&P500	VOO	-0,07	1,00	0,92	0,76	0,02	0,19	0,39	-0,11
NASDAQ	TQQQ	-0,05	0,92	1,00	0,62	0,03	0,18	0,32	-0,08
Real State	VNQ	0,11	0,76	0,62	1,00	0,09	0,20	0,26	-0,14
Gold	GLD	0,28	0,02	0,03	0,09	1,00	0,79	0,10	-0,40
Silver	SLV	0,14	0,19	0,18	0,20	0,79	1,00	0,24	-0,36
Oil	USO	-0,06	0,39	0,32	0,26	0,10	0,24	1,00	-0,12
Dollar	UUP	-0,10	-0,11	-0,08	-0,14	-0,40	-0,36	-0,12	1,00

Source: Portfoliovisualizer.com

In addition to diversification between markets (fixed income, variable income, commodities etc.), we can also diversify between assets within those markets. An example would be, within the stock market, investing in different sectors so that if a negative cycle appears in one of them, there is another to offset it.

Diversification can be taken to deeper levels by implementing different strategies and types of trades depending on timing. As I say, we can complicate it as much as we want.

Lastly, we would also be diversifying if we were to allocate our entire capital to different activities, not just investing. That is, if we had a portfolio that included financial investments, and real estate, as well as other businesses.

Rebalancing

Rebalancing is an attempt to return the portfolio back to its original asset allocation. Over time, some investments will grow more than others, which can cause the weight of each one as part of the portfolio to vary and deviate from set targets. By rebalancing the portfolio we can ensure it is maintained within the initially established risk level.

Retuning the portfolio to its original balance can be done in several ways:

- Selling the assets that hold too much weight and using that cash to buy the ones that hold less weight.

- Modifying the contributions and prioritizing the purchase of assets that hold less weight.

This will all depend on how much the portfolio allocations have deviated. If an asset has appreciated significantly, using the second method to balance the portfolio may take considerable time and it may be more convenient to sell part. You should bear in mind that this option will entail expenses that could be avoided if you simply modify the contributions and use most or all of them to buy the assets that hold less weight.

When to rebalance is at the discretion of the investor. I believe it makes most sense to do so when there is a considerable imbalance in the portfolio that could lead us to incur greater risks.

Withdrawing money from an asset class when it is doing well in favor of an asset category that is doing poorly forces us to buy low and sell high, one of the key premises for investors.

PART 6. EMOTIONAL MANAGEMENT

For some, this is the most important piece of the puzzle. They say that a great trading or investment methodology is useless if you don't master your own emotions and learn about market psychology; that if you don't understand how your mindset can affect your decision making you will never be in a position to beat the market.

I have always been a bit reluctant to attach so much importance to the psychological aspect of the market. Perhaps because of (or thanks to) my having a more rational and objective mind.

The reason why most traders fail is mainly due to two factors:

- They are trading with a bad system that does not give them an advantage.

- They don't have the discipline to follow their own rules.

The point here is that, if you have managed to develop a good strategy, you should "simply" execute it, nothing more. That's what all the preparatory work is for, to make a solid enough trading plan that takes into account all possible situations, so that you simply have to execute what you have already planned. This is why applying automated strategies is the best way to play the markets; because it eliminates the human factor, which, as we know, is the weakest element in a trading system.

This section of the book is largely influenced by the work of Mark Douglas in his book "Trading in the Zone." I sincerely believe that it is the only book you need to study in order to develop the necessary mentality and discipline not to hinder yourself and execute your trading plan effectively.

THE CORE OF YOUR BELIEFS

Think in Probabilities

The most important thing is to understand that trading is a game of probabilities; and therefore, you need to accept the risk and the uncertain result of each trade. This is the only way to eliminate fear and think only in terms of probabilities.

Taking into account that there is no system or methodology that guarantees every trade will be a winner, you should accept that some of your trades will be losers and that this cannot be avoided; this is why risk management plays a vital role.

You must differentiate the uncertain result of each trade individually, with the certain and predictable result of a series of trades to which an edge is applied in the long term. This is what we know as the law of large numbers, which tells us that by repeating a random experiment a number of times, the relative frequency of each elementary event tends to approach a fixed number, called the probability of an event.

Thinking in probabilities is about creating a mindset that incorporates the five fundamental truths that Mark Douglas explains in his book. When thinking about probabilities you assume that:

- Anything can happen in the market at any time.

- You don't need to know what is going to happen next in order to make money.

- There is a random distribution between wins and losses for any given set of variables that define an edge.

- An edge is nothing more than an indication of a higher probability of one thing happening over another.

- Every moment in the market is unique.

By thinking in terms of probabilities, you accept that you don't know what will happen; freeing your mind of any type of emotion, allowing you to remain focused on seeking the edge that puts the odds in your favor and making you less susceptible to making mistakes. Focus on what you can control and ignore what you can't.

Accepting Risk

The road to success is built on risks. People who opt for a safety first approach won't achieve major success.

Accepting risk in the world of investing means that you accept that each trade has an uncertain outcome, that you are accepting the risk that this entails, and that you will bear the possible consequences without emotional distress.

You must accept losses as an inevitable part of trading. Otherwise, any losing trade will damage you psychologically and make you perceive the market as threatening. That sense of threat generates fear, and fear will cause you to make mistakes. By being in the right frame of mind, you won't perceive any information as painful or threatening and you will be in a position to identify an endless number of opportunities. If the information you glean from the market causes you fear, ask yourself if it really is threatening information, or if you are feeling that way due to some bad experience in the past.

Accept losses as a business cost. Every trader suffers them. Incurring a loss does not make you a loser. If you have a methodology that is profitable in the long term, there is no issue with assuming certain losses from time to time, because you will know that it is simply part of the journey toward an overall profit.

You cannot win if you are not willing to lose. You must always be fully prepared to lose the money you risk and not trade unless you are completely confident that you have some sort of edge.

The idea is to not perceive the market as a threat and to be at peace with any result, so that you are not emotionally affected by it. By accepting the possibility of making a mistake or losing money, you won't perceive the market as threatening and you will have a freer and more positive mental state. You will mitigate your fear, doubt and stress, and be able to take advantage of your skills and show your potential as a trader. In other words, you will be able to focus on what you can control, which is the most objective interpretation possible of what is happening in the market.

You must be able to see the market from an objective point of view, because the market provides neutral information. It is your mental structure that determines how you perceive that information.

Taking Responsibility

One of the most important factors in becoming a successful trader is that you take full responsibility for your results. You need to understand that your level of success in trading and the results you obtain are under your control; they are created by you, the result of how you trade the market.

It's easy to find some other cause for our poor performance; diverting attention from ourselves and looking for some external factor to blame. By not taking responsibility for your actions, you impede yourself from reflecting on your actions and on what you could do differently next time. This hinders your development and learning.

Mistakes provide you with a learning experience that guides you on the path to progress. Each error is a puzzle that can provide you with a huge reward if you can solve it. Every mistake is a reflection of something you were doing wrong; so if you can figure out what it was, you can learn from it and improve the way you trade.

While most believe mistakes are bad, keep in mind that most forms of learning come from making mistakes, analyzing them objectively, identifying the mistake, and preventing it in the future. This gives you the belief that you can improve as a trader.

Rules on mistakes:

- Realize that mistakes are a good thing if you end up learning from them.

- Create a culture in which it is okay to make mistakes but it is unacceptable not to identify, analyze, and learn from them.

- Realize that you will make mistakes and have weaknesses. The important thing is how you deal with them. Treat them as learning opportunities that can quickly improve your performance, if you handle them well.

- If you don't mind making mistakes to get things right, you will learn a great deal.

To take advantage of mistakes and learn from them, you must first accept your responsibility.

NEGATIVE EMOTIONS

Fear

This is the emotion which most influences a trader. The fear of risk comes from our upbringing. From a very early age we are programmed to avoid it. The education we receive installs fear in our hearts and holds us back from being successful. The fear of risk paralyzes us and returns us to a structure that we perceive as safe. The way to get rid of fear is to recognize our ability to overcome obstacles: by boosting our self-confidence.

Fear is so strong that it can paralyze a trader. It can be experienced in different ways: fear of rejection, fear of losing money, fear of being wrong, fear of ignorance, fear of missing out on the movement or fear of losing the money already earned.

Fear can manifest itself in various ways:

- Fear of losing money: This can cause a trader to use a tight Stop Loss or close a trade before it has a chance to take place.

- Fear of being wrong: This can lead to the trader not taking on the next trade.

- Fear of missing out on a movement: This can cause a trader who has been out of the market to enter for fear of missing a possible movement in a very bad position when the market is about to turn.

- Fear of letting a profit turn into a loss: In this case, the trader leaves money on the table by taking his profit too early.

The first step in overcoming any of these fears is being aware of them and knowing when they have appeared. When you recognize them, make every effort to continue executing your trading plan.

If you fear that your system will not work, go back to the demo and build the confidence you need to trade with it there. Don't let fear guide your decisions. Follow your plan and never deviate.

One way to keep yourself from getting emotionally involved in a trade is to place the orders and then stay away from the computer.

Trade only with money that you can afford to lose. This way, if that happens it won't entail an economic catastrophe. This is the only way to trade with a calm state of mind, free of negative emotions.

Greed

This is the excessive desire to earn as much money as possible in the shortest possible time. The greediest traders will trade too much or stay too long in the trade; both with negative results. There is no need to be greedy in a trade because another opportunity will always present itself. Don't try to make every trade the big one that will make you rich.

When traders are greedy, they may not even be aware of it. Sometimes greed manifests itself in the form of looking at the profit of an open trade and thinking about how much you have made and how much more you could earn if you keep it open. The truth is that the profits of open positions are not guaranteed until they are closed.

Traders sometimes get confused when looking at those open positions because they see it as money in the bank; and this is why they do things like move the Take Profit level further away as the trade approaches it, because they think the price will continue to move, or they hold positions too long, or set unrealistic targets. All of these things are the result of greed, and they all lead to earning less money in the long run.

It can be difficult to get out of a position when it looks good and is going your way, but most of the time, that's precisely when you should get out.

To overcome this greed, you need to understand that unrealized gains are only potential profits that exist on paper. A trade can only be a winner if the position is closed and the profit is consolidated. Again, be guided by your trading plan, it should tell you where exactly to take the profits on each trade.

Revenge

Trying to get revenge on the market after a loss can lead you to trade based on your emotions and take on more risk than initially planned; generally leading to bigger losses.

You should treat each new trade as independent of the others and realize that trading is not event lasting a day, week or month. What's important is that you draw long-term conclusions.

Hope

This is a (normally unrealistic) sense of expectation and desire for a specific thing to happen. You must trade based on the market, not based on your opinions about it. Hope is a sign that you have not accepted that you hold a bad position, or that you have an unrealistic expectation that something will happen, or a strong desire for it to happen.

Hope can cause traders to move their Stop Loss further away, eliminate it, or even trade without it because they expect the market will turn in their favor and they won't suffer a losing trade. This is how trading accounts go quickly bankrupt.

The hope that a trade will be a winner can be very damaging. When a trader expects a trade to be a winner and this doesn't happen, it can have a negative emotional impact, leading to all kinds of mistakes.

If you want to be successful in your career as a trader, you should know that in the market, hope is for the desperate. Nobody cares what your expectations are. You must trade based on what you see and not what you hope for: develop a strategy and follow it to the letter.

Overconfidence

Being confident in your strategy and your ability to execute it is good,. However, overconfidence can be very damaging. Overconfidence is that feeling of invincibility you get when you are on a winning streak.

Overconfidence makes you feel like you can't go wrong. Because trading is a game of odds, traders will experience winning streaks, but these moments are temporary.

A positive streak increases your confidence and, almost without realizing it, you can become careless and your perception of risk noticeably reduces. An overconfident trader will trade excessively or take too much risk per trade; the results of which are disastrous.

You have to stay disciplined. This is the key to successful trading, constant discipline. Follow your method and the pre-established amount you are prepared to risk. Don't increase it arbitrarily. Many make the mistake of significantly increasing their risk per trade after one or two winning trades, and are still emotionally unprepared to handle that level of risk.

TRAITS THAT WILL IMPROVE YOUR TRADING

Confidence

Confidence is built on the fact that you have a system with a positive edge that has been proven and is profitable in the long run.

Successful traders build good confidence by using their trading plan and method over and over again, over a long period of time, even when they are experiencing tough times in the market. This means sticking with your method and not trading excessively, or risking too much, regardless of your emotions and feelings after a trade.

A sure sign of a lack of confidence is to seek the advice of others. If you don't trust your trading method, go back to the simulation stage and build up your confidence there.

Believe in yourself and your abilities. To be successful, we must overcome obstacles. Most people avoid them because they believe their chances of success are poor.

Lack of belief in yourself indicates a poor level of self-confidence and poor self-esteem. A confident attitude guides you to a positive interpretation of reality.

Self-confidence can be improved through various techniques known as "internal communication":

- This involves the words that go through our minds.

- To improve self-esteem and self-confidence we need to examine our vocabulary and eliminate words that do not contribute positively (maybe, I'll try, I can't...).

- Express positive affirmations about yourself (I am successful, I am sure of myself...).

- The more we use constructive affirmations, the better our perception of ourselves.

Experience

Ultimately, traders will develop good judgment and intuition from their experience. Therefore, do not give up. Your trading will improve with time and persistence.

With hours of screen time you will be able to develop and improve your skills, knowledge, attitudes and behaviors.

Experience will lead you to carry out the process of opening and closing positions mechanically, involuntarily and unconsciously; completely neutralizing emotions and preventing them from interfering with decision-making.

Discipline

Discipline determines the commitment of the trader to follow their trading rules, manage emotions and follow the rules of money management. The market will pay you well for your discipline.

Don't deviate from your methodology. Trade your method over and over again to exploit its edge. Repetition will build your skills.

Don't let a series of winning or losing trades make you deviate from your plan.

The moment you lose discipline, you stop being a trader and become a gambler, and those who gamble their money don't last long in the financial markets.

Independence

You need to be independent. As long as you follow your own style, you will get the best and worst out of your own approach. When you try to incorporate someone else's style, you will end up with the worst of each style.

Successful traders follow a methodology that fits their personality. They have developed a trading style that is consistent with their personality and beliefs. A solid methodology that is very successful for one may be a poor fit and turn out badly for another.

You should avoid trading based on the opinions of others. It doesn't matter how skilled or smart the trader appears to be, because you won't get anything positive out of trading like this.

You should only use your own trading plan as a guide and you should take full responsibility for your trades. Only in this way will you generate the necessary confidence to continue making progress in your development as a trader.

Open Mind

You must be flexible when it comes to changing your mind on a trade when necessary.

Loyalty to an opinion or position can have disastrous results. When the market moves against your expectations, you must be aware that you have made a mistake and the only instinct you must follow is to abandon the position.

Good traders close out their positions when they think they are wrong; great traders reverse their positions when they think they are wrong.

Making your scenario forecasts public can have positive effects; but it can also tie you down to that prediction, and if the market contradicts your expectations, you will be more reluctant to change your point of view. Be very careful with what you share on social networks.

Passion

Regardless of your goals and motivation, if you don't love the world of trading and investing, you will fail. Passion is a fundamental factor since it is partly the reason why certain traders become successful.

Success requires a structured lifestyle and many sacrifices; so if you are not willing to make trading your top priority, it is best to admit that as soon as possible, to avoid being financially and psychologically damaged.

The paradox is that most people who are drawn to trading believe that it is an easy way to make a lot of money; when the reality is that the most successful traders are extremely hardworking.

For successful traders, trading is not a matter of work or of getting rich; it's something they love to do. They do not trade to achieve some other objective. This effort is aimed at finding the thrill of the challenge. A love of trading may not guarantee success, but its absence will most likely lead to failure.

Patience

You need to understand that the way to be successful in the markets in the long term is through slow and consistent profits. You don't have to trade every day to obtain solid returns every month. You must trade like a sniper; wait patiently for the market to give the signal your system is looking for and pull the trigger without emotion.

Patience is a habitual element of trading over longer time frames (H4, daily, weekly); forcing you to have to wait for the candlesticks to develop before executing the trade. If you lose a trade, don't chase after it. Wait for another to appear. Nor should you try to anticipate a trade. Wait for the signal to fully develop before entering.

The lesson is that if the conditions are not right, it is better to do nothing. Bear in mind that the execution of dubious trades is the product of impatience. Being patient is harder than it sounds. It requires resisting the natural human tendency to trade with more frequency. Patience pays off.

MAIN COGNITIVE BIASES

During our decision-making process, there are a series of psychological factors at play that can influence us significantly, known as cognitive biases. Cognitive biases are effects that cause us to distort reality, an illogical interpretation of real information.

This is part of the scope of behavioral finance theory which studies human behavior using elements of psychology, neurology or neurophysiology, and draws the conclusion that people do not always act rationally, they do not always correctly analyze the information available to them and they sometimes aren't even aware of their own preferences.

Below is a description of the most important biases that we must take into account as investors, in order to objectify our analyses and make better decisions.

Overconfidence

Overconfidence bias is a tendency to overestimate our knowledge, to maintain a false and misleading assessment of our abilities, intellect, or talent. It is the belief that we are better than we really are.

Because of this, overconfidence bias can make us take greater risks, because we are not cautious enough in our decision making.

Confirmation bias and anchoring

Confirmation bias occurs when it is difficult for us to consider or accept the evidence that we are wrong in our approaches or decision making;

which leads us to look to other sources for information that corroborate our reasoning.

By not wanting to admit our error, we selectively search for information that is in line with what we think, ignoring any information that contradicts our beliefs. This reinforces our opinion and allows us to continue believing in our initial idea.

Meanwhile, related to confirmation bias, anchoring is based on the idea of giving greater importance to information that was obtained in the first instance instead of any information that appeared later on which contradicts the first.

Authority Bias and Social Proof

These have to do with the influence that other people have on our decision making.

Authority bias has to do with not maintaining the principle of independence and assigning greater importance to the opinions of other people simply because they are (or seem to be) opinion leaders on the subject in question.

Hand in hand with authority bias, social proof involves imitating the behavior of other people who are doing the same thing, believing that if they are doing something a certain way it is because they know something we don't. Classic herd behavior.

Sunk Cost Fallacy, Status Quo And Loss Aversion

The sunk cost fallacy tells us that we are likely to move forward with a decision in which we have already invested a significant amount of time, effort and money.

Within the investment world, it refers to sticking with a losing idea or position with only a minimal expectation that it will improve in the future. It goes hand in hand with loss aversion, which refers to maintaining a bad investment to avoid accepting a loss; and also with the Status Quo bias, which implies that any change from the baseline is perceived as a loss.

Gambler's Fallacy.

This bias that leads us to believe that past events affect future ones. The belief that if an event has not occurred for a certain time, it is more and more likely to happen; or that something that has just happened is less likely to happen again.

Applied to the world of investment, it is the belief that the result of one trade will affect the result of the next one, that if I experience two or three losing trades, the next one will most likely be a winner. Martingale-type management methods are based on this idea.

The truth is that each trade is independent and the result of your last trade really has no bearing whatsoever. Don't increase your risk after a losing streak of trades because there is no guarantee that that next trade will be a winner.

Keeping these biases at bay and relying on a statistical mindset will ensure we don't deviate from correctly applying our plan.

PART 7. BUSINESS MANAGEMENT

Make no mistake, trading is like any other business. It requires resources, planning and review. In this section we are going consider the key aspects that need to be kept in mind when implementing a business model in the market, and the supporting elements that are essential to obtain the feedback we need to improve our results.

TRADING PLAN

The trading plan is a document which sets out two basic aspects of our approach: the system or methodology that generates the buy and sell signals; and the risk management that establishes all rules for capital management rules.

The trading plan must be clearly defined, the more detail the better. As if it were automated by a robot, if possible. No possibility should be left unexplored, no scenario unexplained. It should be a document that tells what to do and how to do it, at all times.

It should be completely objective, so that we don't have to think and improvise in any way. This will ensure that we avoid making decisions based on our emotions.

A trading plan should include and elaborate on at least the following sections:

1. Contingency Management

This first section of the trading plan should include all the instructions for contingency management, a fundamental aspect of the system.

Many traders don't take into account this contingency management section. However, at the right time, when we're in need of an emergency solution, it could literally save us from bankruptcy.

The first thing that should appear in our plan is the telephone number of the salesperson assigned to us, to contact in case of need. If you were not assigned one, call the broker and get one assigned. In the event of any issue when trading in the real world, such as a failure to execute an order, they will be our lifeline.

You should also have a plan B prepared for practically any tool you use, be it hardware or software. You should be able to answer the following questions:

- What happens if the power goes out in the middle of a trade? Do I have an electric generator with sufficient autonomy? Can I resolve this issue using a laptop? Is the battery charged?

- What if the monitor or some other peripheral device breaks? How am I going to solve this? Do I have spare parts? Do I have another computer fully prepared to connect quickly?

- What happens if the internet connection fails? Do I have a second totally independent connection?

- What if the platform doesn't load? Do I have a backup with which to restore it?

These are just some of the questions that you should be able to answer. But there are many other issues that could arise. The questions you need to ask will depend on the circumstances in each case. You need to think carefully about each one to ensure you have a planned solution and to minimize risk should they arise.

2. Defining the Strategy

This involves defining the trading philosophy that we will implement. First, we need a brief and concise description of our strategy, the principles on which it is based, time frames that we are going to use and our objectives, as well as the time frame that our work session will cover.

In this section we should include the set of rules and parameters that would answer the following questions:

- What do we want to do, buy or sell?

- What area will we be waiting for the price to reach in order to find our entry trigger?

- How will the price have to move before it reaches my trading zone?

- What does the price have to do to give me the definitive signal to enter the market?

It is about defining the strategy that gives us the most confidence. The trader should define their own strategy based on their personality. During the course of this book we have presented three trading methods based on technical analysis: Price Action, Volume Spread Analysis and the Wyckoff Method. You may decide to specialize in one of them, or all of them. There are many possibilities.

If you intend to trade using any of these three methodologies, you must at least include:

- Context analysis to determine the direction in which you will move.

- Definition of the market structure.

- Identification of trading zones and levels depending on strategy.

- Scenario forecast based on the current price location

- Types of trades that you are going to look for.

- Definition of our market entry trigger.

- Location of the Stop Loss and Take Profit.

Decide if you prefer to trade in the context of the range or trend; if you prefer to implement a strategy that goes with or against the trend. Whether or not you will incorporate volume analysis and what particular stocks you will look for on the chart.

There are several resources you can use here but you have to be the one to shape your trading plan. During your training process you will learn many things, many different concepts and tools. Over time you must decide what to add to your toolbox and what to discard. It is a process that has no shortcut, since there are multiple options. You should analyze and experiment with each one of them until you determine the option that best suits you.

At first, focus on developing a single trading plan with a single strategy. Over time and as you gain experience, you will be able to trade with more than one system.

3. Choosing Your Markets

What markets will you trade in: Cash equities, futures, options, CFDs, cryptocurrencies, commodities, currencies, etc.?

In the first instance, this will be subject to the hours the trader is available, as well as the funds they can dedicate to their trading. If you currently have a job that takes up part of the day, you should look at which markets are most active during the time period you have available for trading. If, for example, you are in Europe and you have free afternoons, the best markets to trade (understanding these as the ones that offer the most liquidity) can be found in the American market. If, on the other hand, the time slot available to you is in the morning, for traders who operate with volume, the German DAX index is one of the best options.

You may also work full-time and only have a little time at the end of the day. In that case you may decide to be a longer term trader. This offers you a broader set of options since it allows you to cover all markets, though with an increased time frame. You can dedicate less if you are long-term trading, but in exchange you will need to work more on your patience. Cash stocks or ETFs are usually good options.

Another aspect that you should take into account is the nature of the strategy and if it can be applied correctly to that market. For example, if you want to trade under the principles of the Wyckoff Method, you should avoid the forex market since it is a non-centralized market and therefore the volume data is not totally reliable. By default you should look to the stock or futures market. Continuing with this example, if you decide to be a Wyckoff trader, you should look for liquid markets, to avoid possible manipulations. You should avoid illiquid assets such as very small-cap stocks or certain cryptocurrencies, among other things.

4. Determine the Risk Parameters

In the risk management section we have already looked at all the possible risk control implementation options. To put it simply, you must define your rules. Rules that you will feel comfortable with and will consistently execute over and over again without hesitation.

What percentage will you risk per trade; 1%, 2% 3%? Will you establish a trading limit? You won't be tempted to apply a martingale-type approach, right? For each trade you must define exactly where you will place the entry, Stop Loss and Take Profit orders. Will you manage them actively? Will you take partial profits? Where will you take profits? Will you place a Trailing Stop? Up to what point? How? Breakeven: yes or no? Will you be averaging or pyramiding? Or neither?

Absolutely EVERYTHING must be included in the plan. You shouldn't leave anything out. All possible scenarios should be considered. Obviously the trading plan is a living document that you will update over time as you gain experience and live through certain situations, so don't worry if the first drafts are not very complete, this is perfectly normal.

5. Planning Routine

Before our work session begins, we should have our plan prepared: up-to-date charts, identified trading levels and zones, possible scenarios and alarms set.

As well as the trading side of things, we should have checked the news and any fundamental events that might affect us, and we must also ensure that we have to hand all the tools we will need to execute our trades, such as position size calculators.

This is also the time to review any trades we might have open. Analyze the progress of these trades and consider any necessary management of positions that you need to carry out.

If we are going to trade various assets at the same time, we should prioritize them depending on location. The key is to be most aware of those that are likely to emit the entry signal sooner. In the last part of the book we will develop this concept further by discussing the creation of a watchlist for monitoring and classifying assets by lists and tags.

If we have all this under control, we are ready to open the charts and take on the market. Once in it, we will focus on looking for trades for our high priority assets and we will continue to monitor the rest through the use of alerts.

TRADING JOURNAL

We cannot improve what we cannot measure. For this reason it is important to keep a trading journal.

The trading journal is part of the post-market routine which acts as a record that we can use to later review, analyze, draw conclusions and, where possible, implement improvements to our trading approach.

If we don't record absolutely everything we obviously won't be able to improve. Our memory is not just flawed, it's absolutely terrible for remembering certain things. In other words, either we write everything down, or we will lose key information.

By recording everything, we will be able to identify common elements of losing and winning trades. In the first instance, even though we are not aware of the existence of these common characteristics, they may exist. And the only way to identify them is by writing down absolutely all the information we can about the trade. By knowing all these factors, we can limit ourselves to executing only those trades with the highest probability of success.

Pre-Evaluation

In this first part of the trading journal, we will write down the reasons for the trade, the original reasoning that led us to forecast this scenario, without the influence of hindsight and the result of the trade.

This is a detailed summary of the elements that we include in the definition of the trading plan strategy: context, structure, trading zone, type of trade, trigger and location of orders (where and why).

Once in the position, we will note (in real time if possible) any modification that it has undergone during its development: active management of the position, Stop Loss, Breakeven, partial profit taking, etc.

Basic Data Which Must Be Recorded

This includes all the objective data of the trade as well as other data such as the cost of the transactions: Fees, Spread, Swaps etc. It is a necessary part of the business accounting.

At the very least the following data must be recorded:

- Order number.

- Date and time.

- Asset.

- Direction (long/short).

- Type of strategy or type of entry.

- Entry trigger.

- % of risk assumed.

- Risk/Reward Ratio.

- Size.

- Result (Stop Loss, Take Profit, TP1 + BE, TP1 + TP2 etc.).

- Gross result, fees and net result.

- Final balance of the account after the trade.

Although we will mainly focus on recording the objective data of the trade, if we have the capacity to do so, it would be very useful if we could dedicate a section to noting down the emotional state that we have experienced before, during and after the trade. Feelings, intuitions, hunches... you may find a repeating pattern among all that information.

Post-Evaluation

This involves a more in-depth evaluation of trade results. Keeping the trading journal up to date and recording all the data is the first step; but this is only part of the work. If we really want this to be useful we must analyze it afterwards.

When analyzing losing trades the focus should be on identifying if we really did make a mistake, if we were careless in the execution of the system, in the risk parameterization; or if, on the contrary, our actions were correct and the losing operation was simply a product of chance and the randomness of the market.

With regard to winning trades, we are also interested in seeing if we followed the plan strictly and executed it well. Be aware that just because the result of the trade was positive doesn't mean that the trade was well executed. If the trade was a winner but we didn't strictly follow our trading plan, it is actually a bad trade. In fact, it is terrible once. The market has rewarded us for poor performance. In the same way, we may execute a trade well with a negative result: this is what happens when we have done everything we should but the trade is a loser.

Finally, we need to include a column where we can write down what we have learned after evaluating the trade. This is so we can implement any measures according to whether we have made mistakes or not. This aspect is very important, it is about writing down what we should have done; what we then do in the future when a similar situation arises.

PERIODIC REVIEW

As we know, markets are a living entity and are constantly changing. That is why we need to periodically evaluate the results we are obtaining to make sure that the rules that we have established in our trading plan are still appropriate.

Obviously, when reviewing and making necessary changes, you should stay away from the screens. Your mind should be totally clear and focused solely on carrying out a comprehensive and objective review of information.

The documents that we are going to analyze are the trading journal and the trading plan, in that order. With regard to the former, we need to carry out an in-depth review of the performance of our trades as well as our strengths and weaknesses, to try to draw objective conclusions and identify common patterns of behavior between trades. Subsequently we will try to implement any changes that are necessary in the trading plan.

As I have already mentioned, the trading plan will undergo several modifications throughout your career, as you acquire knowledge and refine your trading approach.

The periodicity of the review will depend on the number of trades you execute. Although it is true that mathematicians do not recommend drawing conclusions with less than 30 examples, this number seems too low to me to obtain a statistically significant representation of the results. But you can take it as a minimum number. Obviously the more trades the better.

Based on that minimum number of trades, determine the frequency with which you will carry out further reviews (weekly, monthly, etc.), although you could also do it every time you add 30, 40 or 50 new trades.

Measuring Performance

There are different ratios that can be used to measure the performance of our trades. However, without a doubt the best measure of performance is the profitability chart itself. This chart shows the equity in the account and it can be very useful in alerting us to any significant deterioration in strategy performance.

I have already mentioned that one way to perform a periodic review is after a certain time or number of trades. Well, the profitability chart is another indicator of when might be a good time to reassess the strategy.

A sudden drop could be due to a change in market conditions or a poor implementation of our trading plan. Either way, any unusual behavior is more than enough reason to stop and re-evaluate the situation. You could set your own limits, for example, if curve falls a considerable percentage such as 15 or 20%. In addition you should previously establish the point at which you will execute a definitive stop of the system, which could be when if you reach a Drawdown of 30%, for example.

In addition to analyzing the profitability curve, there are a series of ratios we can use for the same purpose:

Net profit

This is the definitive result of the strategy, after deducting all expenses and fees.

- The formula to obtain the net profit is = net profits - net losses

Although it is a valuable metric, there are others that should be considered alongside it to effectively determine if the strategy is performing well. For example, you may have ended up with a net profit but have incurred huge drawdowns during the process and/or with a low recovery factor, which would indicate a very poor, albeit positive, performance.

Number of trades

This is the first factor you should look at. If the number of trades is not high enough, there is no point in continuing with your analysis of ratios since the reliability of the system will probably not be statistically significant.

Too low a number of trades (50 or less) might indicate a statistical accident which is something we should avoid. Evaluating the performance based on 30 trades is not the same as doing so based on 300. Obviously, the more trades we have executed, the more significant the interpretation of the results.

Percentage of wins and losses

This measures the ratio between the number of winning or losing trades and the total. It is a measure of the system's reliability.

- The formula for obtaining the win percentage is: total number of trades/winning trades.

- The formula for obtaining the loss percentage is: total number of trades/losing trades.

The most interesting thing this tells us is how many times we will win and lose; and it prepares us to expect the performance to sit within those ranges in the future. Therefore, any deviation from these results could be sufficient grounds to re-evaluate the system.

Average profit and loss

This give us an indication about the nature of our trades.

- The formula to obtain the average profit is: total profits/number of winning trades.

- The formula to obtain the average loss is: total losses/number of losing trades.

When analyzing the results of individual trades, we would hope to see that the largest loss is smaller than the smallest profit earned from the winning trades as an indicator of a healthy system.

Winning and losing streaks

This involves analyzing the number of winning and losing trades in a row.

If you know the possible number of consecutive losses you could incur, if they fall within this range you won't then be tempted to abandon the strategy after a few losses. Although, as they say, the biggest losing streak is always yet to come.

An important piece of information about streaks is knowing when they occurred. Knowing this, we could analyze the market to see what conditions might have led to the streak at the time, such as the level of volatility at that moment or some other indicator of market sentiment.

We can do this with both winning and losing streaks. Being aware of when we are going through a winning streak is important, to ensure that we don't relax and that we continue to implement the right risk management.

Drawdown

As we know, this is the difference between the peak and trough values on the capital curve. What we are going to define here is the monetary value of the loss incurred by the system during that fall until its recovery.

- The formula to obtain the Drawdown is: (Maximum capital at the peak - minimum capital in the trough) / maximum capital at the peak.

When it comes to analyzing the Drawdown in backtests, during the development of automatic strategies, this information is important as it indicates the minimum amount of capital we will need to trade using that strategy. We would need to be able to cover three times the value of the worst Drawdown added to any guarantees required by the broker.

Profit Factor

This is the amount of profit per unit of risk; that is, how much profit we get for every euro we lose.

- The formula to obtain the Profit Factor is: sum of all wins / sum of all losses.

For the system to be profitable, the ratio must be greater than 1, which would be the same as saying that the overall profit is greater than the overall loss. Anything over this is a bonus. To give you an idea: a Profit Factor higher than 1.5 can be considered very positive; and anything above 2 would be exceptional. A PF of 1.5 indicates that we have earned €1.5 for every euro that we have lost.

As with the other ratios, the Profit Factor is a good measure of performance, but it is insufficient to assess the merits of the system. The issue with this indicator is that it doesn't distinguish between the results of the trades. A single trade could earn a big profit and a huge PF, and all the remaining trades could be losers and you could still have a positive PF due to that distortion.

Therefore, we would want to see that this profitability isn't just the result of a few trades; rather, that all winning trades generate a stable profit.

Recovery factor

The recovery factor measures how quickly the system can recover from a drawdown.

- The formula to obtain the Recovery Factor is: net profit / maximum Drawdown.

A good system will have a recovery factor of over 5; that is, it will generate 5 times more net profit than Drawdown.

How you analyze all the above is irrelevant. Some might prefer to write it down in a notebook by hand, others in digital format with a simple text editor or a spreadsheet such as Excel. You can even use more advanced tools that have been developed to facilitate this particular task.

Regardless of which medium you decide to use, the important thing here is to do it. Write down and keep a record of all your trades and also attach photographs of everything. This will subsequently allow you to carry out a better quality review.

You can also use specific online software to follow your trading plan, trading journal and perform an in-depth review of the data. Some of the most used by the trading community are Chartlog, Edgewonk, TraderSync or Tradervue.

PART 8. FROM THEORY TO PRACTICE

This last part of the book describes the recommended tools and resources that will allow you to put into practice everything you have learned and to take your first steps in the world of trading and investment with the utmost confidence.

TRADING DESKTOP

Many traders believe they need a special computer to be able to trade or invest. There are indeed specialized companies that offer computers created for this specific function, claiming that it offers a certain edge when trading. Nothing could be further from the truth. In my experience, any commercial computer will be generally enough to run the necessary programs.

Obviously everything will depend on the tools you use. If you decide to be day trader and trade the intraday futures market in real time with advanced volume analysis software such as Volume Profile, FootPrint charts for order flow analysis and even liquidity maps, you will need a significant amount of resources. This means your computer must be equipped with the best hardware to offer you optimal performance.

In general, a decent gaming computer will be more than enough to execute this high-demand form of trading. These types of computers have good processors and high RAM capacity, which is just what you need for more intense trading. At least 8GB of RAM and a 2.5GHz processor.

If, on the other hand, you are going to be medium and long-term investment-type traders for which you will only need a simple platform for chart analysis, a low-end computer, which you can find anywhere, will be perfectly adequate. As you can see, everything will depend on your way of trading and the specific software you are going to work with.

With regard to monitors, 24 inches is more than enough to manage everything perfectly, although my recommendation here is to have two monitors. Two 24-inch monitors is the minimum set up you need to work with the fullest assurances. You can scale up or down depending on the distance at which you place them. Another option, rather than buying two monitors, is to buy an extra wide one.

The reason for more than one monitor is that you will need have several screens open while you are trading. For example, day traders configure their platforms to show several screens, each one offering different information. But you don't have to be a day trader to need these two screens. If you use a platform to analyze charts that is different from the broker's platform, you will need to have both resources available and easily accessible: one monitor to view the charts and the other to send orders to the broker. You may also want to always have open a news calendar, a position calculator, some extra tool, your trading journal to fill in the information on each trade, etc. You will be using a lot of resources and having two screens can be very useful.

Another thing to take into account is the operating system. As a general rule, most platforms have been designed for Windows so if you use macOS for example, the operating system for Apple computers, you will need to use some type of software that emulates the Windows environment such as Parallels, although the option I recommend in this case is to create a partition inside the hard disk using BootCamp and carry out a complete and stable installation of Windows. Remember to bear this in mind if you are buying a computer with an operating system other than Windows.

Another way to access Windows from your Mac is through a virtual private server (VPS). A VPS is a virtual partition of a physical server that enables you to have the operating system and its associated programs installed on the cloud. In other words, it is like having a totally independent computer which you can access remotely from any device. The hosting platforms that offer this service allow for different configurations depending on the processor, ram memory, hard disk, etc.

This is a very good option. Especially if your computer is for personal use. This is another drawback for day traders. Because they use programs and tools which require a huge amount of resources, they need a specific computer just for trading to avoid issues cause by other software or potential vulnerabilities and security threats.

To access a VPS you simply need to set up a remote desktop program. Although there are many alternatives, Microsoft's "Remote Desktop" is a highly recommended free option, and is available for both Windows and macOS and mobile applications.

OPENING AN ACCOUNT WITH A BROKER

As you know, having a broker is essential if you want to participate in the financial markets. At this point you need to choose one that provides you with enough assurances regarding quality and security.

The first basic rule is only use a broker that is regulated by one of the main control agencies such as the FCA (Financial Conduct Authority, the British regulator), the CNMV (the National Securities Market Commission, the Spanish regulator) or the SEC (Securities and Exchange Commission, the US regulator).

And the second rule is avoid at all costs intermediaries whose registered address is in a tax haven, no matter how good the conditions they initially offer you appear to be.

Bear in mind that you need to decide what instruments you are going to trade before you choose your broker. While it is true that some of the most important brokers offer a large number of different assets, there are others that specialize more in specific products.

I won't go into a comparison of the advantages and disadvantages of all the brokers available in the market, but some of the most recommended by traders and investors year after year include Interactive Brokers, TDAmeritrade, TradeStation, AMPFutures, DeGiro and Darwinex, among others.

The process for opening an account is very similar across all brokers. And because it is in their interest that you do so, they make it quite simple for you. The most common steps you need to follow are listed below:

1. Review the minimum requirements that you must meet to open the account. Some brokers offer members of the general public different accounts depending on their qualification or use, and each has mandatory requirements that must be met.

2. Fill in the registration forms. There will be a series of steps in which you may have to verify your email address, select the characteristics of the account, the type of client and provide personal, professional, financial information and contact details.

3. Provide proof of identity and address. At some point you will have to upload a photocopy of your national identity document or driving license; and also proof of your tax address. A utility bill or a bank statement is usually sufficient for this purpose.

4. Sign the agreements and declarations. This the last step to complete the registration process with the broker. Here you simply need to select the documents to be signed and send confirmation that all the information provided is true, giving consent to the applicable laws.

5. Transfer of funds. Depending on the broker, you may be required to transfer a minimum amount. You need to select the payment method and complete and send the order. Be especially careful when identifying the bank transfer and be sure to include whatever you are asked to write in the item line of the transfer to avoid any problems in the receipt of the funds. Some Brokers also allow you to fund the account with your credit card, which makes the process much faster.

I have tried to describe this process step by step as faithfully as possible so you in case you are wary and think you're being asked for unwarranted information. Sometimes the broker may ask us to include the savings we have, where we work and some even ask for the contact address of our work. These are simply measures aimed at trying to minimize the risk they may incur by allowing someone with very little credit to open an account.

Once the process is complete it takes a few days for all the information to be verified and the funds to arrive. In the meantime, download the platform you will be trading with and start researching it.

TRADING PLATFORMS

One of the things that you should consider when selecting the broker with whom you are going to work is what trading platforms they offer.

Be very careful because broker and platform are not the same thing. The broker is the intermediary, the entity; while the platform is simply the tool that is used for that intermediation, which you will use to analyze the charts and launch your trading orders.

There are many options within the world of trading and investing, so it is important that you at least know about some of them and select the one you feel most comfortable with.

There are some brokers that have their own proprietary platforms and others that use external multi-broker platforms. Generally, all brokers allow the use of these multi-broker platforms since they are better known, more used, usually more user-friendly and generally facilitate accessibility for the customer.

Without a doubt, the most popular multi-broker platforms among traders are Metatrader (4 and 5), Ninja trader (7 and 8), VisualChart, Pro Real Time, cTrader, ATAS and TradingView.

These types of platform allow the trader to connect with the broker through a username and password that their own broker will provide. There are no special settings you need for this. By logging onto the platform with the credentials that our broker sends us, we will be able to trade with our external account.

Some of the most popular proprietary platforms include Trader Workstation from Interactive Brokers, TradeStation, xStation from XTB, and Thinkorswim from TDAmeritrade. They are usually very powerful although most of them only incorporate certain basic indicators and do not allow more advanced ones to be imported. This is one of the great advantages of multi-broker platforms; because their use is more widespread, it attracts more developers who dedicate more resources to creating more complex tools and indicators.

After trying a few, the one I have been using recently is TradingView. TradingView has the great advantage of being a web application and therefore doesn't need to be installed on the computer. You can connect from any computer and keep your settings thanks to its storage in the cloud. It also has a desktop version that you can download and install on your computer if you wish, and it even has applications for both IOS and Android. It is a very friendly, accessible and intuitive application, and because it is open source it has attracted the attention of many tool and indicator developers, making it one of the most recommended trading and investment platforms on the market.

Preparing the Chart

Below is a description of the basic tools that we will find on our platforms. For this example we are going to use Tradingview. Below is a brief description of how to set up the chart so that you can start analyzing it. This platform has also been incorporated into many trading data websites as well as in some broker proprietary platforms, so I recommend you learn the basics.

The first thing we need to do is register on the platform. We can choose from several plans, from a free one with certain limitations to several paid packages. You can start with the free plan and if you continue to advance in your career as an investor sooner or later you will need to subscribe to a payment plan.

Once in the platform we will see something like this. We need to know how to use the following tools:

This is not the place to go into a comprehensive presentation of the platform. It is simply a matter of knowing what a trading platform is and what we can find in it. We will focus on the main screen since all platforms more or less have the same menus. The price chart will always be in the center surrounded by different tools for chart and drawing settings.

Since we are traders that analyze supply and demand, we need to prepare the chart with at least the two resources we need for this purpose: price and volume. As you can see, the price is already shown in candlestick format. To add the volume we need to incorporate it from the indicators menu. In most platforms, the volume is shown using colored bars, generally red and green, depending on the type of candlestick to which it is associated. If the candlestick is bullish the volume bar is shown in green, while if it is bearish the bar is red. This doesn't make much sense and can even lead to error since volume has no upward or downward direction. The volume bar simply indicates the number of trades so a neutral color might be a better option so we can analyze the information as objectively as possible.

With this done, we now have our chart set up with the minimum configuration of price and volume necessary to be able to start analyzing:

Depending on how much complexity we want, we can add more indicators. My trading approach is based on the analysis of price action, VSA, Wyckoff and Volume Profile. I try to use the minimum tools necessary that allow me to perform my analysis with the utmost guarantees. This is what my basic screen looks like and the indicators that I currently use:

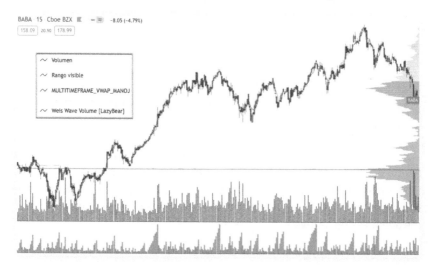

Price and volume chart

We have already looked at everything related to price and volume data. This information is what we fundamentally rely on for our analysis.

Weis Wave

Located in the lower part of the chart. The Weis wave indicator collects and analyzes volume data to graphically represent the accumulation of transactions made per price movement. That is, depending on the configuration we assign to it, the first thing the code does is identify the start and end point of a price movement. Once this is determined, it adds up all the volume traded during the development of that movement and represents it in the form of waves. In short, it measures the accumulated volume per wave.

All waves start from a baseline set at 0 (just like the standard vertical volume). Green waves correspond to bullish movements and red waves to bearish movements. This is very useful for knowing the level of participation in each movement. It allows us to analyze whether there is harmony or divergence based on the law of effort vs result.

Volume Profile

Located on the right side of the chart. It shows us the volume traded per price level. The vertical axis represents the price and the horizontal axis the volume.

It is an essential tool for knowing the degree of interest represented by the different levels and zones. A higher volume will be represented as a longer horizontal bar and will suggest greater interest; while a lower volume will be displayed as a trough and will indicate a lack of interest on the part of the agents at those levels.

There are different types of profiles:

- **Fixed range**. This allows us to manually launch profiles on any particular price action.

- **Session**. This is the profile for the day. Especially useful for day traders.

- **Composite**. Created to try to eliminate the noise of short time frames and thus obtain a better understanding of the longer term, of the context. There are two types:

  - **Fixed**. Shows the volume distribution over a predetermined time period. It does not change unless the selected period is underway.

  - **Variable**. This is the one we see in the chart. It characteristically shows the traded volume of all the price levels currently on the chart. It is important to keep this in mind because if you move the chart, the profile will change.

Weekly and monthly VWAPs

VWAPs are very important institutional levels. It represents the average price of all contracts traded during a specific time period and is shown on the chart as a moving average, whose position varies as transactions are executed. Depending on the time frame we can make use of different VWAP levels. The most commonly used are the session VWAP for intraday traders and the weekly and monthly VWAP for medium and long-term traders.

The last chart shows the specific names of each of the indicators in case you want to look for them in Tradingview and incorporate them into your template. My YouTube channel contains videos in which I comment in more depth on these indicators. I recommend that you follow me both on YouTube and on my other social networks to monitor what I am doing in real time.

DEMO TRADING

Once we have the chart ready, it is time to move forward and start the demo trading stage; that is, with real market data but with fictitious money.

Personally, I don't recommend spending too much time on this. A lot of traders only consider switching to real money once they have obtained a certain amount of profit during demo trading. But think about it. Trading real money has absolutely nothing to do with trading fake money. Not in the slightest. You may think, after spending a long time in the demo phase, that you have everything under control, and after starting to trade with real money you find you're making every mistake in the book and end up bankrupting your account.

Why does this happen? Simply because the emotions we are exposed to in a real and a fake environment are not the least bit alike, and when you start risking real money, things change significantly.

What I recommend is that you go through this demo trading phase as quickly as possible and use it for what it really is, to check the operation of the platform, see its characteristics, the chart tools you are going to use, memorize where everything is located, see the types of orders and their operation, etc.

Nothing more. It is about adapting to this new work environment. And this is important because you may realize that the platform is not what you expected, that you have specific needs that it doesn't meet, that it is too simple or too complex for you, or that you simply don't like it. This is the time to check all these kinds of things.

Of course, in addition to familiarizing ourselves with the software, it is at this stage where we must learn to look for and recognize the market behavior on which our trading plan is based. But this has nothing to do with trading. What I mean by this is investing hours of screen time looking at historical prices to discover past opportunities for our strategy and what we would have done to enter or exit the market. It is what is known as analyzing "in hindsight", with the chart on pause.

Ultimately, this is the stage in which we should focus on gaining a deeper understanding of the platform and more experience with the method.

TRADING WITH REAL MONEY

Once everything is in order you can open your account with real money. The best way to learn is by trading in real situations and observing your emotions and how they affect you when making decisions.

But don't go too fast. Starting to trade with real money doesn't mean immediately following the risk management stipulated in our trading plan.

Let's divide the real money trading process into several stages. The first stage is about limiting ourselves to gaining experience with the application of our strategy while maintaining an exposure to risk that is as low as possible. In other words, taking a risk per position of even less than 1 or 2% of the account. We should start by opening positions which in the result of a Stop Loss would suppose a loss of cents or at most a few euros (or dollars).

This is where we are going to truly cut our teeth as traders. A latent loss in demo mode of €10,000 is not the same as losing €2 of real money. That two euro loss will make you experience emotions that you never knew you had, I can assure you. This is the key. Demo trading is of no use to us once we have everything under control. To build our emotional foundations we must start trading in real situations.

Over the course of the following stages we will try to take on an ever increasing risk in our trades. If we started by risking pennies or a few euros, now we are going to try trading with several tens or hundreds of euros. This, as we know, is something very personal and will vary greatly depending on the trader. During these later stages there will be many traders who feel comfortable losing €40 or €50 per trade, while others who are more risk averse will feel uncomfortable with losses of €15 or €20.

The key is to continue moving forward with this process, little by little, until we reach the initial risk that we have established in our trading plan.

To carry out this strategy of adapting the real market there are certain products we can use such as CFDs that allow us to open very small positions. Some brokers allow trading with micro lots, with position sizes made up of very few units. Although CFDs tend to have a very bad reputation among some, if you trade them with a good broker it is a very interesting option for this type of learning environment.

In summary, the goal here is to continue implementing our strategy in the market in real time; take real risks and gradually increase these as we consolidate our strategy and emotional management.

There is no set time this process should last for. For some it will take a few weeks while for others it may last months or even years. Everything will depend on the strength of the strategy, how defined the trading plan is, the time that the trader can dedicate to it and their degree of risk aversion and emotional control.

WHERE AND HOW TO LOOK FOR IDEAS

As you know, there are a huge number of assets that can be traded. This section details those resources that we will use to find those assets that we will later include in our watchlist.

Both this section and the next one on the organization of our watchlist are oriented more towards medium and long-term trading. For those traders who are going to operate intraday these two concepts don't really apply, because they don't need to scan the market as they will have already decided in advance which asset or assets they are going to focus on; ad nor will they need to create a watchlist to classify these assets according to the priority level of possible entry since they will already be monitoring them very actively during the hours they decide to be in front of their screens.

The first thing we are going to do is scan the market, looking for those assets that meet our specific trading criteria. This means knowing where and how to look for ideas. This is one of the great problems investors face on a day-to-day basis. Below are a number of resources that are useful for this purpose:

Scanners

Several different websites offer this service. These websites track the markets based on specific filters. One of the most used finviz. This platform allows you to include both fundamental and technical filters, and even combine them together, which is of great benefit to the trader.

The idea is that you set your filters in line with what you intend to trade. You therefore need to have a well-defined strategy and a specific trading plan. What is your approach going to be, range or trend trading? If it is based on trends, will it be with or against the trend? Until we have a basically defined plan, we won't be able to scan the market because essentially we won't know what to look for.

Let's suppose you decide to follow a strategy based on the ideas of the Wyckoff method. And that in particular you are looking for assets that are in a potential Spring position (bearish false breakout to the lows of the structure). Well, a very simple idea that might allow us to find potential actions in this situation is to include a technical filter that shows us a traditional chartism pattern known as a "double bottom". This pattern identifies a market in a support zone, that is, the price is interacting with a relevant previous low. And there we have it; a potential bearish false breakout situation.

Similarly, a "double top" pattern could alert us to a possible Upthrust situation (bullish false breakout), and put us in a position where we might consider selling.

Obviously, not all actions that comply with the filter criteria will present trading opportunities, but we will almost certainly get some good ideas by implementing this type of strategy.

These types of scanners allow us to include several filters at the same time, so the more creative we are when coding the particular situation we are looking for, the closer we will be to identifying the best stocks.

Continuing with the Wyckoff method, another technical filter that we can use to identify a potential distribution structure in progress is the chartism pattern known as "head and shoulders". In essence this pattern is an accumulation or distribution structure (depending on whether the pattern is normal or inverted). All we need to do at this point is check the stocks that have been identified one by one and carry out our price and volume analysis to check the quality of the signal.

You may want to implement a strategy in which the price is already in an uptrend after you have identified a signal of underlying strength. In this case there are two filters that we should look for. In the first place, a sign of underlying strength and secondly, that the market is already moving with the trend. One way to confirm these would be to add the technical filter of the "double bottom" and also another filter looking for the price to be above a moving average of, for example, 20 periods. Now we have our two ingredients. If 20 is not enough, we can increase it to 50 or more periods. The more periods, the further it will have traveled. In other words, the more reliable the signal will be but the less profit we will be able to obtain.

This is exactly what is happening in the attached screenshot. This filter is capable of identifying a potential accumulation structure and moreover in a potential break and retest (BUEC) position. This platform is just great. When hovering over the tickers, a small price graph appears which offers a preview of the market situation, so you don't have to open a new tab for each of the identified securities.

Let's suppose now that we want to execute a trade against the trend. The most obvious filter we would apply here is for the price to be far from a moving average. For example, if what we want is to identify a possible over-bought condition to look for an opportunity to sell, we could configure the filter to show those securities that are 40 or 50% above the 50-period moving average. The market may not yet be ready to revert to the mean, but when this happens it will be an essential condition that the price be quite far from this type of moving average, so this can be a good premise.

In addition to price filters we can also include volume filters as well as other variables. We could easily identify a climax if we look for those securities where the volume has increased by X times compared to what was seen recently. And if we also combine it with a filter in which the price is hitting a new low, it would be the right situation to identify a potential Selling Climax. Interesting, right?

We can also play with the time frame and look for these types of patterns and filters for daily charts and subsequently look at a shorter time frame to look there for our entry trigger. As we can see, the imagination has no limits. The more experience you gain, the more good ideas you will have that you can take advantage of.

Insiders

To prevent certain types of conduct among those with insider information, regulatory bodies oblige directors and major shareholders to disclo-
se their holdings, transactions and any changes in ownership of shares in
their own companies.

This information is available to the public and is clearly very useful to
us as traders. We're talking about monitoring the actions of those who actually handle insider information. The fact that they are forced to report it does
not diminish its significance, since we can be sure that they wouldn't report
it otherwise.

finviz

Search ticker, company or profile

Home News Screener Maps Groups Portfolio Insider Futures Forex Crypto Backtests Elite

Latest Insider Trading | Top Insider Trading Recent Week | Top 10% Owner Trading Recent Week

Filter [All Transactions]

Ticker	Owner	Relationship	Date	Transaction	Cost	#Shares	Value ($)	#Shares Total	SEC Form 4
YORW	Rasmussen Steven P	Director	Sep 20	Buy	45.63	13	600	2,727	Sep 20 02:36 PM
AMCR	Roegner Eric V	President,Amcor Rigid Plastics	Sep 08	Option Exercise	11.16	303,000	3,381,480	452,135	Sep 20 02:11 PM
AMCR	Roegner Eric V	President,Amcor Rigid Plastics	Sep 08	Sale	12.30	303,000	3,726,900	149,135	Sep 20 02:11 PM
SOL	SHAH CAPITAL MANAGEMENT	CFO	Sep 20	Buy	6.75	6,000	40,500	11,613,298	Sep 20 02:01 PM
AIS	CARY RICHARD C	Controller, CAO	Sep 16	Option Exercise	53.53	4,583	245,330	39,743	Sep 20 01:58 PM
AIS	CARY RICHARD C	Controller, CAO	Sep 16	Sale	150.32	4,583	688,917	35,160	Sep 20 01:58 PM
RAPT	HO WILLIAM	Chief Medical Officer	Sep 17	Sale	38.97	2,000	77,930	63,106	Sep 20 01:58 PM
REFL	Omega Fund IV, L.P.	Director	Sep 16	Sale	32.55	5,537	180,229	5,002,708	Sep 20 12:53 PM
REFL	Omega Fund IV, L.P.	Director	Sep 17	Sale	33.02	94,463	3,118,770	4,908,245	Sep 20 12:53 PM
MGC	KENNEDY DOUGLAS L	President & CEO	Sep 17	Sale	32.61	5,000	163,063	70,723	Sep 20 12:52 PM
PCF	HAFRES BEN H	Director	Sep 17	Buy	10.00	1,675	16,750	1,675	Sep 20 12:47 PM
SMH	SILLS PETER J	Director Emeritus	Sep 16	Sale	40.84	2,841	116,026	714,350	Sep 20 12:36 PM
MGNX	BIOTECH TARGET N.V	10% Owner	Sep 16	Buy	20.94	400,000	8,376,800	8,675,564	Sep 20 12:21 PM
MGNX	BIOTECH TARGET N.V	10% Owner	Sep 17	Buy	19.93	200,000	3,986,680	6,875,564	Sep 20 12:21 PM
MTEM	BIOTECH TARGET N.V	10% Owner	Sep 16	Buy	6.13	100,000	613,000	10,042,003	Sep 20 12:17 PM
BHLB	Mhatre Nitin J.	President and CEO	Sep 13	Buy	24.64	3,800	93,632	33,880	Sep 20 12:00 PM
PBHC	Rusmat Walter	Senior Vice President, CFO	Sep 16	Buy	16.50	1,000	16,500	21,000	Sep 20 1:58 AM
BCG	STAHL MURRAY	Director	Sep 17	Buy	37.50	150	5,625	1,425	Sep 20 11:29 AM
TPL	STAHL MURRAY	President and CEO	Sep 17	Buy	2.46	675	1,660	181,825	Sep 20 11:25 AM
TPL	STAHL MURRAY	Director	Sep 17	Buy	1300.40	3	3,901	1,322	Sep 20 11:00 AM

We should therefore try to use this information to our advantage.
Again, finviz offers us the possibility of doing so within its web platform. The
"Insider" tab shows a list of company tickers, the position in the company or
the relationship of the party in question, as well other information on the
executed transaction.

But we need to be careful with this and continue to apply common
sense, independence and objectivity in our analysis. We should simply treat
this information as one more sign of strength or weakness that confirms or
rejects our trading hypotheses; in no case should we take action solely and
exclusively based on this information, however relevant it may be.

In other words, after seeing the report, what we have to do is go to the
chart and analyze what is really happening there. We should be looking for
some signal from the price that is in line with the insider action. An interesting and practical application of this would be if we were to see in this list a
large purchase from a major company insider and at the same time see the

price developing into a potential accumulation structure. This is the power of using these kinds of tools.

But as I say, everything is always subject to the chart, to the price action and the volume. It is the chart that will ultimately confirm or reject our trading idea.

Professional Manager Portfolios

Just like the positions of insiders, the portfolios of actively managed funds are also relevant sources of information for the investor. Although with some delay, these institutional investors are required to inform their participants periodically about the positions held by the fund.

Although we aren't dealing here with the important members of companies, we can also consider professional managers in some way as the owners of insider information with respect to the companies they analyze. The logic is simple; these institutions usually allocate a huge amount of resources to analyzing the fundamentals of companies in great detail. They have direct contact with company directors and may have access to detailed knowledge of the company's plans. All of which makes them among the most knowledgeable of agents when it comes to the corporation in question.

Therefore, knowing that a certain investment fund has allocated a large amount capital to a certain stock should send up a flag and compel us to technically analyze the situation. We may at times come across a stock with signs of underlying strength that suggests future price rises, so our job as technical analysts is to identify a trading zone in which we can join them.

Fund Type

💡 Fund group: `All` ⬍

💡 Morningstar Category: `Mid-Cap Value` ⬍

💡 Manager tenure greater than or equal to: `Any` ⬍

Cost and Purchase

💡 Minimum initial purchase less than or equal to: `Any` ⬍

💡 Load funds: `All` ⬍

💡 Expense ratio less than or equal to: `Any` ⬍

The majority of funds or the most capitalized ones will ultimately have many of the large companies in their portfolio. In terms of the types of funds to look for, a good idea are funds whose investment philosophy is Value Investing. As we have seen, this investment approach identifies securities that are undervalued by the market and which have good future prospects.

To carry out these searches, we need an analysis supplier such as Morningstar or YahooFinance. We need to go to the funds tab and there filter by the type of fund that we want. In this case, we are interested in an active management style. Regarding the category, small and mid-cap funds could be of interest, although here we can search for any type.

Options Market

The options market is another resource that can provide us with very good ideas if we have at least some basic knowledge about how this type of market works.

As we discussed in the early pages of the book, several types of trades can be carried out in the options market, each with different sentiments and expectations. If you remember, buying a CALL option has bullish sentiment, buying a PUT has a bearish sentiment, a selling a CALL has sideways/bearish sentiment and selling a PUT has sideways/bullish sentiment.

Our task now is to get very basic reading of that which is in line with what we are looking for.

There are basically two problems with trying to get an understanding of what the flow of options means:

- We cannot know if the contracts are purchases or sales. When we see the **Open Interest** at a certain price, we cannot know if those active contracts are purchases or sales.

- Based on the premise that institutions will also eventually take some losses, just because we believe there is a bullish or bearish sentiment in the market does not necessarily mean that the market will go in that direction.

Open Interest is the total number of contracts that are open, pending execution. It is a value that is used to get an idea of the sentiment of investors. It is updated at the end of the day and revealed the following day. It is done this way so that we cannot know whether these contracts are purchases or sales. Despite these issues with Open Interest, we can use it to reach certain conclusions:

- If there is an Open Interest of X and we see a much larger order come in, it is most likely a position opening = intentionality.

- If there is an Open Interest of X and we see that a similar order enters at the same price, it is most likely a position being closed.

- If there is an Open Interest of X and a new position is opened with the same amount with a later expiration, it is most likely the roll of a position, so the sentiment would remain the same but the time frame would be extended.

An options roll is a change to a position and is carried out by closing the current position (CALL/PUT sale) and opening a new position (CALL/PUT purchase). You can roll the price, expiration or both.

It may seem complicated, because it is, so this source of ideas should only be considered by those traders who understand the way the options market operates.

To try to make things clearer, one way to use this information is to look for any unusual activity that suggests positions have been opened or to look at the Open Interest, in both cases where the strike price is Out of The Money.

Unusual Options Activity refers to an imbalance between the Open Interest and the entry of a new order. A large order as we know is by definition an action originated by institutional traders, and this is the type of information that the retail trader is interested in assessing: Why is there a large trader interested in entering there? What are they most likely doing (buying or selling)?

For example, if we have a possible accumulation structure under development, or we have seen some signal that denotes underlying strength and we also see that in the options chain of that company there are a large number of open CALL contracts at a price that is above the current price level, this is a sign that would reinforce the scenario. In this case we would assume that these CALLs are purchases and with the strike price that is out of the money, the sentiment and expectation is bullish, especially if what we see in the chart reinforces this idea.

And now we have to overcome the next problem, which is that the largest companies have large numbers of both CALL and PUT contracts open. If we look at Apple's options chain, for example, we will see a huge Open Interest on both sides. Given this scenario, it is advisable to simply ignore these types of assets since it does not allow us to make any kind of reading about what is most likely to be happening there. It seems much more logical to look for those stocks in which this unusual activity is significantly noticeable and which we can interpret more intuitively. This would be the case for medium and low cap companies.

To analyses the options market, I use the proprietary TradeStation platform, although there are software applications available that are exclusively dedicated to this task.

The advantage of having an account with this broker is the other utilities it offers us: in addition to providing us with the expected brokerage services, it gives us access to the options market and is a broker that we can link with TradingView, allowing us to access this platform in real time and to trade directly in it. It is certainly a good option.

The Trading Community

There is a very large trading community out there and with a bit of research we can find members who like to share all sorts of relevant information about the market on a multitude of platforms and websites.

Independent company analysts, radar alerts on unusual activity in the options market, futures traders who analyze based on some form of supply and demand methodology, experts who share micro and macroeconomic analysis, relevant fundamental news and events, economic results, etc. There are many options, but all this presents a big problem and that is that most of these resources are just smoke and mirrors or of poor quality.

As a result we need to carefully analyze any information we find on the internet, maintaining the principle of independence above all else. If you are going to use these types of resources, you must be able to remain totally objective to ensure the information doesn't skew your perspective in any way, regardless of where the information comes from.

Unlike those resources that scan the market which can offer us signals that confirm or reject our analysis, these sources may for example claim a company offers a trading opportunity based on their valuations or their method; but you must bear in mind that their valuations or method may not be in line with what you are looking for a security to do before trading it.

Ultimately, this resource is there to save ourselves time and to leverage the work of others in the process of searching for ideas. But as with any other resource, it must always be dependent on our own analysis.

Where can you look for these resources? Specialized websites, forums, private communities, Twitter profiles, YouTube channels, Telegram etc.

CREATING A WATCHLIST

As we scan the market for ideas we need to organize our database in such a way that we can access these quickly. To do this, we can organize them into lists by asset type or organize them by label according to their priority.

Organization by Lists

This is optional. Although I do recommend creating several lists according to the type of asset, it is not a really necessary for the purposes of effective organization.

What I do with this type of organization is to group together assets listed on the same type of market You can use the asset classification that we looked at in the first part of the book: Stocks, funds, derivatives, indices, currencies, cryptocurrencies, commodities. Or you can create your own. How you organize things doesn't matter as long as it makes sense to you.

Organization by Labels

Organizing by labels will allow us to indicate the location of the assets.

This means assessing the urgency with which the market may develop the signal that we are looking for as our entry trigger. I suggest using three different labels depending on the priority:

- **High priority**: Assets that are in the trading zone or level and directly waiting for the entry trigger.

- **Medium priority**: Price heading towards the zone. Waiting for a movement to develop to start looking for the signal.

- **Low priority**: Price far from the area of interest. We still need to see two movements before reaching the trading level.

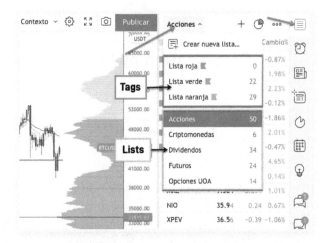

The image offers an example of how we might organize our watchlist. This one in particular is mine. As you can see, I have 5 different lists depending on the type of asset (stocks in general, cryptocurrencies, stocks that distribute good dividends, futures in general, and stocks from the options radar). And at the same time my labels identify the priority using three colors: red for low priority, orange for those that according to the analysis are medium priority, and in green the positions that I have open and those that are high priority.

This allows me to periodically review my sources of ideas and in general, when I identify an interesting security, it is because it falls within the medium priority category. My day-to-day work then involves checking to see if they can be moved into the high priority list where I do a more exhaustive analysis and with greater periodicity in search of signals that offer me the opportunity to enter the market.

Setting alerts

The final tool that we are going to use to help us better keep track of our watchlist is alerts. Whether we have a lot of assets on our watchlist, or we are away from our screens, alerts are a very valuable resource that can be of great use in the task at hand.

Alerts are going to be especially useful for two purposes:

For **medium-priority** assets that are developing a trend that is moving towards the trading zone. There is no big secret here. The market is developing a trend towards the zone in which we are going to look for our entry trigger.

The next two charts show two examples of this idea. We identify our trading zone and place the alert on it. When the price reaches it, the asset is raised to high priority and from that point on we simply wait for our entry trigger.

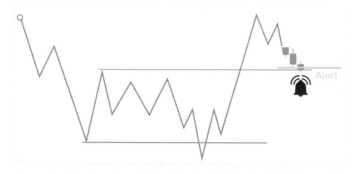

For **high-priority** assets when we want our trigger candlestick to reach a certain level before giving us the definitive signal to enter. With this action, we are looking for the market to show aggressiveness, and for this to be significant enough to reliably cause a change of character. And this means that it should be able to break the dynamic in the opposite direction such as a trend line or a previous pivot point.

Be very careful with this type of alert because the market will still have time to change and consider the problems you might face if you don't wait for the close of the candlestick to make your decisions.

We would receive the best assurances if said candlestick finally closes above a previous pivot point and also breaks its current downward dynamic, as shown in the example chart. At that moment we would be in a position to launch our orders to enter the market.

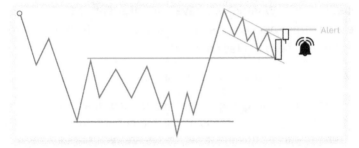

In Tradingview it is very simple to add an alert to the chart. Simply right click on the level at which you want to place the alert and select "add alert". A new options box will be displayed that allows you to configure the alert with other variables, as well as to select the means of notification, expiration, etc. Once you have configured it, click on "create" and the alert will be automatically active on your chart.

ACKNOWLEDGEMENTS

Congratulations. After reading this book you have now taken the first step. I sincerely hope that it has been of value to you and helped you build the foundations that will allow you to reach higher levels of performance as a trader or investor.

The content is dense and nuanced. It is very difficult to acquire all the knowledge after a single reading, so I recommend that you review it again and take personal notes for a better understanding.

As you know, I continually carry out research and share additional information, so please write to me at **info@tradingwyckoff.com** so that I can include you in a new list and send you future updates of the content totally free of charge.

See you on social media!

Twitter: twitter.com/RubenVillaC

YouTube: youtube.com/RubenVillahermosa

Website: tradingwyckoff.com/en

Before you go, I wanted to ask you for one small favor. **Could you please consider posting a review on the platform? Posting a review is the best and easiest way to support the work of independent authors like me.**

Your feedback will help me to keep writing the kind of books that will help you get the results you want. It would mean a lot to me to hear from you.

ABOUT THE AUTHOR

Rubén Villahermosa Chaves has been an independent analyst and trader in the financial markets since 2016.

He has extensive knowledge of technical analysis in general and has specialized in methodologies that analyze the interaction between supply and demand, reaching a high degree of training in this area. In addition, he is passionate about automated trading and has dedicated part of his training to how to develop trading strategies based on quantitative analysis.

He tries to bring value to the trading community by disseminating the knowledge acquired from principles of honesty, transparency and responsibility.

BOOKS BY THE AUTHOR

Trading and Investing for beginners

Stock Trading Basics, High level Technical Analysis, Risk Management and Trading Psychology.

The financial markets are controlled by large financial institutions which allocate enormous resources and hire the best engineers, physicists and mathematicians to appropriate the money belonging to the other participants. And you're going to have to fight them.

Your only chance is to somehow level the playing field. Instead of fighting them you need to try to trade alongside them. To do this, you need to become the complete trader and develop and follow the 3 main principles that will largely determine whether you are successful or not:

WHAT WILL YOU LEARN?

- Basic and advanced concepts on **Financial Education.**

- Theoretical fundamentals on **Financial Markets.**

- 3 high level **Technical Analysis** methodologies:

    - Price Action.

    - Volume Spread Analysis.

    - Wyckoff Methodology.

- Advanced **Risk Management** Techniques.

- Principles of **Emotional Management** applied to trading.

- How to make a professional **Business Management.**

- How to start from scratch, **from Theory to Practice.**

All this knowledge will allow you to:

- Improve the health of your **economy.**

- Understand **how the stock markets work.**

- Learn 4 **winning trading strategies.**

- Implement **solid money management methods.**

- Develop a **statistical and objective mindset.**

- Make step by step your own **trading plan.**

- Implement **trade record** and periodic evaluation.

- Discover resources for obtaining **investment ideas.**

- Manage the organization of assets through **watch lists.**

The Wyckoff Method in Depth

How to trade financial markets logically

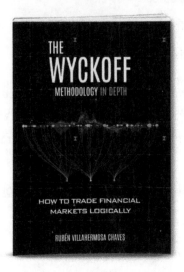

The Wyckoff method is a technical analysis approach to trading in financial markets based on the study of the relationship between the forces of supply and demand.

The premise is simple: When large operators want to buy or sell, they execute processes that leave their mark that can be seen on the charts through price and volume.

The Wyckoff method is based on identifying this intervention by professionals to try to elucidate who has control of the market in order to trade alongside them.

WHAT WILL YOU LEARN?

- **Theoretical principles** of how markets work:

    - How price moves.

    - The 3 fundamental laws.

    - The processes of accumulation and distribution.

- Exclusive t**rading elements** of the Wyckoff methodology:

    - Events.

    - Phases.

    - Structures.

- **Advanced concepts** for experienced Wyckoff traders.

- Resolution of **frequent doubts**.

- **Trading and position management**.

All this knowledge will allow you to:

- Identify **institutional money** participation.

- Determine market **context and sentiment**.

- Knowing the **high probability trading zones**.

- To propose scenarios on the basis of a defined **roadmap**.

- Manage **risk and trade** appropriately.

Wyckoff 2.0: Structures, Volume Profile and Order Flow

Combining the logic of the Wyckoff Methodology and the objectivity of the Volume Profile

Wyckoff 2.0 is the natural evolution of the Wyckoff Methodology. It is about bringing together two of the most powerful concepts of Technical Analysis: the best price analysis together with the best volume analysis.

This book has been written for experienced and demanding traders who want to make a quality leap in their trading through the study of advanced tools for volume analysis such as Volume Profile and Order Flow.

The universality of this method allows its implementation to all types of traders, both short, medium and long term; although daytraders may obtain a greater benefit.

WHAT WILL YOU LEARN?

- Advanced knowledge of how financial markets work: **the current trading ecosystem.**

- Tools created by and for **professional traders.**

- Essential and complex concepts of **Volume Profile.**

- Fundamentals and objective analysis of **Order Flow.**

- Evolved concepts of **Position Managemen**t.

All this knowledge will allow you to:

- **Discovering the B side of the financial market**:

  - The different participants and their interests.

  - The nature of decentralized markets (OTC).

  - What are Dark Pools and how they affect the market.

- How the **matching of orders** takes place and the problems of their analysis.

- Knowing the Trading principles with **Value Areas.**

- How to implement **Order Flow** patterns in intraday Trading.

- Build step by step your own **trading strategy**:

  - Context analysis.

  - Identification of Trading areas.

  - Scenario planning.

  - Position management.

BIBLIOGRAPHY

Adam Hayes y Eric Estevez. (2021). What Is Behavioral Finance? Obtenido de https://www.investopedia.com/terms/b/behavioralfinance.asp

Al Brooks. (2012). Trading Price Action Reversals: Technical analysis of price charts bar by bar for the serious trader. John Wiley & Sons, Inc.

Al Brooks. (2012). Trading Price Action Trends: Technical analysis of price charts bar by bar for the serious trader. John Wiley & Sons, Inc.

Al Brooks. 2(012). Trading Price Action Trading Ranges: Technical analysis of price charts bar by bar for the serious trader. John Wiley & Sons, Inc.

Andreu Guilanyà Mercadé. (2006). La perfecta imperfección de los mercados. BOLSA.

Bank for International Settlements. (2019). Triennial Central Bank Survey. Foreign exchange turnover in April 2019. Monetary and Economic Department.

Bespoke Investment Group. Talk Markets. (2017). 2017 Sector And Asset Class Correlations. Obtenido de https://talkmarkets.com/content/us-markets/2017-sector-and-asset-class-correlations?post=153247

Bolsas y Mercados Españoles. (2010). Estrategias Stock Picking.

Charles D. Kirkpatrick y Julie R. Dahlquist. (2011). Technical Analysis: The complete resource for financial market technicians. Pearson Education, Inc.

CME Group. (2013). A Trader's Guide to Futures. Thought Leadership with a Global Perspective.

CME Group. (2020). Self-Study Guide to Hedging with Grain and Oilseed Futures and Options.

CNMV. (2015). Los fondos cotizados (ETF): Guía Informativa.

CNMV. Conozca su perfil como inversor: Guía rápida.

CNMV. El mercado de valores y los productos de inversión: Manual para universitarios.

CNMV. Los productos de Renta Fija: Guía.

CNMV. Opciones & Futuros: Guía.

CNMV. Psicología económica para inversores: Guía.

CoinMarketCap. (2021). Today´s Cryptocurrency Prices by Market Cap. Obtenido de https://coinmarketcap.com

David H. Weis. (2013). Trades About to Happen: A Modern Adaptation of the Wyckoff Method. John Wiley & Sons Inc.

Ekanshi Gupta, Preetibedi Preetibedi y Poona mlakra. (2014). Efficient Market Hypothesis V/S Behavioural Finance.

Gregorio Hernández Jiménez. (2011). Educación financiera avanzada partiendo de cero.

Gregorio Hernández Jiménez. (2016). Opciones y futuros partiendo de cero.

Hank Pruden. (2007). Top Trading: Behavioral Systems Building, Pattern Recognition, and Mental State Management. John Wiley & Sons.

Instituto MEFF. Suba o Baje la Bolsa, con Opciones de MEFF dormirá tranquilo.

Investing. (2021) Horario de los mercados bursátiles y de Forex. Obtenido de https://es.investing.com/tools/market-hours

Jack D. Schwager. (2014). The Little Book of Market Wizards: Lessons from the Greatest Traders. John Wiley & Sons Inc.

John J. Murphy. (1999). Technical analysis of the financial markets: A comprehensive guide to trading methods and applications. New York Institute of Finance.

Magner N, Lavin JF, Valle M, Hardy N (2021) The predictive power of stock market's expectations volatility: A financial synchronization phenomenon. PLoS ONE 16(5): e0250846. https://doi.org/10.1371/journal.pone.0250846

Mark Douglas. (2001). Trading in the Zone: Master the Market with Confidence, Discipline, and a Winning Attitude. Prentice Hall Press.

Minding The Data. (2020). Simulating Roulette Betting Strategies with Python. Obtenido de https://mindingthedata.medium.com/simulating-roulette-betting-strategies-with-python-61bf40fc4a1c

Nathaniel Jaye. (2017). The Adaptive Markets Hypothesis: A Financial Ecosystems Survival Guide. Obtenido de https://blogs.cfainstitute.org/investor/2017/12/18/the-adaptive-markets-hypothesis-a-financial-ecosystems-survival-guide/

Peter Carleton. (2021). 20 Key Financial Ratios. Obtenido de https://investinganswers.com/articles/financial-ratios-every-investor-should-use

Portfolio Visualizer. (2021) Asset Correlations. Obtenido de https://www.portfoliovisualizer.com/asset-correlations

Raynor de Best. (2021). Statista. Most traded currency pairs on the forex market in 2020. Obtenido de: https://www.statista.com/statistics/1203453/most-traded-currency-pairs/

Robert D. Edwards, John Magee, W.H.C. Basseti. (2019). Technical Analysis of Stock Trends. Taylor & Francis Group, LLC.

Robert T. Kiyosaki. (2011). Rich Dad, Poor Dad. Plata Publishing LLC.

Rubén Villahermosa. (2018). La Metodología Wyckoff en Profundidad: Cómo operar con lógica los mercados financieros.

Rubén Villahermosa. (2019). De trader discrecional a cuantitativo. The Ticker: Trading e inversión cuantitativa. N6. Instituto Wyckoff España.

Rubén Villahermosa. (2021). Wyckoff 2.0: Estructuras, Volume Profile y Order Flow.

SEC. Asset Allocation. Obtenido de https://www.investor.gov/introduction-investing/getting-started/asset-allocation

SEC. Office of Investor Education and Advocacy. (2011). SEC Pub. 009. Saving and Investing: A Roadmap To Your Financial Security Through Saving and Investing.

SEC. Stocks. Obtenido de https://www.investor.gov/introduction-investing/investing-basics/investment-products/stocks

Sergio Fernández. (2019). Libertad financiera: los cinco pasos para que el dinero deje de ser un problema. Plataforma Actual.

TendenciasFX. (2015). Introducción a la Especulación de divisas: Cómo aprovechar los ciclos Económicos Globales, Preservar tu Patrimonio y Multiplicar tus Ahorros.

The Nippon Technical Analysts Association. The First Step Guide to Technical Analysis. Kakuya Kojoh. Toshiki Aoki.

Thomas J. Stanley y William D. Danko. (2010). The Millionaire Next Door: The Surprising Secrets of America's Wealthy. Taylor Trade Publishing.

UKEssays. (2018). Adaptive Market Hypothesis and Behavioural Finance. Obtenido de https://www.ukessays.com/essays/economics/adaptive-market-hypothesis-behavioural-3916.php?vref=1

Víctor Monfort. (2016). La guía The Tradingway: Introducción y teoría básica.

Printed in the USA
CPSIA information can be obtained
at www.ICGtesting.com
LVHW021136121124
796387LV00003B/25